94-2863

Dedicated to the Members of Crafted With Pride.

"No great improvements in the lot of mankind
are possible, until a great change takes place
in the fundamental constitution of their
modes of thought."

John Stuart Mill.

QUICK RESPONSE IN APPAREL MANUFACTURING

A Survey Of The American Scene

Alan Hunter
College of Textiles
North Carolina State University.

THE TEXTILE INSTITUTE
10 Blackfriars Street
Manchester M3 5DR

THE TEXTILE INSTITUTE
10 Blackfriars Street
Manchester, M3 5DR,
United Kingdom

© The Textile Institute 1990

First published 1990

Reprinted 1993

ISBN 1 870812 30 1 Paperback

Printed by Hobbs the Printers, Southampton

Preface

This book attempts to pull together the work carried out over the past five years or so by a large number of people in the U.S. textile and apparel industries to develop methodologies and systems whereby they can become more competitive in world markets. The need for such systems is great and it is urgent. At stake is the survival of a viable industry which is the largest employer of labor in the U.S.A. and, by far, the largest employer of minority and female workers.

The social and economic costs of displacing this work force would be enormous and to speak of retraining them for other work, as do the proponents of free trade, is much easier said than done. There is a high level of manufacturing concentration in regions of the country which have few job alternatives. Further, most of the workers are second or third earners in the family and they have a relatively limited education. Also, it should be remembered that the alternative to plant work - so called service jobs - would pay considerably less than the industry wage scale.

It is popular to think of textiles and apparel as sunset industries that are a kind of drag on the overall economy. In fact, both industries have, for the past 10-15 years, been in the forefront of manufacturing in terms of productivity increases. Together they invest close to two billion dollars each year in new equipment - much of it with a very high technology content. However, their products, and this is particularly true for apparel, have a high labor content which puts them at a tremendous disadvantage vis-a-vis the low wage countries of the world which see textile and garment manufacturing as the prime route to economic growth.

It is the purpose of this book to show that the U.S. industry can become competitive with much of the rest of the world without the need for miracles. Changes in management mind-set and priorities, full use of the new technologies, the realization that fiber making, textile manufacturing, garment making and retailing are not separate businesses, but must operate as parts of an integrated, consumer responsive supply system are the essential ingredients for success.

The work presented here should be of interest to other industries which compete globally. The apparel pipeline is the longest and most complex of manufacturing supply systems. Like many older industries, it developed in times when off-shore competition was limited, when the time value of money was not a major concern and when the end-product had a long life. Such environments encouraged practices which are no longer permissible. Economically sophisticated nations, when competing with the newly industrialized countries, such as Taiwan or South Korea, must take full advantage of every managerial and technical development if they are to compete and prosper.

In one sense, this book is premature. It was only in 1984 that any coordinated effort was made to develop a comprehensive Quick Response (QR) methodology. Elements of it had, of course, existed for several years but the systematic fitting together of all the pieces is a very recent endeavor. Despite the progress made to date, detailed feasibility/cost/benefit studies are still urgently required and, in many cases, management attitudes lag industry potential. But there is a need to assemble and disseminate the available information and to do it now. Thus, one target audience is the management group operating the pipeline.

The second reason for writing the book is to provide an educational tool. It is mandatory that an understanding of QR be built into the knowledge base of graduating students; it is too important a subject to be left to chance encounter. At the time of writing, the U.S. industry, has been given a breather from the relentless pressure from imports as a result of the weakening of the dollar. This currency situation cannot last indefinitely and, if we are wise, we will put our house in order while we can.

The author of this book is not really an author - he is an editor. Although heavily involved in the formative years in the development of QR methodology and its dissemination throughout the trade, his contribution is small compared with those of many others. However, in the later chapters, where opinion plays a greater role and where future research directions are the subject, the author is solely responsible for the content.

QR is a complicated subject and describing it involves a certain amount of repetition; topics appear and reappear in different contexts. Although every effort was made to keep repetition to a minimum, it still exists. Having at least two types of audience also presents problems. To industry people, some of the material will be well known, while students, on the other hand, may find themselves wishing for more basic explanations. Instead of footnotes, references and asides are reserved for the end-of-chapter notes and the need for a comprehensive index is minimized by having a comprehensive Table of Contents. Also, the Appendices are very extensive. There is a real need to "prove" the worth of QR and this entailed making the data available to the reader who likes to check things. Students and the research community will also benefit from this data base. Finally, students have found the many acronyms confusing and they suggested the addition of a Glossary of terms.

The membership of Crafted With Pride In U.S. Inc., (CWP), under the leadership of Roger Milliken, made research into QR possible through its generous financial support and Robert Swift, their Executive Director, drove everyone relentlessly. Among the prime movers in the development of QR, Peter Butenhoff and Richard Cotton of the duPont Company warrant special mention; Bob Frazier led the Kurt Salmon Associates consulting team - the prime contractors for the study - and was ably supported by Peter Harding and others from the firm. The contributions of other industry consultants were indispensible; Charles Farris of the BCG, Nathan Katz and Bill Summerour. And behind them were the dozens of people from all branches of the industry who gave of their time to answer all the questions and criticize all the assumptions and hypotheses.

The list of acknowledgements would be incomplete without the inclusion of what may be called the disseminators. An essential part of the CWP strategy was that of bringing the results of the various studies and trials to the attention of the industry at large. Notable among the people who tirelessly gave of their time were the staffs of AAMA, Apparel Industries Magazine, Bobbin Magazine and such trade consultants as Bob White of IBM, Emmanuel Weintraub and Smiley Jones. Thanks to them, Quick Response became an industry catch phrase in a matter of months instead of years.

On a personal level, thanks are due to John Fennie of Celanese Textile Fibers and to the faculty of the College of Textiles at North

Carolina State University who allowed the author to join them. Their kindness has led to the teaching of QR and provided the time to write about it.

Finally, thanks are due to Stafford Swearingen for his preparation of the Figures while a student at NCSU and Gloria Supino Hunter for much of the typing, including the copious Appendices, and all of the moral support.

Table Of Contents.

Introduction.

Every effort has been made to develop the need for, and the methodology of, Quick Response in as logical a flow as possible and, to a large extent, the sequence is historical. However, this is not a detective story and there is merit in showing the scope of QR early on. Students find a definition helpful in that it provides a road map of what is to come.

QR has been defined in many ways. The briefest is probably:

"Having the products the customer wants, in the right place, at the right time and at the right price."

A more complete version follows:

"QR is an Operational Philosophy and a Set of Procedures Aimed at Maximizing the Profitability of the Apparel Pipeline.

• QR depends on the integration of all the parts - fiber, textile, manufacturing and retail - into one consumer responsive whole.

• QR is driven by comprehensive and rapid information transfer between the sectors in the pipeline from retail point-of-sale back upstream

• QR requires the highest standards of product quality at all stages to allow significant reductions in safety stocks and product specification testing times.

• QR demands frank and open dialogue between supplier and customer and relies on high levels of mutual trust.

• QR calls for the use of up-to-date hard and soft technologies to minimize work in process, maximize customer responsiveness and to off-set the added costs of increased product diversity in the system.

• QR employs as its principal elements:

        – rapid development of sample fabrics and garments,

        – Computer Assisted Design,

        – flexible, short-run spinning, weaving, dyeing and finishing operations,

        – Just In Time shipping of fiber and fabric,

        – highly engineered manufacturing, including such elements as Unit Production Systems, computerized marking, laser cutting, automated sub-assembly sewing and modular work groups,

        – Electronic Data Interchange,

        – standardised bar-coding of fabric and garments,

        – pre-ticketing and drop-shipping of garments,

        – planned, frequent shipments of garments,

        – pulling back open-to-buy dates,

        – point-of-sale tracking at retail,

        – reducing initial retail orders to less than 50% of requirements,

        – flexible merchandise planning,

        – continuous re-estimation of customer demand,

        – frequent in-season reorders of of merchandise with short order-to-delivery times."

....

The purpose of this book is to show that if QR is applied to the manufacture and distribution of apparel products, enormous benefits will accrue to the industry in the form of:

- Increased sales volumes.

- Reduced markdowns.

- Reduced stock-outs.

- Reduced costs and prices.

- Greater price validity at retail.

- Improved financial performance.

- Increased competitiveness with off-shore suppliers.

The book is divided into four parts:

Part I puts the subject of QR in perspective. Chapter 1 gives the background to the biggest problem the U.S. textile and apparel industries have ever had to face; the rapid increase in the share of the market going to imported products. In round numbers this share now amounts to over 35% if only finished apparel imports are counted, but well over 50% if fabrics imported for conversion into apparel in the U.S. are included. More serious is the potential for further deterioration of the industry as the dollar returns to historical strengths unless tighter controls are placed on imports. Chapter 2 describes the traditional apparel supply system and its excessive cost of operation in some detail; a necessary pre-requisite for an understanding of what must change if the industry is to recover its health. Chapter 3 adds to the background picture by describing the early attempts by various U.S. trade groups to do something about the problems they faced.

Part II of the book develops the QR methodology and its impact on U.S. competitiveness. Chapter 4 relates to collapsing the length of the pipeline; the time taken for fiber raw materials to reach the consumer as finished apparel. The adoption of well understod Quality Management and Industrial Engineering techniques make it possible to pass goods through the pipeline in one third the traditional time. The move to a contracted pipeline has a drawback,

3

however, and that is the need for shorter production runs which increase unit costs unless steps are taken to off-set this diversity effect. Chapter 5 treats of this problem. Chapter 6 is concerned with one of the most important aspects of QR; the electronic transfer of information between trading partners. In the last 2-3 years a number of trade groups have set out to develop voluntary industry standards for Electronic Data Interchange (EDI) and their programs are described. Chapter 7 - QR Macroeconomics, together with the material in Chapters 10 and 11, is the heart of the book. The concept of retail re-order is developed, the information contained in earlier chapters is assembled into a quantitative picture of QR and the potential savings to the system are estimated. The title "Macroeconomics" was chosen to differentiate the material in Chapter 7 from the later cost/benefit studies of Chapters 10 and 11. The earlier results, although they considered specific fabric and garment types, were based on broad assumptions and only a hazy understanding of the costs and benefits of EDI, bar coding, etc. The two models should be thought of as complementary, with the former being a necessary forerunner to the latter. Also, the earlier model both has intrinsic interest as part of the development of QR and because it allowed the broad estimates of increased world competitiveness treated in Chapter 8 to be generated.

Part III is concerned with the industry trials carried out in the U.S. in 1985-86 to verify the results of the studies described above (Chapter 9), the cost/benefit studies mentioned above (Chapters 10 and 11) and descriptions of the specific pieces of technology needed to operate a QR program (Chapter 12). The material on technology is, of necessity, far from complete. New developments occur almost daily and it was not considered practical to devote a great deal of space to anything but the broadest outlines of where specific classes of equipment fit into the manufacturing and supply pictures.

Part IV is devoted to the major research programs being carried out in various parts of the world. The results of the efforts described in Chapter 13 will have a pronounced impact on the further stream-lining of QR supply methodologies as well as the ways in which the economically developed nations combat import pressures from the low wage exporting nations. The final Chapter addresses the question, "Is QR Enough?", and the answer is, "No". Simply applying the methods of QR without consideration of the problems inherent in actually applying Quality Management precepts or managing technological change in an organization is a waste of everyone's time. The problem of raising the level of design for U.S. manufactures is also addressed, as is the issue of the need for more agressive import substitution practices.

As stated earlier, the Appendices are voluminous. Providing this level of detail is an attempt to preserve the work done in the first five years by an industry in transition.

PART I

BACKGROUND TO QUICK RESPONSE - THE PROBLEM.

Chapter 1. Textile And Apparel Imports.

The primary purpose of this book is to explore the development and content of consumer responsive apparel supply systems.
However, an appreciation of the political and economic environments in which the industry found itself in the early to mid-1980's
is a prerequisite to full understanding of why there is a need for the
industry to change quickly to what must become a new way of life
if it is to survive.

The complexities of international trade in textiles and apparel
are discussed only briefly, as are the ins and outs of international
apparel sourcing. The emphasis here is on those aspects of the
rapidly worsening trade imbalance that are related to QR.

Trade Balance.

In 1987, the U.S. trade deficit in Textiles and Apparel
amounted to $24.8 billion dollars; approximately 15% of the total
trade deficit.[1] Ten years previously, in 1977, the deficit was $3.9
billion and as recently as 1980 the figure was still not a matter of
major concern - $4.7 billion dollars. In the space of only seven years
the deficit increased by $20 billion, an average rate of increase of
27%/year. The situation is illustrated in Figure 1.1.

The gross trade deficit conceals a variety of contributing factors. Of the $20 billion increase noted above, $15 billion came from
apparel and only $5 billion from fabric and other textile products. In
growth rate terms, the increases in imports for the two groups
amounted to 19%/yr. and 14%/yr. respectively. It should also be
noted that the trade in textiles swung from a surplus of almost $1
billion in 1980 - the previous time the dollar was weak - to a deficit
of $4 billion by 1987.

A clearer idea of the real increase in the import/export balance
is obtained by examining the volumes in terms of square yard
equivalents (SYEs). Table 1.1 shows selected import data for the

7

key years. Export figures are not shown in the Table as changes were relatively small over the period under study. Further, no correction was made for changes in the "shopping basket" mix within the broad trade categories.

Figure 1.1
U.S. Textile & Apparel Trade
1971 - 1987

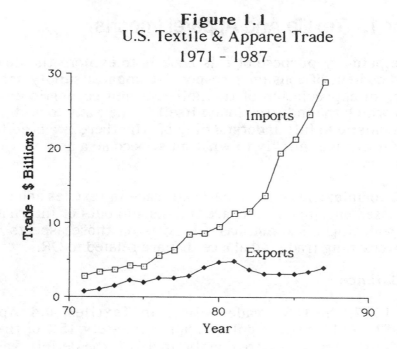

The growth in physical volume between 1980 and 1987 was 15%/year compared with 27%/year for the dollar volume. 40% of the increase came from apparel and 20% increases from each of the other three categories. The patterns of growth in Table 1.1 reflect continuing shifts in the opportunities for exporting to the U.S. Many of the newly emerging countries concentrate initially on spun yarns and fabrics and then move on to simple garments where styling and quality are not as important as price. When manufacturing skills have improved, and the distribution infrastructure developed to a level acceptable to importers, there is movement toward higher price point apparel. It is worth noting that imports in 1977 were almost identical with those three years later; 5000 million SYE.

When exports to the U.S. reach a level large enough to cause a measure of disruption, quotas start to be applied and at that point, the exporting nation naturally shifts its manufacturing emphasis to higher added value products.

Table 1.1
U.S. Imports Of Textile Manufactures
(Million SYEs)

	Yarn	Fabric	Apparel	Misc.	Total
1980	380	1217	2884	403	4884
1981	443	1706	3136	490	5775
1982	496	1478	3382	579	5935
1983	868	1871	3875	1093	7707
1984	1280	2547	4707	1674	10207
1987	1814	3079	6125	2134	13152
AGR - %/yr.	25	14	12	27	15

Most of the growth in imports since the mid-1970s has come from the export activities of a small number of Far East nations that saw textile manufactures, at very low cost, as the quickest route to economic development. Prior to that time, the major exporters were Japan and Hong Kong, both of which placed heavy emphasis on fabric exports. The 1970s saw the emergence of Taiwan and South Korea, first as fabric and then, increasingly, as garment suppliers. Other countries were quick to follow - Thailand, Sri Lanka, Macao, Pakistan and Brazil among them - with the latest major entry being the PRC.

To meet this competition, Japan undertook a program of exporting high skill content, high quality textiles such as the silk-like low weight polyester fabrics and Ultrasuede that have been built into global businesses. Hong Kong, for its part, deemphasised yarn and fabric manufacture and concentrated on high quality, higher price point apparel. When quotas impacted the scale of its export activities, Hong Kong simply contracted manufacture in low wage countries without quota problems, often supplying equipment and management to ensure high manufacturing standards. The low capital intensity of apparel manufacture makes it easy to move rapidly to other sites. One example of the speed with which an emerging nation can penetrate the U.S. market is provided by Indonesia, which, from a standing start in 1980, shipped $250 million worth of textiles and apparel in 1984.

9

Labor Rates.

Developing nation wage rates and the competitive advantage they provide, is the single greatest contributing factor to the surge in imports, more than off-setting freight costs, tariffs and lower worker productivity.

At the textile level, the rates provide a 15-35% cost advantage.[2] This is multiplied as the fabric moves into the garment phase where there is roughly a 50% cost advantage at cutting, sewing and finishing. At close to $7.00 and $6.00 per hour, respectively, for textile and apparel workers, the U.S. cannot compete with the $0.20-0.30 per hour paid in the PRC or the majority of the smaller Far Eastern countries that pay less than $1.00, and in some cases, no more than $0.50 per hour.[3] Partially off-setting the labor rate advantage in the newly emerging nations are productivity levels of 50-65% of those in the U.S. but these increase, with experience, to the 85% level of the major exporters.

The Multi-Fiber Arrangement (MFA)

Under GATT, the MFA provides the ground rules for international trade in textiles and apparel. Taken at face value, it offers fair and rational procedures for both importing and exporting nations, but like any other arrangement, it assumes that all the signatories will play by the rules and that all parties will administer them with equal firmness. This has proven not to be the case.

The major low-cost exporting countries consistently exceed the 6%/yr. growth rate suggested by the MFA, while simultaneously erecting non-tariff barriers. Further, Taiwan, South Korea and Hong Kong, which between them account for around 50% of all U.S. imports, can no longer be considered as developing nations, yet they have virtually frozen out the poorer countries for which the MFA was designed - see Figure 1.2.

An example of the speed with which the Big Four can adapt to new threats or opportunities is provided by their handling of the non-MFA fibers. Prior to 1986, the MFA covered only cotton, wool and the man-made fibers. It was not possible, therefore, to impose quotas on products containing such fibers as silk, ramie and linen. Imports of these products were insignificant through 1983 (2 million units in 1982, 3 million in 1983), but as quotas on MFA gar-

10

ments tightened, attention was turned to them. In 1984 such imports had increased to 8 million units i.e. $50-60 million, and by 1987 the Big Four had increased non-MFA exports to $1.8 billion or 17% of their total apparel exports to the U.S. Most other exporters were too slow to take advantage of this opportunity that ended when these classes of goods were incorporated into the MFA on its renewal at the end of 1986.

Figure 1.2
U.S. Imports Of Apparel
From Developing Regions

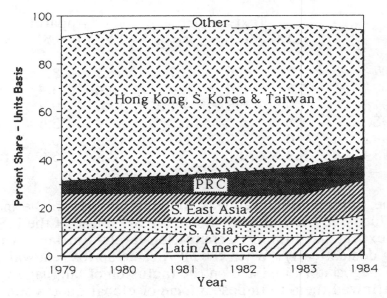

The situation becomes even less balanced, and further from the aims and ideals of the MFA, when U.S. imports are compared with those of the EC and Japan. Table 1.2 shows the changes in imports of textiles and apparel by the three largest market groups from the developing nations over the period 1974-1984.[4] The data are in dollars per capita and, even allowing for differences in the ways that different countries allocate their disposable income, they illustrate several important points.

• Japan has the lowest import levels for both textiles and clothing. These and the low ratio of clothing to textile imports, demonstrates Japan's concern over its trade balance, which is

11

strongly positive for textiles and slightly negative for apparel. More detailed data also show the sharp fluctuations in Japan's imports which give every indication of being firmly managed.

• The EEC lies between Japan and the U.S. in terms of both textile and apparel imports, but there are two distinct parts to the importing patterns, with 1980-81 the break point.

Table 1.2
Trade With Developing Countries
Imports In Dollars Per Capita

	Textiles			Apparel		
	EEC	U.S.	Japan	EEC	U.S.	Japan
1974	4.7	3.6	3.7	6.1	8.1	5.2
1976	5.8	3.4	4.4	10.4	13.4	5.1
1978	7.9	3.8	7.1	13.6	19.9	7.4
1980	11.8	5.1	6.3	22.4	25.6	7.3
1982	8.0	5.0	6.3	19.3	30.7	9.6
1984	8.3	10.1	7.1	18.5	56.6	10.4

The European market was the first on which the major exporters focussed their efforts. Some 5 years ahead of the U.S. crisis, Europe experienced import penetration levels similar to those now existing domestically. When the MFA came up for renewal in 1981, the EEC negotiators insisted on the inclusion of language which, in effect, allowed them to impose a form of global quotas and to limit imports of goods classified as "sensitive". [5]

Denied the earlier freedom of access, the exporters turned to the only other market available - the U.S. Figure 1.3 shows clearly the consequences of the European initiative[6] and Figure 1.4 provides deficit data for the major importers for the period 1974-84.

The U.S.A., together with West Germany and the Scandinavian countries, appear to be the only nations that not only respect the MFA, but often carry its philosophy to extremes. The administration of import regulations is heavily influenced by free-trade philosophy, despite the lack of reciprocity among trading partners. Further, the Customs Service, which is probably the only government agency apart from the IRS to turn a profit, is under-staffed to the point where only 2-3% of shipments can be inspected – this despite the many cases of infringement and outright fraud that come to light each year.[7]

Figure 1.3
Apparel Imports, U.S. & EEC
Unit Basis – 5 Major Suppliers

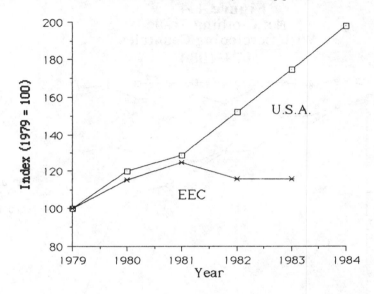

Currency Fluctuations.

In the past, textile and apparel imports have correlated well with the appropriate trade weighted value of the dollar against other major currencies. In 1980, when the dollar was last weak, exports benefitted and there was a pause in the growth of imports. Since early in 1986, however, when the dollar began an extended slide, the impact has been slow to emerge. Three of the major reasons for this are:

• The length of time needed for the major importers to locate equivalent domestic resources

• The high mill and manufacturing operating rates of 1987. These were a result of the mill closings that followed the earlier surge in imports, and they reinforced the habitual reluctance of U.S. industry to sell off-shore on a continuing basis.

This "ratcheting down" has had a severely handicapped the ability of U.S. firms to take advantage of currency fluctuations.

• The high proportion of imports that come from countries whose currencies are, or were, tied to the dollar in one way or another.

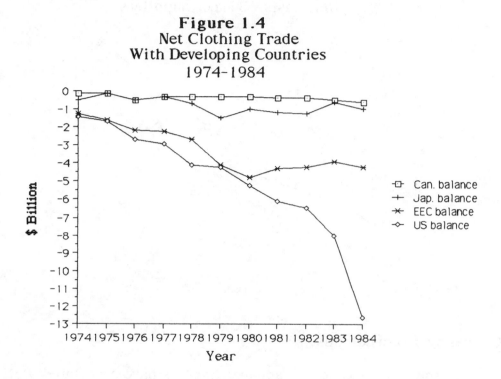

Figure 1.4
Net Clothing Trade
With Developing Countries
1974-1984

The Importers.

As noted earlier, imported, finished apparel accounted for roughly 35% of all the garments sold at retail in 1987. A further 15% was made in the U.S. from imported fabrics - for a total of over 50%. It is reasonable to ask, "What is imported and who does the import-ing?"

The import penetration of domestic consumption varies with the type of garment. Quotas, seasonality, tariff rates and labor con-tent all play a part in determining the penetration level. Table 1.3 shows the level of consumption and the break-down of sourcing for ten major garment lines in 1986. Import penetrations range from

14

22% for all dresses to 63% for all sweaters. The latter number ex-
cludes the 144 million ramie sweaters imported in 1986; if these are
included, the import share jumps to 71%.

In 1983, The Philadelphia College of Textiles and Science carried out a survey, the results of which suggested apparel importing
was divided approximately evenly between retailers and job-
ber/designers on the one hand and apparel manufacturers themselves on the other. KSA, for its Annual Sourcing Breakfasts, carries
out similar surveys which give a finer break-down; about a 2:1:2
ratio for retailers: importers: manufacturers.

Table 1.3
U.S. Production and Imports
Selected Apparel Lines - 1986.
(Millions of Garments)

	Production Plus Imports	Imports %
M&B Knit Shirts	887	30
M&B Trousers, Shorts	802	27
WC&I Slacks & Shorts	771	40
WC&I Knit Shirts	724	61
WC&I Woven Blouses	592	51
M&B Woven Shirts	552	59
All Sweaters	341	63
All Coats	299	51
All Dresses	268	22
All Suits	34	37

The retailers are interested in the higher margins achievable
with imported goods, particularly those from the low wage countries, as well as the variety and exclusivity of many of the garments
originating in Europe. Over the last decade, the Far East has developed sophisticated manufacturing and support systems, making it
easy and attractive for the retail buyer to source off-shore. This applies particularly to private label merchandise which is of increasing
importance to both department stores and mass merchants. The
drawbacks associated with importing, that have only recently been
documented, will be discussed in the next chapter, but the fact remains that the Far East has built up an attractive, one-stop-shop-

ping system. A type of jobber, or "marriage broker", has developed over the years; one who can lay out quickly and easily the types and costs of yarns and fabrics available in a given season, together with color and style guides. The more sophisticated of them also provide economic forecasts for the buyers.

The manufacturer situation is more complicated. Garments are imported because, in many cases, it is cheaper to contract or to set up plants abroad. Off-shore sourcing also provides a way of avoiding large capital investment in new capacity. A third reason is to broaden the product line for the benefit of the retail customer. Another route finding increasing favor with the manufacturer is to cut fabric in the U.S. and send the parts abroad for assembly. In this way, the imported garments are assessed for duty only on the added value, under article 807 of the Tariff Schedule. Incidentally, 807 manufacture introduces a complication into the Census trade data; the cut parts are counted as apparel exports - thus inflating the export data - and, after assembly, appear again as apparel imports.

One important class of imports is designer labelled apparel. Many design houses rely exclusively on the Far East, particularly Hong Kong, to produce high quality goods at mark-ups which will fund their marketing programs.

Fabric importing, though less lucrative because less labor intensive, is carried out by a large part of the supply system. Retailers can import for contractor manufacture; manufacturers, to supplement domestic mill offerings or because certain fabrics are not made in the U.S.; convertors and jobbers, for reasons of cost or differentiation; mills, to supplement lines or to make use of surplus wet processing capacity.

Impact On Employment.

The material discussed so far in this chapter has had to do with the trade environment in which the U.S. industry must operate. It should be clear that the off-shore supplier has a great deal going for him, providing a wide range of options for the domestic manufacturer or buyer. International trading protocols exist, but they are not universally observed and in the U.S., enforcement is particularly weak. These facts became painfully clear to industry leaders in the early 1980's and they initiated a number of projects in an attempt to improve the competitive position of the industry before its position weakened to the point where it was no longer viable. These initiatives all had a central belief; the loss of jobs had to be slowed and then reversed.

Table 1.4 gives some idea of the impact of textile and apparel imports on domestic employment.[8] The total is low. No account was taken of fiber manufacture, imports of non-MFA fiber products or miscellaneous imports such as handkerchiefs, down-filled garments, hosiery, coated fabric apparel etc. If these are included, the number for 1984 was around 800,000 jobs lost to imports. Import increases since 1984 suggest that by the end of the decade, of the order of one million jobs will have been lost.

Table 1.4
Labor Content Of Imported Apparel - 1984

Item	1984 Imports 1000 Doz.	Job Equiv.
Coats	12,072	139,000
Woven Shirts	39,096	114,500
Trousers/Slacks	31,278	144,500
Suits	995	22,300
Dresses	3,713	18,200
Skirts	3,805	14,000
Knit Shirts	47,640	78,200
Sweaters	15,737	54,600
Gloves	25,687	59,600
Other		66,400
TOTAL		711,300

The economic and social cost of this loss is enormous and there is little evidence to suggest that the consumer at large has benefitted, despite claims that import controls cost the consumer up to $27 billion per year[9] and that without imports, domestic producers would have no restraints on implementing price increases. However, apparel prices rose at only half the general Consumer Price Index for much of the period in which imports were growing rapidly, and this can be attributed more to the competitive nature of the domestic industry than to the presence of imports. The implementation of the new technology now coming on stream, will ensure that further cost containment is passed on to the consumer. It is

17

widely believed that imported products hold down price inflation, but this is not usually the case; regardless of cost, the retailer takes a higher markup on imports. Further, imports are increasingly taking the higher price-point markets and have a decreasing impact on basic goods.

Notes - Chapter 1.

1. The industry data used in this section are based on U.S. Dept. of Commerce and Census Bureau information.

2. Du Pont estimates.

3. Werner International, "Apparel Sourcing Analysis", 1985. This two volume study of the factors affecting apparel sourcing is an excellent country by country reference.

4. "The Textile And Apparel Trade Crisis", a study prepared for FFACT, Alan Wolff et. al., 1985. Figure 11.

Other good sources of information are, "The U.S. Textile and Apparel Industry - A Revolution in Progress", a Special Report published by the Office of Technology Assessment and "The Global Textile Industry, Toyne, Arpen et al, George Allen & Unwin, 1984.

5. "Liberal Protectionism: The International Politics Of Organized Textile Trade", Aggarwal, University of California Press, 1985 gives an excellent account of what actually took place during the 1981 MFA negotiations.

6. Wolff, Figure 14.

7. The Daily News Record does a good job of reporting infringements.

8. Study by A. Hunter for the MMFPA, Apparel Industry Magazine, April 1986.

Chapter 2. The Traditional Supply System.

The U.S. apparel supply system of today is extremely complex. It is characterized its unusual length - fiber to yarn, yarn to fabric, fabric to garments and retailing, with many specialist variations on each of the major components - and the enormous variety of end-products. At one end is a handful of large chemical companies; at the other, thousands of apparel manufacturers and retail outlets. The number of different fibers used in apparel is relatively small; the variety of garments enormous, being measured in the millions. The characteristics of the participants also vary widely; high capital intensity at the man-made fiber stage to high labor intensity for the apparel manufacturer. With such large numbers of players, it is not surprising that competition is intense and the financial performance of the industry overall is less than satisfactory when compared with all manufacturing.

Much of the complexity and many of the American industry's problems are of recent origin. Textile manufacture was the first of the industrialized commodities and, for much of its life, cloth was the end-product; the clothing was mainly home sewn. The 19th century saw the introduction of mass manufacture of basic garments which were distributed through much of the country via dry-goods stores. For both these industries, cost was of the utmost importance as most of the rapidly growing population had neither the time nor the money for fashionable clothing, most of which was imported from Europe. This emphasis on low cost basic goods dominated the business until recently and still influences much of the supply pattern.

Pipeline Inventories.

Each sector in the supply system has traditionally regarded itself as a separate business with its own strategies and, at best, thought of itself as a link in a chain of supply. With a heavy emphasis on manufacturing efficiency in a highly competitive industry and with a history of low interest rates on money borrowed for working capital, it is not surprising that management and operational patterns were developed which were at

19

odds with the rapid changes in the needs of the consumer in the 1950s and 1960s. This applies particularly to the emphasis on long manufacturing runs and substantial minimum order quantities which necessitate large raw material and finished goods inventories. Table 2.1 gives some idea of the length of the supply chain as it existed for most woven fabric apparel until very recently.

Table 2.1
Apparel Pipeline Inventories
And Work In Process
(Weeks)

	Inventory	WIP
Fiber		
Raw Material	1.6	
WIP		0.9
Finished Fiber @ Fiber	4.6	
Fiber @ Textile	1.0	--
	8.1	0.9
Fabric		
WIP - Greige		3.9
Greige Goods @ Greige	1.2	
Greige Goods @ Finish	1.4	
Finishing		1.2
Finished Fabric @ Textile	7.4	
Fabric @ Apparel	6.8	--
	16.8	5.1
Apparel		
WIP		5.0
Finished Apparel		
@ Apparel	12.0	
Ship To Retail	2.7	
Apparel @ Retail		
Distribution Center	6.3	
Apparel @ Store	10.0	--
	31.0	5.0
TOTALS	55.0	11.0

For apparel made from woven fabrics, the pipeline represented above is 66 weeks, and of that, only 11 weeks are taken up with processing; the balance of over one year is storage time. For knit goods the pipeline length is shorter - 6 to 7 months, including time in the store - because of processes that are faster, simpler and more flexible than those for wovens. But, even for knits, the time in inventory accounts for over 2/3 the pipeline length.

The term "work in process" is itself misleading. A large proportion of WIP time is, in fact, that spent by the product between process steps. It has been estimated that less than 1% of WIP time is spent on actual conversion of a product. Perhaps the best example of this is to be found in apparel manufacturing. Most companies use the progressive bundle method for moving cut parts through the plant as they are sewn into garments. Bundles of identical parts are tied together, moved around in carts and held until the sewing operator needs them. Following the specific sewing operation the parts are again tied into bundles for passing on to the next operator. The actual sewing time is measured in minutes; the total WIP time is measured in days or weeks as can be seen in Table 2.1.

The Table also shows the remarkable level of inventory duplication. Product is held by the supplier as finished goods and further large stocks are held by the customer as raw material. Why the latter? Because experience has taught the customer that he must cover his operations against late deliveries, a tight market, unacceptable quality etc.

The high levels of finished goods inventories maintained by the supplier have three components; batch, seasonal and safety stocks. Batch stocks are a function of the perceived economic order quantity or manufacturing run length. Changes in the run length policies of the organization or consolidations of process steps can have a sharp effect on batch stocks.

Apparel retailing is a seasonal business. Close to 40% of men's apparel is sold in the three months of June, November and December and half of that is bought in the Holiday season - see Figure 2.1. The purchase pattern for women's wear is similar, but less pronounced. These are average data; for specific garment types, e.g., fleece goods, the seasonality can be extreme. To meet this variable demand, producers must build stocks and then draw them down as customer activity increases. Such stocks can never be eliminated, but if modern flexible manufacturing techniques are applied to the increasing proportion of fashion goods, a levelling of seasonal inventories would result.

There are two kinds of safety stocks; external and internal. External safety stocks are dictated by the level of customer service desired by vendor and supplier and are functions of the accuracy of demand forecasts as well as the replenishment times. As customers come to demand higher and higher service levels, the challenge is to maintain these stocks at current levels through WIP reductions and closer liason with the merchandising and purchasing agencies of the customer.

Internal safety stocks are really an admission that all is not well with the manufacturing operation. They can be held because of poor quality, machine down-time for repairs or because of uncertainty over batch processing times. As manufacturing management skills improve, these stocks can be reduced with no adverse effect on the business.

Figure 2.1
Retail Sales by Month - Menswear

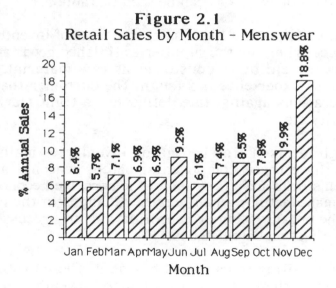

Month

During the past ten years or so, both the textile and apparel industries have achieved productivity gains substantially above the average for all manufacturing. To do this, the textile industry has invested new capital at a rate of over $1 billion per year; the apparel industry at $600-700 million per year. These investments have had a beneficial impact on the rate of product cost inflation, but at the expense of decreasing product line flexibility - longer runs of fewer products at a time when the public is asking for product diversity. It should be noted here that the high technology equipment in which the investments have been made have had little impact on global competitiveness. The newly developed economies of the Far East have also been quick to invest in new technology, without the need for the level of financial returns necessary in the U.S. But in their case, the low cost of labor has allowed them to retain the flexibility of older equipment.

The lack of progress in improving the fiber through apparel inventory situations, is demonstrated by Figure 2.2 which gives both average inventory in weeks and the number of times the inventory has turned in a year.

Figure 2.2

U.S. Fiber, Textile & Apparel
Finished Goods Inventories

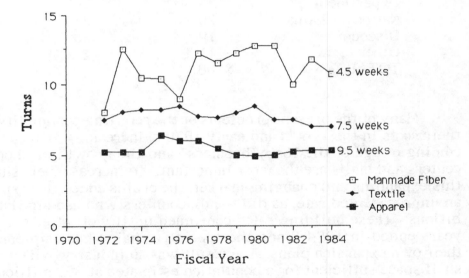

The Retail Scene.

Retail sales of apparel were about $100 billion in 1984 when many of the QR analyses were carried out. Today's equivalent figure is about $150 billion. These estimates relate to outerwear, underwear and nightwear; they do not include furnishings of one kind or another. Detailed data are not readily obtainable and, considering the complexity of the retailing operation, this is not surprising. The 1984 values used here are practical in that they equate % shares and dollars.

23

There are many types of retail store and no general agreement on terminology. The broad division used here - Department and Specialty Stores vs. Mass Merchants - divides the business into two roughly equal blocks. Table 2.2 gives a finer break-down and also shows the importance of apparel sales to the different types of store.

Table 2.2
Apparel Sales By Store Type

	Apparel Sales ($ Bill)	Apparel % of Total
Apparel Specialty	25	75
Department	25	66
National Chains	20	33
Discount	19	33
Other	11	--
TOTAL	$100	50

Many of the present problems of the retailing community have their roots in the 1960's and early 1970's; increasing affluence, the coming of age of the "baby boomers" and the growth of shopping centers and malls are the most important. To increase their share of this expanding and changing market, the chains added floor space at an unprecedented rate, as did the discounters who had similar ambitions. These building rates continued until well after the boom years ended in 1974-5 and the specialty chains had implemented their own expansion plans. The result was an industry-wide level of shelf space sufficient for a population estimated at 500 million and, thus, unsatisfactory profits per square foot - a basic measure of retailing performance.

This profit situation, together with the constant drive to take share from the department stores, increased the propensity to import lower cost but higher margin goods, drove the chains and the discounters to offer higher price point merchandise and led to increased use of sale pricing to maintain volume.

While this was going on, two other destabilizing factors increased in importance; the growth of fashion goods, with their

24

shorter shelf life, and the proliferation of both new brand names and private label business.

Retail Inventories.

Of prime concern to the retailer is the number of times the store inventory can be turned. Figures 2.3 and 2.4 show how both department stores and mass merchants have handled the problem.

Figure 2.3
Inventory Turns - Department Stores

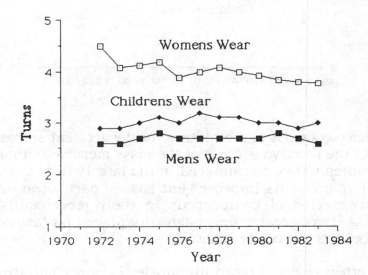

Clearly, department stores were slow to respond to the problems facing them in the 1980's. In women's wear, which accounts for over 60% of the sector's apparel sales, the position deteriorated over the 12 year period. Reduced profitability has often forced cutbacks in the level of customer service, which was one of the hallmarks of the department store, but such gains have been off-set by the increasing level of price markdowns. Being required to carry a wide variety of higher priced merchandise in times of relative fashion chaos also complicates their inventory management problems.

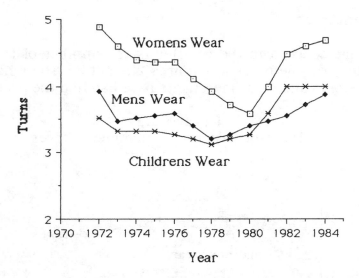

Figure 2.4
Inventory Turns – Mass Merchants

In sharp contrast to the picture for department stores, Figure 2.4 reflects the relative success of the mass merchants in overcoming the problems they encountered in the late 1970's, though there is still far to go. This improvement has, in part, been due to the greater proportion of basic goods in their merchandise lines. Maintaining it, as greater dependence is placed on fashion goods, will call for strong inventory control.

One other aspect of retail inventories is important; their cyclicality. The high proportion of a year's retail sales which occurs during the Holiday season and, to a lesser extent, at mid-year, requires large build-ups in stocks. The patterns of inventories for retail establishments is shown in Figure 2.5, where they are compared with the relatively constant level that characterizes the textile mills.

This cyclicality has two important aspects. First, the pattern means that control is inherently more difficult. The second aspect centers around the unpredictability of sales. Should demand be less than was planned for, the surplus is difficult to move unless prices are sharply reduced and/or future deliveries are cut back. In the former case profits suffer; in the latter there is a severe impact on the suppliers which increases in magnitude as the impact is felt further upstream. Thus, a relatively small reduction in retailer orders can have a significant impact on textile mills and an even greater one on their fiber suppliers.

Figure 2.5
Pipeline Inventories

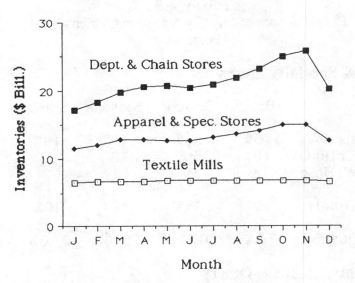

Retail Product Seasonality & Markdowns.

Several times already, the influence of fashion on retailer operations has been mentioned. As this aspect of the pipeline is central to the development of a QR methodology, a number of terms will be defined more closely.

By seasonality is meant the normal shelf life of a product. Basic goods have a year-round life i.e. one season. Apparel items which can be differentiated by the weather patterns - Spring, Summer, Winter - are referred to as "seasonal" goods and have a shelf life of 2-3 seasons. Fashion garments have shorter shelf lives and are classified as either 4-6 seasons or 7+ seasons (High Fashion). Designers have led the way in increasing the seasonality of their goods and the department stores have given them strong support as a steady flow of new merchandise onto the shelves attracts customers and strengthens their fashion image.

Markdowns are reductions from first price, or sale prices, expressed as a percentage of first price.

27

Table 2.3 gives a break-down of the seasonality of apparel by major category for the two broad groups of retail outlet. More detail, including estimates of inventory turns, is shown in Appendix A. Estimates of markdowns are also included in the Table.

Table 2.3
Retail Apparel Mix By Number Of Seasons
(Percent)

Department & Specialty Stores

		Basic	2-3 Seasons	4-6 Seasons	7+ Seasons	Total
% Total						
48%	Women's OW	5%	36%	45%	14%	100%
35%	Men's/Child OW	10	50	30	10	100
17%	UW, NW, Hose	78	19	1	2	100
	Weighted Total	19%	38%	32%	10%	100%
	Est. Markdowns	7.5%	20.5%	26.0%	27.0%	20.1%

Mass Merchants, Chains & Others

		Basic	2-3 Seasons	4-6 Seasons	7+ Seasons	Total
34%	Women's OW	7%	58%	30%	5%	100%
48%	Men's/Child OW	15	62	20	3	100
18%	UW, NW, Hose	85	13	1	1	100
	Weighted Total	25%	52%	20%	3%	100%
	Est. Markdowns	5.0%	13.0%	19.0%	22.0%	12.1%

Total Retail

	Basic	2-3 Seasons	4-6 Seasons	7+ Seasons	Total
Est. Markdowns	6.0%	16.7%	23.6%	28.0%	16.1%

The above are 1983-4 data and the markdown estimates are, no doubt, now understated. The pattern over time for the department stores has been one of a steady increase for all merchandise categories - see Figure 2.6 - and has reached the point where prices, as first posted, have little validity.

Figure 2.6
Markdowns As % Sales
<u>Department Stores</u>

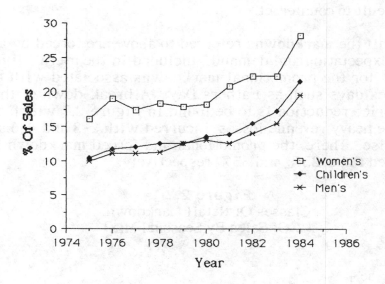

<u>Mass Merchants</u>

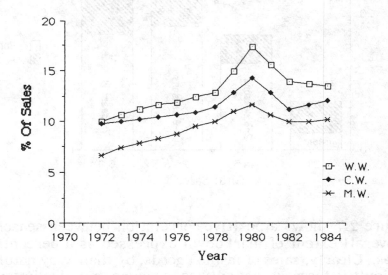

The situation with the mass merchants is more satisfactory. As was the case with inventory turns, the situation was brought under greater control early in the 1980's. Again, though, as the reliance on basic goods decreases, the markdown syndrome will be more difficult to counteract.

Not all the markdowns referred to above are forced by a mismatch of expectation and demand. Included in the overall figure of 16% is 6% for the promotional markdowns associated with traditional sales days such as Fathers Day. A break-down of the two types of price reduction is to be found in Figure 2.7 which shows clearly the heavy revenue losses incurred with 2-3 and 4-6 season merchandise. There, the promotional and forced markdown levels are assumed to be 25% and 35% respectively.

Figure 2.7
Classes Of Retail Markdown
(% Of Sales By Seasonal Mix)

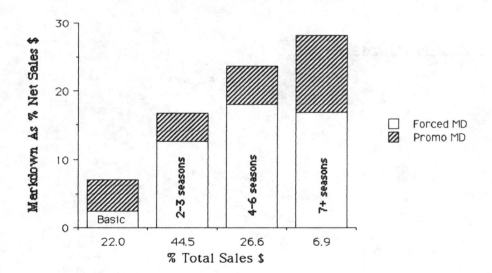

Figure 2.7 shows a positive correlation between seasonality and the overall extent of markdown expressed as a percentage of retail sales. Clearly, sales of fashion goods, by their very nature, are more difficult to forecast, not only as to voume, but also in terms of the mix of styles and colors. The somewhat lower sensitivity of High Fashion goods to forced markdowns, when compared with 4-6

30

season garments, is a reflection of the better grasp of fashion trends and tighter control of distribution.

At this point one other retailing problem should be introduced. This is the "stock-out", which occurs when the store runs out of a particular Stock Keeping Unit (SKU), be it in size, color or style, as a result of innaccurate buyer forecasts. Their impact on the store's business is not well understood, and only rough estimates have been made of the revenues lost because of them. Their frequency increases with markdowns and they contribute both to potential customers leaving the store empty handed throughout most of the season and to the "white elephant" character of end-of-season sales.

Summary Of Pipeline Revenue Losses.

The shortcomings of the traditional apparel pipeline discussed in this chapter are by no means exhaustive. The ones that were chosen have a common property; they can be quantified. Table 2.4 gives the revenue loss equivalents of the excessive inventories, the stock-outs and the forced markdowns for each of the major sectors in the pipeline. They add up to 25% of retail sales, most of which occurs at the retail and manufacturer levels.

Table 2.4
Revenue Losses In The Apparel Pipeline
(% Retail Sales)

	Fiber & Textile	Apparel	Retail	Total
Forced Mkdns	0.6%	4.0%	10.0%	14.6%
Stock-Outs	0.1	0.4	3.5	4.0
Inventory @ 15% Carrying Cost	1.0	2.5	2.9	6.4
Total	1.7%	6.9%	16.4%	25.0%

Clearly, no manufacturing system can exist without inventories and forecasting consumer demand is notoriously difficult. Of the 25%, then, some part will always remain, no matter how efficient the system becomes. One of the objectives of the book is to demon-strate that it is possible to improve systems revenues by up to half of this amount by changing the way the apparel business is con-ducted.

Key to this change is making the manufacturing process more responsive to consumer demands by shortening the pipeline and moving the retailer buying process closer to the season for which the garments are intended. Adopting these changes will not only improve the financial performance of the industry, but will also make it more competitive with imports.

Notes - Chapter 2.

Much of the information used in this chapter is to be found in the usual U.S. Department of Commerce publications. The inven-tory data come from the Bureau of Census.

The information on categories of apparel and their markdowns is based on NRMA statistics and market research panel data anal-ysed by KSA.

There is a great need for more research into apparel retail trends. Data are difficult to obtain and there are consistency prob-lems, but the rewards would be considerable, especially in view of the rapid changes in the average seasonality of garments. Point-Of-Sale tracking by SKU, when it is in general use, will provide the op-portunity for this type of analysis.

Chapter 3. Industry Initiatives.

Given the problems facing the textile and apparel industries, the next step is to answer the question, "What did the industry do about them?"

The soft goods industry is made up of many trade associations, some of them large and generic, e.g., the American Textile Manufacturers Institute (ATMI), and the American Apparel Manufacturers Association (AAMA), the others specializing in one or another market or production sector. Traditionally the trade organizations had little to do with each other except when a government action or proposal required a joining of forces. As imports to Europe and then the U.S. started to increase in the late 1970s and early 1980s, however, several cross-industry programs were developed. The purpose of this chapter is to examine the most important of these initiatives and to show how the industry has developed unified approaches to R&D, Marketing and political activity, all aimed at making the U.S. industry more globally competitive.

Textile/Clothing Technology Corporation – (TC)^2

In 1979, a joint study by Fred Abernathy, the former director of engineering and head of energy research at the National Science Foundation and John Dunlop, a former Labor Secretary, recommended that, because of its labor intensity, the apparel industry should explore the use of automated manufacturing. Acting on this recommendation, in 1980, Hartmarx, Burlington and du Pont founded (TC)^2, with the automation of tailored clothing as its first priority. A contract was let to the Draper Laboratories, an advanced technology spin-off from MIT, to design equipment capable of making a man's jacket sleeve without operator assistance. The choice of a sleeve was deliberate – if the machine could perform that operation, it could do almost anything in the way of clothing manufacture. A draw-back to the choice was that most of the U.S. garment industry is concerned with "apparel" or non-tailored products and this group was slow to join the corporation. However, by 1985, membership included most of the fiber producers and large textile companies and several of the larger apparel companies. With the help of matching Department Of Commerce funds, the project has continued to make progress and its present position will be discussed in a later chapter.

$(TC)^2$ undertook its second major project in 1988, with the opening of a demonstration center for state-of-the-art garment manufacture.

In 1987, the AAMA formed an alliance with $(TC)^2$, whereby the technical leadership of AAMA will participate in the operation of the Corporation, will recommend projects for its consideration and will urge the AAMA members to join $(TC)^2$. Past experience suggests that the sign-up queue will be short. With a few exceptions, the apparel companies are small when compared with members of the other industry sectors. Little of their research is either fundamental or long-term in outlook and the majority of companies have no R&D budget. It is devoutly to be hoped, however, that every advantage will be taken by the AAMA membership to share in the cost of developing the new technology that will help them to survive.

$(TC)^2$ has its equivalents in both the EC (the BRITE Program) and in Japan (the MITI Project). These programs, both of which are extremely well funded, and $(TC)^2$ will be discussed, in terms of their technology content, later in the book

The Fiber, Fabric & Apparel Coalition for Trade - FFACT.

The second industry joint venture was the formation in 1985 of a lobby group - FFACT. FFACT has proved to be extremely effective in monitoring and disseminating trade information and in generating Congressional support for new trade legislation. The Presidential veto of The Textile & Apparel Trade Reform Bill of 1985 passed both houses in 1986, but was vetoed by the President and Congress allowed the veto to stand. In 1987 a second bill, The Textile & Apparel Trade Act was successfully introduced but again fell to a Presidential veto late in 1988.

The only unfortunate side-effect of FFACT was that it encouraged the formation of an opposing group, the Retail Industry Trade Action Coalition (RITAC), a coalition of retailers and importers, that undertook a strong lobby action of its own based on the premise that imported apparel offers substantial savings to the consumer. As was noted earlier, there is very little practical evidence to support this point of view. Analyses of mail order catalogs and retail store surveys both suggest the principal advantage to the retailer of importing medium to high price apparel is that of allowing higher markons.

Crafted With Pride In U.S.A. Council Inc. - CWP.

In the Spring of 1984, under the strong leadership of Roger Milliken, an association was formed to handle the marketing needs of the industry. Its Mission Statement was:

> "The Crafted With Pride In U.S.A. Council, Inc. is a committed force of U.S. cotton growers, labor organizations, fabric distributors and manufacturers of man-made fibers, fabric, apparel and home fashions whose mission is to convince consumers, retailers and apparel manufacturers of the value of purchasing and promoting U.S. made products."

With a rapidly growing membership, CWP undertook extensive market research to learn more of consumer attitudes to domestic and imported apparel and to decide on the most effective way of affecting purchasing decisions. The resulting advertising and PR campaigns, which were launched late in 1985, are widely recognised as models of their kind and did much for the morale of the industry. Dozens of smaller groups with related regional and special interests sprung up, including the well publicized America For Kids organization. CWP programs are discussed here, however, only to the extent that they impact QR methodology.

Under the direction of what is now called the Competitiveness Committee, an early focus of CWP research was to determine the true cost to the retailer of importing garments. This is not a trivial problem and some explanation of retailer costing practices is necessary for an understanding of its importance.

Until very recently it has not been possible for a retailer to keep track of either the costs or the profitabilities of individual Stock Keeping Units (SKUs). A large store can offer literally thousands of apparel SKUs, which differentiate between different sizes, colors and styles. Before the advent of low cost computers and computerized point-of-sale (POS) tracking systems, the only available financial measures of a buyer's performance were the Gross Margin (sales value at first price less cost of goods) and the Gross Margin Return On Inventory (GMROI). Many of the cost items required to calculate a Net Margin; discounts, markdowns, promotions, operating costs, cost of inventory, etc., were allocated and among these were most of the costs of importing - the so called "hidden" costs. This is still the case for all but a handful of large retailers, though the adoption of detailed, on-line stock-keeping is picking up speed as bar coding of apparel, similar to that used for groceries, is implemented.

The first serious study of the full cost of importing was carried out early in 1984 by The Nathan Katz Company on behalf of the National Knitwear and Sportswear Association and was limited to womens sweaters. The study involved 73 retailers, and found that, despite larger markons for imports - 61% vs. 52% - the median gross margin was only 4% larger than for domestic sweaters because of less favorable discount terms, greater markdowns and other price adjustments. Off-setting this gross margin advantage were operating and merchandising costs that were substantially higher for imports than for domestic goods. The major components of such costs were as follows:

- Inventory turns (sales divided by average inventories) significantly lower for imports, with stocks being held an average of 5-6 weeks longer.

- Imports financed for about 15 weeks longer than domestic goods because of Letter of Credit (LC) payment and longer shipping and storage times. An LC is the standard way of guaranteeing payment for contracted off-shore services. The buyer's funds are frozen until shipment of the goods, thus losing interest, and there is also a processing fee.

- Sales limitations because of the difficulty in adjusting the open-to-buy mix to meet changing fashion and the reduced ability to reorder goods. Open-to-buy is the timing of purchases by the retail buyer. Not only do off-shore OTB's come earlier than the domestic equivalent, but there is little chance of ammending the volume or product mix, as can happen, partially, with domestic suppliers.

• None of the co-op advertising allowances that are frequently made by domestic vendors exist for imports.

• Foreign travel costs.

• Import processing and merchandising services such as brokerage fees.

• Additional handling and processing associated with opening and refurbishing garments that have been in transit for many weeks. The impact of these hidden costs was to reduce the higher apparent profitability of imported sweaters to around the same level as that of domestic goods.

Clearly, it was important to the CWP effort to verify the above results, to extend the analysis to a wider range of garments and to present the findings to the retail community. The analysis was carried out by the Boston Consulting Group who reported the results in the Spring of 1985.

Boston Consulting Group Studies.

BCG analysed the total system costs of importing vs. domestic sourcing for six specific garments. To remove the impact of fashion and design, the following simple, low cost garments were selected. The retail first prices are shown in parentheses. A man's sport shirt ($17), a woman's blouse ($24) and a woman's skirt ($19) had relatively short selling seasons, around 2-3 months of retail shelf life. The remaining three garments had shelf lives of 6 or more months - a man's casual slack ($18), a man's dress slack ($28) and a woman's slack ($22). Table 3.1 shows the Planned Gross Margins for the garments on an imported and a domestic basis.

The first step taken by the BCG was to determine the Realized, as opposed to the Planned Gross Margin. The longer order lead times associated with imported merchandise decrease the accuracy of the buyer's sales forecast and the result is either greater forced markdowns, in the case of over-supply, or substitution of lower margin goods, should supplies run out.

Table 3.1
Planned Gross Margins By Garment & Source
(Percent)

Garment	Domestic	F. East	Difference
Men's			
Shirt	43	67	(24)
Casual Pant	48	53	(5)
Dress Slack	54	61	(7)
Women's			
Skirt	50	54	(4)
Blouse	52	62	(10)
Pant	50	56	(6)

The impact of these markdowns were found to vary with the seasonality of the garments and, as expected, womenswear was marked down more than men's garments. In terms of reduction of gross margin, the import advantage - the right hand column in Table 3.1 above - decreased by 1-4%, with the woman's blouse and skirt changing 4% and the other garments 1% (see Table 3.2).

Several importing costs are normally included in the gross margin calculation on an allocated basis; agency fees, shipping duties and tariffs and buying office expenses are the major items handled in this way. Other costs, not normally allocated to specific garment types, were found to be similar to those identified in the Katz study of sweater imports and were carefully quantified:

• Additional warehousing for an extra month; 5¢ to move garments in, 5¢ to move garments out; space costs of 2-7¢ per garment per month, depending on the garment type, slacks being the most expensive. The extra storage added 14-17¢ to the cost of imports. When importing, retailers would rather err on the side of goods arriving too early rather than late.

• Inventory carried for an additional 3 months - 2 months for shipping and 1 month for the warehousing discussed above - at 1.2% of landed cost per month prior to store floor - an importing cost of 15-37¢.

• Re-separation and refurbishing costs of 3-5¢ per garment greater for imports than for domestically produced goods. Not all garments need refurbishing, but the probability of imports requiring attention is twice that of domestic goods, in part because of the greater use of hang-packing by domestic manufacturers.

• The greater cost of travelling to the Orient compared with domestic buying trips was estimated to add an additional 4¢ per garment. In calculating this figure, it was assumed that two people would visit the Far East twice per year for 21 days each trip - a cost of $16,000 - in order to buy 20,000 dozen garments. In contrast, domestic sourcing of 40,000 dozen garments was calculated to cost $13,000 (8x3 day trips to New York).

• De-consolidation of imported garment lines at the retail distribution center costs an additional 4¢ per garment.

The total of these "hidden" costs amounted to between 40¢ and 67¢ per garment, depending on the type. The impacts of both the forced markdowns and the unallocated logistics costs listed above, on the planned Gross Margin differences are shown in Table 3.2. This Table is an extension of Table 3.1. It takes the right hand column - the import advantage - and reduces the values by the "hidden" costs just discussed. The right hand column of Table 3.2 shows the effect of cost reductions readily obtainable to the domestic producer through the application of a minimum of plant engineering and technology. These reductions are discussed in greater depth later in the book.

The results supported and extended the Katz findings for sweaters by demonstrating that when full costs are applied to several important classes of imported apparel, the apparent large margin advantages of imports are significantly reduced, some to the point where they do not justify the risks associated with importing. In addition, the preliminary BCG estimates of potential improvements in domestic manufacturing costs agreed well with earlier work by du Pont and a number of industry consultants and prompted more detailed analyses of the impact of new technologies on apparel costs. Finally, by relating order lead time to buyer forecast error, the door was opened to later work on re-order response times and the potential for supply system savings. In other words, the stage was set for the development of QR methodology.

Table 3.2
Realized Gross Margins
Domestic vs. Imports
(Percent Difference)

Garment	Planned	After Markdown	After Logistics	With Improved Costs
Man's				
Shirt	(24)	(23)	(20)	(16)
Casual Pant	(5)	(5)	(1)	5
Dress Slack	(7)	(6)	(4)	-
Woman's				
Skirt	(4)	-	(2)	7
Blouse	(10)	(6)	(3)	6
Pant	(6)	(5)	(2)	3

Notes – Chapter 3.

"Retailers' Profit and Performance on Imported vs. Domestic Sweaters" was prepared by Nathan Katz and Co. for the National Knitwear and Sportswear Association.

"Analysis of Garment Sourcing Economics" was prepared by the Boston Consulting Group for Crafted With Pride In U.S.A. Inc., May 1985.

PART II
THE QUICK RESPONSE PROCESS

Chapter 4. Collapsing The Pipeline

The first aspect of QR to consider is the shortening of the traditional pipeline by eliminating unnecessary inventories and Work In Process (WIP) times. Other components will be discussed in later chapters. Among these are the new technologies that allow further collapsing of the traditional supply timetables.

Table 2.1 showed a rough break-down of the inventories and WIP for the major industry sectors. These were average data and for any given product, process or company, the numbers are different. The method used by the Crafted With Pride analysts was to break the pipeline down into approximately 40 pieces and then to question sample groups of appropriate industry managers as to what was standard and what was possible. Kurt Salmon Associates then applied their own background knowledge to develop industry averages. Feed-back of the final estimates to industry revealed very little disagreement with those used here. It should be noted that the practices of the major companies have changed substantially since the analysis was undertaken; for them, the pipeline has already been reduced. However, the picture presented here still holds for much of the business.

Inventory Reduction.

A firm committment to change by top management is the single most important step to be taken by any company intent on introducing new procedures, operating philosophies or strategies. Objectives can be clearly stated, technology provided and methodologies made available, but little will happen until the senior managers insist on and fully support the changes. Learning to operate with significantly lower stocks of raw materials and finished goods is no simple matter because so many new disciplines must permeate the organization.

In its broadest sense, all the component companies forming the supply system should have a common objective; to operate as a single factory by reducing the randomness of material flows.

The obvious point of attack on inventories is duplicate stocks, i.e., finished goods held by the supplier and raw materials held by the customer. There are two parts to the problem; how to manufacture in a more flexible manner so as to get rid of the inventories associated with long runs of individual products and how to persuade the customer that he need not hold safety stocks, i.e. to adopt a Just In Time (JIT) supplier relationship.

It is frequently the case that complex equipment and systems are developed with insufficient thought on how to do what is needed at the right time without error. The objective should be to eliminate unnecessary activity and complexity. Material should be moved as directly as possible from its existing state to its finished state so that every move adds value to it. This is the basic precept of industrial engineering, but traditional methods often obscure it. In aiming for minimum stock levels, operations must be examined in detail with the objective of eliminating:

• Wasted time. Nothing sits longer than is absolutely necessary.

• Wasted energy. Equipment is operated only for productive purposes.

• Wasted material. All raw material is converted to useful product. A very simple, back-of-the-envelope calculation of the effect on profits of a single point gain in first quality production is all the persuasion anyone needs.

• Errors. No rework and no repeating of tasks.

The same messages can be expressed in positive terms:

• Produce products the customer wants.

• Produce only at the rate the customer wants. This means producing to order and not to inventory; pretending there is no warehouse.

- Produce only goods that meet specification.

- Produce with no unnecessary lead time.

- Produce with no waste of labor, materials or equipment.

A frequently used analogy is that of water flowing in a stream. Before clearing the stream, water (material) is flowing but much of it is sitting in deep pools (inventory) at the bottom. Once the channel has been cleared (industrially engineered), the bottom is clearly seen throughout its length. The total volume of flow is the same, but all the water is moving at the same speed.

Techniques have been developed to help achieve these improvements - Operations Research for queueing and optimization, MRP, Kanban, MRP II, etc. - and Japanese companies claim that their application has made a significant contribution to business success. The last of these techniques, Manufacturing Resource Planning (MRP II) is relatively new on the manufacturing scene and is a much broader in scope than Materials Requirement Planning (MRP).

MRP II dictates that all the elements of planning - business, sales and production - be balanced simultaneously in a closed loop system. The key is a Master Schedule used to develop a long term manufacturing plan that takes into account product families, sales forecasts, actual orders, plant capacity, delivery schedules, etc. MRP itself is one component of the process. As new information is fed into the system, the whole Master Schedule changes; it is flexible.

Quality Management.

Application of Industrial Engineering principles and techniques has been successful, but is often limited to manufacturing operations. To achieve an all-embracing change in corporate culture, a broader based philosophy is needed and none has been more successful than the Quality Management methodology first developed by Deming and marketed as a structured program by Philip Crosby. Several of the leading fiber and textile producers have adopted the program and adapted it to their own environment. Adoption is time and energy consuming, but the results are well worth the effort. Crosby estimates that the cost of quality in most corporations amounts to as much as 20% of sales dollars and half this amount can be transferred to earnings. Industry experience supports this estimate.

The Quality Management philosophy of a corporation is simple to express and the following, formulated by Celanese Corp. in the early 1980s, is a good example:

"Celanese will deliver to its customers products and services that conform exactly to requirements.

This requires that we design our manufacturing, marketing, technical and administrative processes to prevent deviations and that we perform all operating and staff functions right the first time."

The techniques and mechanics of the Quality process include Statistical Quality Control, systematic Error Cause Removal procedures, formal Problem Solving training, Interruption Free Processing and, above all, a Zero Defect mentality at every level in the organization. Once adopted, Quality Management is, of necessity, accompanied by a change to a more participative management style, an increase in employee involvement and a marked improvement in employee morale.

The external objective of the process is to operate with suppliers and customers through partnership programs which set up agreed on product specifications and allow certification of the product. Certification is at the heart of QR; it means the following:

• Quality is the responsibility of the supplier.

• Incoming products meet agreed upon specifications.

• Incoming inspection is eliminated.

• No production delays due to substandard materials.

• Cushion inventories eliminated.

• Buyer-seller relationships of full confidence and trust.

• Integrated production planning, including free exchange of plans and consumption and inventory data.

Milliken and Company was an early exponent of Quality Management and it is now the dominant theme in their business style. The company has quantified the savings to its customers of implementing product certification, i.e. guaranteeing that the customer's specifications are rigidly adhered to. They are shown in Table 4.1.

To a customer using a million yards of fabric per year, certification can increase profits by up to $200,000 and at the same time, contribute to the contraction of the pipeline.

Table 4.1
Cost Reduction At The Textile/Apparel Interface.
($ Per Yard Of Fabric)

	$/Yd.
Greater width utilization - 2% of fabric	0.0500
Discontinue fabric inspection at apparel	0.0400
Discontinue color/shade control testing	0.0800
Provision of longer roll lengths	0.0195
Reduced fabric inventory at apparel	0.0125
TOTAL	0.2020

The importance of Quality Management is paramount. In one sense, QR is an off-shoot of QM; certainly the former is impossible without the latter. When, in later chapters, the financial implications of QR are discussed, it should be remembered that they are understated; they exclude the improvements in a company's profit performance resulting from the adoption of QM.

The next sections will quantify, by sector, the inventory and WIP reductions believed to be achievable through application of Quality Management procedures (or a reasonable facsimile), currently available technology, and free and rapid exchange of information between partners.

Man-Made Fiber Producers.

The reductions in inventories that can be achieved by the fiber producer are shown in Table 4.2, with more detail provided in Appendix B. Two sets of improvements are displayed; Quick and Very Quick. The former come from application of the techniques outlined earlier and which lead to certification of product by the customer. The second level calls for very close ties with the raw material suppliers and for both technical and human resources innovation.

As with textile inventory reductions, a major contribution is made by cutting back on the times taken to change over equipment from one product to another. These "down times" have in the past limited plant flexibilty and it is only in recent years that attention is being paid to the profit improvement and increase in customer satisfaction inherent in rapid change-overs.

The second kind of innovation, which applies to management of the work force is associated with plant flexibility. In an industry that is seasonal, and if production is to order and not to inventory, work loads can vary significantly. Cross training and flexible staffing both contribute to optimal operations.

Table 4.2
Man-Made Fiber Inventories
(Working Weeks)

	Trad.	Quick	Potential Very Quick
Raw Materials	1.6	1.0	0.2
WIP	0.9	0.7	0.6
Finished Fiber @ Fiber.	4.6	3.1	1.3
Finished Fiber @ Text.	1.0	0.5	0.2
TOTAL	8.1	5.3	2.2

The inventory levels above are average values; variations will occur depending on such things as the package or put-up, e.g beams versus cheeses, or the ageing time for a product to stabilize physically. But, these variations are small compared with the reductions that can be achieved.

Textile Mills.

The biggest reductions in textile inventories come from avoidance of duplicate stocks of finished fabric at the apparel customer's plant. Table 4.3 shows there is the potential for as much as a 2/3 reduction if duplicate testing and JIT shipping are combined with highly engineered, well planned and flexible manufacturing operations.

The essential ingredient in reducing duplicate stocks is information. Electronic order and invoicing procedures, shipping status, defect mapping and width and shade data are crucial, as is the playback of the finished apparel sales information. This last is of critical importance for the correct scheduling of both greige manufacture and finishing operations.

The data in Table 4.3 refer to woven fabrics, of which there is a large variety. Specific fabric types each have their own characteristics and Appendix B provides data for both a spun poplin and a textured polyester pongee.

Table 4.3
Textile Fabric Inventories
(Working Weeks)

	Trad.	Quick	Potential Very Quick
WIP Greige	3.9	2.7	2.0
Greige @ Greige	1.2	1.0	0.8
Greige @ Finishing	1.4	1.2	0.8
WIP Finish	1.2	1.0	0.8
Fin. Fabric @ Textile	7.5	5.0	2.5
Fin. Fabric @ Apparel	6.8	3.4	0.5
TOTAL	22.0	14.3	7.4

Knit goods have not yet been analysed in the same detail as wovens. Knitting is inherently faster than weaving and flexibility is greater because of shorter down-times and computer patterning. Off-setting this advantage, however, is the high level of seasonality of much knit apparel, e.g. fleece wear.

There are other problems. Late in 1985, at the request of the Knitted Textiles Association, representatives of the knit pipeline, from fiber through retail, answered a questionaire designed to high-light the QR issues facing them. The purely qualitative results re-vealed the lack of new products, the low level of supplier/customer dialogue and the absence of both Electronic Data Interchange (EDI) and cooperative planning. In general, each supplier had a higher opinion of his performance than his customer found realistic.

Apparel & Retail Inventories

A glance at the data in Table 4.4 shows even greater potential for inventory reductions at the manufacturer/retailer interface than was the case for textile products.

The technology of garment manufacture, both hard and soft, has made tremendous advances in the last ten or so years, and it is this change which makes possible much of the inventory reduction shown below.

Table 4.4
Apparel & Retail Inventories
(Working Weeks)

	Trad.	Quick	Potential Very Quick
Post Cut WIP	5.0	2.5	1.0
Fin. App. @ Apparel	12.0	11.1	1.0
Transport To Retail	2.7	1.4	1.0
App. @ Retail Distrib. Center	6.3	1.1	--
App. @ Ret. Store	10.0	10.0	8.0
TOTAL	36.0	26.1	11.0

By using sophisticated Unit Production Systems (UPS), mod-ular manufacturing, optimal sub-assembly operations, highly engi-neered traditional manufacturing flow systems with "intelligent" sewing machines and computer shop floor controls, what used to take weeks now requires days or hours to manufacture. The types of equipment and software available will be discussed in more de-tail later in the book. As is so often the case, however, the problem is not one of technology availability, but of the management attitude to technology investment and implementation. With these greatly reduced manufacturing times, it becomes possible to make more to order and less to stock, thus taking up to 11 weeks out of finished goods inventory.

Another contribution comes from retail ticketing by the manufacturer - a simple procedure - replacing a time and labor consuming operation by the retailer at the warehouse. Pre-ticketing not only reduces system costs by 12-13¢ per garment, it allows merchandise to be drop-shipped at the store, thus by-passing the retail distribution center entirely.

Logistics.

The traditional shipping times, manufacturer to retailer, are noteworthy. The extraordinary time of 2.7 weeks found in Table 4.4 is a carry-over from the days of basic merchandise and low interest rates, when the shipping cost was the only criterion. Today, delivery can be made anywhere in the U.S. inside of three days. There is an additional charge for this kind of service, but it is more than off-set by the saving in time. In the traditional system, the time taken from fabric leaving a finishing plant to its arrival at the manufacturing plant, plus the shipping time to retail and through distribution to the sales floor can amount to 50-55 days. A QR system can shorten this logistics time to 15-30 days while cutting $0.40-0.60 per unit from the system cost.

The times and costs involved in the movement of fabrics and garments, from the receipt of an order at the fabric finishing mill until the garment reaches the store, are shown in Appendix C. They apply to ladies blouses sold through a department store. Other items and types of store each have their own characteristic times and cost, but the differences do not affect the end result to any significant extent. The data are arranged to show various logistics options open to the manufacturer, who is assumed to have a separate, centralized cutting plant. The principal message contained in Appendix C is that by rethinking the whole transportation problem, it is possible to reduce costs very significantly.

Inventory Summary.

When all the potential inventory and WIP reductions are added together, the picture looks like Figure 4.1.

Figure 4.1
Fiber, Fabric, Apparel & Retail Inventories
(Working Weeks)

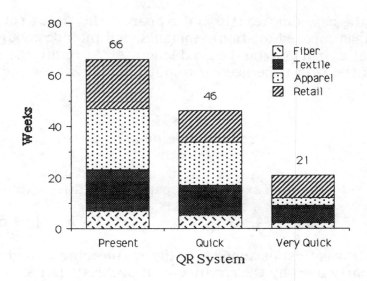

From the traditional pipeline length of 66 weeks, it is possible to go to 46 weeks using Quality Management and Industrial Engineering techniques. The further step, to 21 weeks, is more difficult. It involves the full use of available technology, rapid and open information exchange up and down the pipeline and close, trusting partnerships between suppliers and customers. It also involves substantial investment by the retailer and his suppliers in EDI and bar coding equipment as well as in point-of-sale tracking at the Stock Keeping Unit (SKU) level, so that the buyers, vendors and their suppliers can be kept informed of "real" consumer demand.

Product Development.

One other and vital part of the QR system is the use of more rapid and accurate techniques for the development of new products. Table 4.5 gives an indication of typical development times for each of the industry sectors before the use of Computer Assisted Design (CAD) softwear. As was the case for inventories, the incompatibility of the short shelf life of fashion products and these development times is clear.

51

The time span for Fibers covers the range from simple modification of existing products to the development of totally new fibers Examples of these might be a change of luster and, say, a new cross-section or dye variant fiber, respectively.

In the cases of Textile and Apparel, the times refer to new products, as opposed to simple variants, and include enough experience to get a firm grip on the product costs. At retail, the 5-7 month figure is the lead time needed to put together a new merchandise plan.

Table 4.5
New Product Development Times
(Months)

Fiber	Textile	Apparel	Retail	Total
3 - 50	4 - 5	6 - 7	5 - 7	18 - 69

CAD was first developed for the engineering draughtsman and subsequently used by the architectural profession. Its use in fabric design became possible when sophisticated high resolution color monitors were made available. In a recent development, spun yarns can be built up from colored fiber images and the desired twist inserted on-screen. CAD systems tailored to both woven and knit, plain and novelty fabrics are available and the finished designs can be printed out in very high resolution, simulating the surface texture.

The transition to garment design was slower for the very good reason that the problems facing the programmer were much more compex than in any other field. The depiction of garments in two dimensions presents few difficulties - it is the building up of a three dimensional image, the rotation of the image with the depiction of the correct drape and fabric folding and then the translation of a three dimensional image to the subtly curved pieces of fabric in a two dimensional pattern that have taken the time. The technology is still under development, but has made enormous strides in the past 3-4 years.

The major CAD systems available to the industry will be discussed in a later chapter, but three aspects of the technology have important effects on QR:

• First, the speed with which new designs can be developed has been cut from weeks or days to hours.

• Many of the commercially available CAD units are linked to Computer Assisted Manufacturing systems - CAD/CAM. In this way the translation of an on-screen design to knitting, weaving, pattern and marker making and cutting is simple and rapid. Further, this exact knowledge of the location, shape and orientation of each cut piece, will one day contribute to automation of the cutting and sewing operations.

• The third important aspect of CAD is that it not only allows vendor/customer design interaction, it positively encourages joint efforts. It takes so little time to modify a design that the direct input of the buyer becomes possible and desirable.

Style Testing.

Another string to the designer's bow has recently become available. This is Style Testing. When a group of consumers with similar socio-economic backgrounds is shown, say, a variety of styles and/or colors of blouse, there is a high level of agreement on the preferred garments. Further, the expressed preference is found to hold at retail check-out. The research is usually carried out in shopping malls and is quickly done once the target customer has been defined.

Style Testing allows an early screening of design alternatives and concentration on the preferred garments. These are precisely the needs of the fashion markets with their short shelf life and relative unpredictability of demand. Reorder has limited value for this class of merchandise and Style Testing has a great deal to offer. The opportunities for simplifying manufacturing schedules, compacting the range of offerings and increasing the accuracy of the merchandise plan are obvious but, to date, the industry has been slow to take advantage of them.

Style Testing was developed by Cambridge Opinion Associates using sample garments. The possibility of using CAD print-outs in place of garments is now being explored and early indications are encouraging. One sector of the industry for which this approach should have a strong appeal is the mail-order catalog houses, whose targeted customers make choices entirely based on photographs. A further simplication would be to test artist's sketches such as those produced for fashion forecasts 15 or so months ahead of a season. A preliminary investigation into this technique has been carried out at NCSU and the results are promising. If confirmed, the whole product development schedule could be drastically reduced.

From the view-point of the apparel manufacturer, CAD and Style Testing, together with inventory and WIP reductions, allow the apparel calendar to be moved closer to the season by several months. The major changes can be summarised as follows:

- Concept of line - 3 months later.

    - Benefit of current style trends.
    - Use of Style Testing.
    - Better fabric shopping.

- Samples designed using CAD - 4 months later.

    - Sample garments not produced until the line is firmed.

- Order sample fabric - 3 months later.

- Order greige fabric - 3months later.

    - Color specs for up to 2/3 of fabric.
    - Final specs on retail feed-back.

- Sell to retailer - 1 month later.

    - Use computer generated color prints and actual fabric.
    - Orders for no more than 50% of projected sales of seasonal goods.

- Apparel manufacturing starts - 2 months later.

    - Less than 50% of projected sales produced.
    - Balance produced against retail sales experience.

The operational elements that are basic for textile, apparel and retail QR are summarised in the next sections. Several of these have not yet been introduced systematically, but they will be covered in later chapters.

54

The elements fall into one of five categories: pre-season planning and adjustments; real time information exchange during the selling season; rapid product design and development; manufacturing and product delivery systems and Quality Management precepts.

Textiles Quick Response – Basic Elements.

• Tracking of consumer sales and sell-through, retail inventories and apparel manufacturer inventories by fabric, color and style.

• Close working relationships with manufacturers and retailers on line development and planning.

• Shortened new product development cycle using computer-aided design and line editing through style testing.

• Direct order status, availability schedule and assortment specification with apparel customers.

• Forecasting/re-forecasting system using input from customers' forecasting programs.

• Linked finished and greige goods planning systems.

• Lot tracking systems using in-plant data input procedures.

• Process control, measurement and monitoring procedures to minimize off-quality production and rework.

• Rigorous quality control systems to support above.

• Plant scheduling using linear programming models.

• Through-put time reduction through process consolidation programs/technology.

• Improved short-run economics through set-up time reduction programs.

- Close liason with customer on optimum roll size and make-up to minimize dock to spreader times.

- Electronic transmission to customers of detailed packing list information and specifications (width, shade, defects).

- Logistics systems to ensure on-time, pre-scheduled delivery of goods.

- Direct entry to raw materials suppliers of forecasts/reforecasts and shipping requirements.

- Linkage of supplier test results on quality with process control and management systems.

Apparel Quick Response - Basic Elements.

- Consumer style testing, point-of-sale tracking and post-season analysis of consumer/retail sell-through, turns, stock-outs and forced markdowns.

- Based on the above, participation in Retail Assortment Planning.

- Involvement of key retailers and fabric suppliers in style design (CAD), editing and forecasting.

- Working with key retailers and fabric suppliers in development of the retail sales and receipt forecast adjustments and lead times.

- Sharing retail order entry and availability information with fabric suppliers and fabric order and availability information with retailer.

- Master schedule capacity utilization planning integrated with forecasts, forecast corrections, fabric order and cut plan.

- Block scheduling of production flow (perhaps by retail order).

- Full use of technology for short-cycle sewing, finishing and price ticketing.

• Rapid internal movement of goods from cutting to sewing and sewing to apparel distribution center or store.

• Cut planning from fabric supplier inventory records and rapid receipt and processing of fabrics into cutting.

• Shorter seasonal calendar with more compact design/sampling schedules and smaller initial orders.

• Quality Assurance sampling to permit direct receipt of fabrics and shipments of finished garments.

Retail Quick Response – Basic Elements.

• Seasonal Assortment Planning by department, category, style and store.

• Weekly Sales, Inventory and Receipt Planning by store and SKU.

• Firm vendor order and receipt planning, communicated to vendors with agreed lead times and boundaries for change.

• Recording actual sales, inventory and receipts daily, by SKU with statistical smoothing.

• Adjust store sales forecasts based on actual daily sales.

• Adjust store receipt plan based on the above.

• Direct order communication to vendors available daily, including actual sales and inventory.

• Vendor price ticket systems.

• Store receipt procedures, from D.C. and/or direct from vendor.

• Rapid incoming transportation, cross-dock processing and store distribution systems.

• Markdown information, promotional and forced, by style, shared with vendor.

• Stock-out information, by store and SKU, shared with vendor.

• Pre-season planning with vendor, holding open-to-buy for later initial orders and re-orders.

• Quality Assurance sampling plan to permit store shipments (direct or cross-dock).

Notes – Chapter 4.

Many of the data contained in this chapter come from the CWP studies. Although unpublished earlier, the material has been summarized in the trade press. The Milliken estimates of customer cost reduction have also been widely used in seminars and articles.

The KTA questionnaire was prepared and analyzed by P. Harding of KSA and the author.

An excellent introduction to Quality Management is Philip Crosby's "Quality Is Free", a Mentor paperback and excellent value.

The Style Testing methodology is summarized in a paper given by Kenneth Frato at the 13th Annual International Apparel Research Conference in Atlanta GA., November, 1986. The 1985, 1986 and 1987 Conferences papers also include valuable material on inventory reduction and the management of change in an organization.

"Production Flexibility; Changing Perspectives On Operations Management For The 1990's", presented in June 1989 at the Limerick Conference on "The Future of the European Clothing & Footwear Industries" by David J. Tyler of Manchester Polytechnic. This very thoughtful study discusses many of the topics central to QR.

The listings of the basic elements of QR were prepared by KSA for CWP.

Chapter 5. Product Diversity

There is a cost penalty associated with collapsing the pipeline. Making to order, or producing a wider variety of goods, means shorter runs and more styles in work at any one time. This occurrence is referred to as diversification and it adds substantially to the cost of goods unless steps are taken to minimize the impact of frequent change-overs. It impacts all sectors of the industry, tending to add, as it does, to work in process and inventory levels.

Textile Operations.

Figures 5.1 and 5.2 show the effect of diversity on textile operations. They are based on the inventory data for the pongee and a poplin fabrics discussed in the previous chapter and displayed in Appendix B. Under traditional, long run conditions, the time needed for the pongee, feed yarn through finishing, is 42 days or 8.4 weeks. Short runs and small dye lots can increase this figure to 70 days or 14 weeks. The equivalent times for the poplin are 43 days, increasing to 62 days or 12.4 weeks. The levels of diversity described as Very Low, Low, Medium and High correspond to the seasonality of the goods - Basic, 2-3 Seasons, 4-6 Seasons and 7+ Seasons, respectively.

Shown alongside the traditional, are the QR times which, although they off-set some of the diversity impact, cannot overcome all of it. No plant, however, will suddenly move from a low to highly diverse mix of fabrics. Changes will be small and they will be made slowly, accompanied by the appropriate operational procedures.

In the last 2-3 years, the major textile companies have made great progress in their handling of short runs. Minimum order sizes, which were measured in thousands of yards, are now measured in hundreds of yards. Further, in those cases where closer partnerships have been established with the apparel manufacturer, the response times to orders against agreed upon fabric programs have been sharply reduced. Milliken and Company have cut such response times – fabric order processing, dyeing and finishing and shipping, through receipt and quality check at the manufacturer – from 7 weeks to 1 1/2 weeks or less.

The cost of carrying additional inventory is only one of the costs of increased diversity. Decreased equipment utilization, less efficient use of materials and reduced worker productivity are other penalties. Appendix D contains data on the inventory impact and also gives the manufacturing costs of the poplin and pongee fabrics under varying diversity conditions. These costs are summarised in Tables 5.1 and 5.2.

Figure 5.1
Textile Inventories – Through WIP Finishing

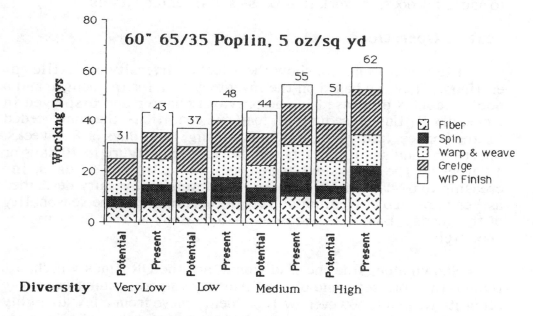

Given the magnitude of the variations shown in Tables 5.1 and 5.2, the mills are concentrating on short run procedures and have little incentive to complicate matters by broadening significantly their fabric lines – unless they can get prices to support such a step. A great deal of process research is needed to develop methods to minimize these cost penalties and allow domestic mills to become more competitive with the fabrics now being imported.

60

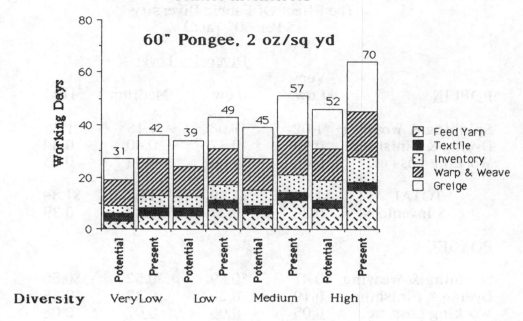

Figure 5.2
Textile Inventories

60" Pongee, 2 oz/sq yd

Legend:
- Feed Yarn
- Textile
- Inventory
- Warp & Weave
- Greige

Diversity: Very Low, Low, Medium, High (Potential / Present)

Apparel Manufacture.

The effect of diversification on apparel manufacture is similar to that for textiles; most operations show better costs, the longer the run. An example of this is fabric cutting costs which are sensitive to both the units per cut and the cuts per week for a given style. These relationships are shown for a lady's blouse in Figure 5.3.

A second important effect of diversification is that it affects fabric utilization. Fabric can account for up to 40% or more of the total garment cost and the extent to which the marker maker can minimize waste in cutting is of great importance. For simple garments such as T shirts, fabric utilization will exceed 90%. As more shape is put into the blocks, the utilization drops off. For a mass produced fitted blouse, material utilization can be as high as 85%, but the waste factor can increase by 5% or so as the number of units decreases.

Table 5.1
Textile Manufacturing Costs
The Effect Of Fabric Diversity
($ Per 60" Yard)

POPLIN	Diversity Level			
	Very Low	Low	Medium	High
Spinning & Weaving	1.02	1.08	1.18	1.35
Dyeing & Finishing	0.35	0.37	0.40	0.44
Working Loss etc.	0.03	0.04	0.04	0.05
TOTAL	$1.40	$1.49	$1.62	$1.84
$ Inventory	0.24	0.27	0.32	0.39
PONGEE				
Spinning & Weaving	$0.47	$0.49	$0.52	$0.56
Dyeing & Finishing	0.19	0.20	0.22	0.25
Working Loss etc.	0.05	0.06	0.07	0.08
TOTAL	$0.71	$0.75	$0.81	$0.89
$ Inventory	0.13	0.14	0.16	0.19

In the last few years, technological progress in marker making, the development of sized patterns, or grading, and fabric laying and cutting has been rapid. As computers take over more of these skilled tasks, the impact of diversification will decrease. Low ply cutting has had an impact. Automatic pattern making for yarn dye or printed fabric that allows the print to continue through the sewn seam is becoming a reality.

Further gains will be made as fabric quality improves. The leading mills are now signalling, prior to delivery, the minimum fabric width within a roll and streaming production so that the variation about the mean width is kept small. Fabric defects are also being mapped and transmitted electronically to allow the computerized marker maker to avoid them optimally. Tightening side-to-side and along-the-length shade control will also place fewer restrictions on the making of markers and increase material utilization.

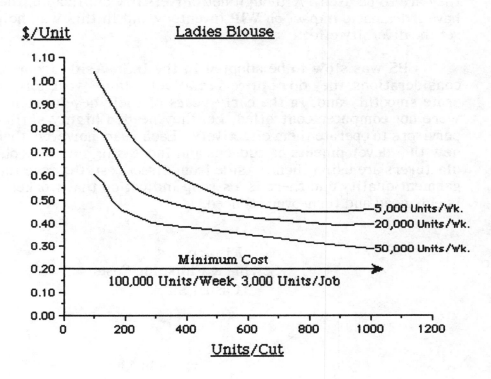

Figure 5.3
Cutting Cost Per Unit

$/Unit   Ladies Blouse

5,000 Units/Wk.
20,000 Units/Wk.
50,000 Units/Wk.

Minimum Cost
100,000 Units/Week, 3,000 Units/Job

Units/Cut

The remaining problem has to do with people. With long runs, a low skill sewing machine operator can learn quickly to handle the same seam over and over again. Frequent changes of style slow down operations significantly and this is especially the case when the labor turn-over rate is high and a constant stream of novice operators is entering the shop. Recently, the problem has been compounded by the development of "intelligent" sewing equipment which can perform several operations simultaneously or perform a series of specialized sewing tasks, e.g. collar making, at high speed. Unfortunately, the skill levels required to make the best use of this equipment are of a higher order and take longer to master. One answer to these problems is, undoubtedly, a greater use of automation, with fewer, higher paid and more stable workers.

In the chapter on technology, the use of Over-Head Rail or Unit Production Systems (UPS) is discussed in some detail. These replace the traditional movement of bundles and deliver individual pieces of cut fabric in pre-set sequences to designated operators as they are to be used. Although not universally applicable, they can have a dramatic impact on WIP inventory and in this way help off-set the diversity effect.

UPS was slow to be adopted in the U.S. Aside from capital considerations, they do require a relatively stable work force to operate smoothly and, in the early years of their development, they were not computer controlled, i.e. they needed highly skilled supervisors to operate them effectively. Each year, however, there are new UPS developments or add-ons and increasing numbers of manufacturers are using them. Aside from direct cost, they can improve garment quality and there is a strong indication that worker moral is enhanced and turn-over reduced.

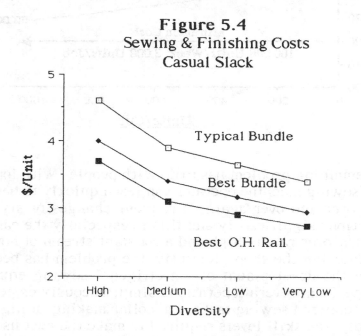

Figure 5.4
Sewing & Finishing Costs
Casual Slack

Figure 5.4 shows the impact on sewing and finishing costs of UPS used for casual slack manufacture - the benefit is much less marked for blouse manufacture. The data show clearly that for a given $/unit cost, an operation can sustain a significant increase in the level of garment diversity by using Over-Head Rail equipment.

The data used in this section are shown in Tables 5.2 and 5.3. For the sake of continuity, the poplin and twill in their slack and blouse connotations, respectively, were used. Detailed break-outs of the sewing and finishing costs for Typical Progressive Bundle Unit, Best PBU, and Best UPS are given, for reference, in Appendix E. "Best" simply means a highly engineered plant in the Industrial Engineering sense.

Table 5.2
Textile/Apparel Costs & Diversity
Men's Casual Poplin Slack- Best PBU
($ & Linear Yards)

Diversity Level	V. Low	Low	Medium	High
Textile				
• Fabric Cost/Yd $	1.40	1.49	1.62	1.84
• Margin @ 20%	0.35	0.37	0.41	0.46
Total	1.75	1.86	2.03	2.30
Apparel				
• Δ Material Usage		0.5%	1.5%	3.0%
• Yds/Unit	1.25	1.25	1.27	1.29
• $/Unit – Fabric	2.19	2.34	2.58	2.97
• $/Unit – Trim	0.65	0.65	0.67	0.69
Total Materials	2.84	2.99	3.25	3.66
• Cut	0.21	0.26	0.33	0.43
• Sew & Finish	2.95	3.17	3.39	4.01
Sub-Total	3.16	3.43	3.72	4.44
Total Cost	6.00	6.42	6.97	8.10
• Margin @ 25%	2.00	2.14	2.32	2.70
Best PBU Cost	$8.00	$8.50	$9.29	$10.80
Typical PBU	$8.68	$9.29	$10.11	$11.73
Best UPS	$7.73	$8.27	$8.98	$10.42
Typical PBU/Best UPS	1.12	1.12	1.12	1.12

Table 5.3
Textile/Apparel Costs & Diversity
Women's Pongee Blouse - Best PBU
($ & Linear Yards)

Diversity Level	V. Low	Low	Medium	High
Textile				
• Fabric Cost/Yd $	0.71	0.75	0.81	0.89
• Margin @ 20%	0.18	0.19	0.20	0.22
Total	0.89	0.94	1.01	1.11
Apparel				
• Δ Material Usage		0.5%	1.5%	3.8%
• Yds/Unit	1.38	1.38	1.40	1.42
• $/Unit - Fabric	1.22	1.30	1.41	1.57
• $/Unit - Trim	0.26	0.26	0.27	0.28
Total Materials	1.48	1.56	1.68	1.85
• Cut	0.20	0.26	0.32	0.45
• Sew & Finish	2.34	2.51	2.68	3.30
Sub-Total	2.54	2.77	3.00	3.75
Total Cost	4.02	4.33	4.68	5.60
• Margin @ 25%	1.34	1.44	1.56	1.87
Best PBU Cost	$5.36	$5.77	$6.24	$7.47
Typical PBU	$6.24	$6.69	$7.23	$8.68
Best UPS	$5.25	$5.65	$6.11	$7.31
Typical PBU/Best UPS	1.19	1.18	1.18	1.19

Notes – Chapter 5.

The material used in this chapter was drawn, for the most part, from the studies carried out by KSA on behalf of CWP.

A great deal of work is required to find ways to minimize the impact of diversity on dyeing and finishing operations. A recent paper (as yet unpublished) by Tomasino and Sommerville, NCSU College of Textiles, examines in some detail the impact of batch size on dyeing costs using a variety of process methods.

Some idea of the impact of increasingly frequent style changes on both the purchasing of fabrics and the production of garments on a medium sized company can be gained from the data below.

	Number Of Seasons Per Year		
	2	4	6
Lines Per Season	2	3	5
Fabrics Per Line	2	5	8
Colors Per Fabric	4	6	8
Fabrics/Colors/Yr.	32	360	1920
Styles Per Line	6	12	20
Sizes Per Style	6	6	6
Colors Per Style	4	6	8
SKU's/Year	288	1728	5760

Chapter 6.   EDI/Linkage.

The importance to QR of collecting and transmitting information backwards and forwards in the pipeline speedily and with a high order of accuracy cannot be over-emphasized. It is fundamental to the concept of changing apparel supply from a manufacturing driven to a consumer driven system. For this reason, the subject of Electronic Data Interchange in its various forms is treated separately.

It is convenient to think of EDI as having two main components as it applies to the apparel pipeline. The first of these is the electronic transmission of transactional information such as forecasts of requirements, purchase orders, shipping notices and invoices. The second aspect relates to information accompanying the physical transfer of goods, i.e. fiber, fabric and garments, by means of bar coding of the merchandise, as well as the recording of retail sales information at the cash register by means of Point Of Sale (POS) scanning of bar codes.

The main impediment to early implementation of EDI by the apparel industry was that each pipeline sector considered itself a separate entity and developed its own way of doing business, using its own language. The advantages of using electronic communication and product identification had to mark time until the various industry groups could agree on common information formats and protocols to be used across the interfaces.

A number of individual companies had set up varieties of EDI with their own suppliers and customers in the late 70's and early '80's, but it was not until 1984 that the first set of meetings took place between a few progressive textile and apparel companies with a view to establishing industry-wide standards. These led to the formation of TALC - the Textile Apparel Linkage Council - in May of 1986.

TALC

TALC is a volunteer organization composed primarily of textile and apparel manufacturers together with other interested parties. Its principal objectives are to develop voluntary standards for use by the industry and to promulgate and encourage the use of these standards by means of seminars, meetings and publications.

TALC has been enormously successful. Virtually all major textile and apparel companies became members in its first year of operation and there has been rapid progress toward establishing standards of communication between the two industry groups. Its activities have the endorsement of both the AAMA and the ATMI.

The following are brief summaries of the voluntary standards adopted in the first two years of the Council's operations.

- **EDI Format.** TALC has endorsed the use of ANSI X12 standard formats. ANSI X12 are the American National Standards Institute's standards for the electronic transmission of data for such business transactions as purchase orders and invoices and are widely used in many industries. To facilitate their use, TALC has developed an ANSI standards conventions document entitled Textile Apparel Manufacturers Communications Standards (TAMCS). The communications links between trading partners may take the form either of direct connection between their computers or via a third party networking service. The use of the latter service greatly simplifies the task of linking to many suppliers or customers without loss of confidentially of information.

- **Roll Identification.** Each roll of fabric shipped by the textile producer will be uniquely identified by means of a 15-character identifier, consisting of a 6-digit producer number followed by a 9-digit alphanumeric producer-assigned number. The roll identification number is to be represented in both human and Universal Product Code (UPC) bar code readable forms on a hang-tag or pressure sensitive label accompanying the roll. A recommendation has also been approved for the layout of the information on the ticket.

With an industry-unique roll identification, the apparel manufacturer no longer needs to re-ticket each roll for his own inventory identification which is made more accurate and simpler to handle. The other, and major, benefit is that the standardised ticketing opens the door to the transmission of other quantitative and qualitative information by the fabric producer.

• Width/Length Measurement. By obtaining accurate dimensional information in standard form, the apparel manufacturer is in a position to reduce costs and improve efficiency through better fabric utilization, elimination of duplicated measurements and speeding up the marker making and cutting processes. The standards call for widths to be expressed in $\frac{1}{4}$" increments, rounded down; the length of the roll is to be given in 0.1 yard increments.

In a growing number of textile/apparel partnerships, these and other measurements are being transmitted ahead of the actual shipping of the fabric. In this way, computerization of the cutting process takes place while the fabric is in transit and the roll can be taken directly to the spreading table.

• Shade Measurement. To eliminate duplicate measurements of fabric shade, the standard calls for each roll to be identified with either delta values or the 5-5-5 shade sorting convention agreed to by the trading partners.

• Identification and Flagging of Fabric Defects. Based on buyer/seller agreement, defects to be flagged by the producer have been established for four categories: Critical, Denim, Standard and No Flagging Required. The principal method for flagging defects for automated detection is the use of metallic stick-on devices, but several textile companies are now using more sophisticated mappings of defects that record the distance of the fault from the edge of the fabric. Such methods, of course, allow greater fabric utilization by the manufacturer.

• Packaging of Rolls Within Cartons. This standard established sets of packing specifications for individual rolls within a carton, including weight classifications, packing recommendations, and carton and strapping specifications.

• Packaging for Individually Wrapped Rolls. This standard, adopted in May 1988, established a set of packing specifications including: weight classifications, types of packaging, as well as the fit, material, clarity, and end closure specifications for each weight classification.

• Order Status. The items of information necessary for the seller/buyer interface on delivery data relative to order status are provide by this standard. Communications on delivery non-conformance are also being reviewed.

In addition to the above, TALC committees are working on a number of other topics for possible standardization. These include questions of distribution and transportation: sequential loading and unloading of rolls, recommended materials handling equipment, guidelines for determining cost effective roll size and recommendations for core tube size and strength.

Another study area is that of forecasting. A committee is examining ways to define the items of information and their timing, to be transmitted by manufacturers to textile suppliers projecting future demand. This is a subject of great importance to the textile producer because of the long lead times associated with fabric manufacture.

The need to make use of the voluntary standards is widely accepted by TALC members but it will be some time before adherence is wide spread. In the summer of 1987, TALC surveyed AAMA member firms to assess actual or intended use of the standards. Of the 136 respondents, only 25% were linked electronically with their suppliers though others affirmed their intention of moving in that direction within the year. The survey yielded invaluable information on the progress being made in such areas as acceptance of supplier width, length and shade information. The responses showed clearly that testing duplication is still deemed necessary by far too many manufacturers, but that steady progress is being made. Future surveys will allow TALC to focus on those areas where industry acceptance is lagging.

VICS.

At a meeting held in Chicago on June 24th. 1986, major retailers, manufacturers and textile producers formed the Voluntary Inter-Industry Communications Standards (VICS) Committee whose aim it is to provide leadership in the use of standards for the capture and transmission of product related information between manufacturers and retailers. The Committee has identified two areas on which to concentrate its efforts:

• Standard Item Identification. Here the the first of the objectives was to gain general agreement among retailers and manufacturers on the use of the UPC system to identify products so that automated point-of-sale devices can be employed efficiently to capture accurate information on consumer purchases at the SKU level. Currently, retailers use a variety of methods for product ticketing including pen, magnetics, Optical Character Recognition (OCR) Font and, in some cases, UPC. Until such time as UPC is universally implemented, the trade has agreed to use Dual Technology Vendor Marking (DTVM) which involves both UPC and OCR A.

The second objective was to encourage the establishment of common item identification standards for yarn and fabric products used in the production of consumer goods. Clearly, this was a direct reinforcement of the TALC activities.

• Standard Data Transmission Format. Again, two objectives were identified; to establish a single set of communication formats and protocols for EDI between manufacturers and distributors and to encourage the development of equipment to record and make available to producers information about consumer purchases.

Having made substantial progress in these areas, VICS has moved into a third action area, that of promoting and monitoring implementation by the industry. Focus is on relating to industry trade associations, providing training and educational programs, stimulating equipment and software vendors and providing leadership in identifying and overcoming barriers to progress.

Most recently VICS and the governing body of UPS, the Uniform Code Council, co-sponsored the VICS Retail Cost/Benefit Study to be carried out by Arthur Andersen. This research was designed to quantify the benefits to the retailer of participating in EDI despite the high initial costs of implementation. The Study paralleled a similar investigation by KSA of the cost/benefit relation for apparel manufacturers. The results of both investigations are given in Chapter 11.

As with TALC, the progress made by VICS has been extremely rapid and in one sense it has even greater importance for the future of the pipeline. There is little question that the rate of adoption of EDI by producers will be determined, in large part, by the speed with which the retailer insists on vendor compliance with his needs. It is, therefore, encouraging to note the increasing number of influential retailers who are applying EDI to their basic product lines for automatic re-stocking of merchandise. Already, one of the most important advantages to be gained from such systems is being reported; that of the sharp reduction in stockouts accompanied by higher sales volumes.

The use of standard formats for product identification has helped speed the implementation of an important aspect of QR. Ticketing of merchandise by the manufacturer rather than the retailer allows substantial reductions in Distribution Center handling. It also reduces the system costs. Ticketing at retail costs 15¢ to 25¢ per item, compared to the 2¢ to 3¢ incurred by the manufacturer.

The challenges facing the retailer are formidable. The grocery industry has used bar coding with point-of-sale tracking for several years, but the number of suppliers and SKU's they must handle is small compared with those of the apparel world which measures its offerings in the millions and is supplied by 15-20,000 vendors. Further, the apparel industry is becoming more and more fashion-goods oriented. In line with this, a variety of third party systems has sprung up and there is increasing interest in "electronic catalogs" that will allow the buyer to scan rapidly each vendor's offerings and to handle the increasingly difficult task of relating bar coded information to merchandise descriptions. The more progressive buyers are already calling for such catalogs to contain visual displays of the garments, which, in addition to requiring immense amounts of computer memory, increases the need for information security.

Another kind of problem centers around the vast amount of information generated by point-of-sale tracking at the SKU level. Turning this body of data into information of use to the buyer is one of the next barriers to be overcome by the industry. However, once the basic problems have been overcome, not only will automatic rapid re-ordering of best selling garments be possible because of real time inventory control, but the whole new field of style trend analysis will be opened up for study.

SAFLINC & FASLINC.

In the first quarter of 1987, two more linkage organizations were born, making a full set for the apparel industry. The first of these was the Sundries and Apparel Findings Linkage Council (SAFLINC) which, as its name suggests, concerns itself with all the components, other than fabric, that go into the manufacture of apparel - thread, buttons, zippers and the like. The second group, the Fabric and Suppliers Linkage Council (FASLINC), was organized to develop voluntary standards and protocols for transactions between fiber suppliers, dyestuffs and chemicals producers, yarn spinners and textile mills, thus completing the EDI network for the whole apparel pipeline.

Both SAFLINC and FASLINC are close to TALC in terms of objectives and strategies for achieving them, though they each address areas of special concern to them. SAFLINC members have a strong interest in the forecasting aspect of their interface with customers and also a concern over the optimum methods for handling large numbers of small items such as buttons. In the case of FASLINC, fiber and chemicals quality certification is of great interest and, of course, the distribution and varying standards of cotton fiber present many unique problems.

SAFLINC was intended to handle the needs of suppliers of such non-woven items as linings and interfacings, but members of the industry were slow to participate. In the Fall of 1987, however, the non-woven industry set up its own study groups to determine the EDI needs of its members when linking to both suppliers and customers. The first step being taken by these committees is to make the greatest possible use of the work done by TALC and the other linkage councils.

Computer Integrated Manufacturing (CIM).

The linkage organizations described so far have had as their principal focus the interchange of information and goods with customers and suppliers. There is, however, another part of the apparel supply system where linkages are increasingly needed; apparel manufacturing itself.

Computerized cutting equipment, Unit Production Systems, and programmable sewing machines are all driven electronically and, as the use of technology increases, the progressive apparel manufacturer will rely increasingly on the computer. The problem is that as these islands of automation spring up, there are few linkages allowing the transfer of information among them. Most machinery manufacturers are concerned with optimizing their own equipment and there are no industry accepted guidelines for information transfer to and from other pieces of equipment. There are exceptions to this generalization, the most important being the integration of CAD with marker making and cutting by such companies as Gerber, Investronica and Lectra which manufacture all the units themselves.

The industry is addressing this need. Between August 1987 and February 1988, four meetings were held by an increasing number of interested industry members. Initially, the idea was to adapt the TALC procedures under the acronym of CIM/LINC, but the specialized nature of the project and the extended time frame over which the teams would have to operate led to the work being transferred to a newly formed AAMA CIM Committee.

There are three other CIM related initiatives that show considerable promise. The first of these forms part of the overall AAMA research program and involves the University of Louisiana at Lafayette. In September of 1988, representatives of the two organizations initiated a joint effort to create an Apparel Computer Integrated Manufacturing (A-CIM) Laboratory. The initial project has as its objective the definition and establishment of the system(s) and standards required to implement data driven manufacturing and enable optimum utilization of both existing equipment and equipment under-development for the apparel industry. Cooperative efforts with (TC)[2] and other universities and agencies will be examined once the first project is underway.

The textile and apparel machinery makers have also seen the clear need for standards rationalization. The newly formed Textile and Apparel Machine Modernization Foundation (TAMMF) has been funded by the Trade Adjustment Assistance office of the U.S. Department of Commerce. Its first project will be devoted to computer communication standards to enable "textile mills to reduce the need for specially designed protocols for each type of machine and each vendor and to tie all machinery together in one plant".

In a third endeavor, the Apparel Manufacturing Technology Center of Georgia Tech Research Institute is studying the fundamentals of CIM architecture using IDEF modelling methodologies. The U.S. Air Force established the Integrated Computer Manufacturing (ICAM) program in the 1970's. From this program grew IDEF (ICAM DEFinition) which comprises three related manufacturing modelling methodologies: IDEF0, the Function Architecture; IDEF1X, the Information Architecture; IDEF2, the Dynamics Architecture. The progress being made on the Georgia Tech program is reported regularly; see Notes.

With this broadening of effort devoted to CIM, there is a clear need for some group to review all activities and ensure that duplication of effort is kept to a minimum.

Notes – Chapter 6.

"Delivering The Right Stuff", an excellent account of the importance of EDI to the QR movement, is to be found in AAMA Apparel Research Notes Vol. 5, No. 3 August 1986. It was written by Robert White, IBM Apparel Industry Consultant.

Bobbin Magazine gives full coverage to the activities of the various linkage committees. Two reports in particular are worth examination: "TALC Official Standards Implementation Guide", July 1987 and "The Talc Report Card", December 1988.

"Getting Started With Piece Goods Linkage" was published by TALC in conjunction with AAMA in September 1988.

"Electronic Data Interchange In Apparel - A Guide To Solutions And Software" was produced by the Management Systems Committee of AAMA in October 1988.

VICS produces a series of Newsletters describing the activities of the organization. These can be obtained from the Corporate Information Systems group of K mart Corporation.

The December 1988 issue of Retail Technology & Operations, published under the banner of Womens Wear Daily, contained several articles relating to linkage activities, including one on bar code catalogs.

The AMTC Quarterly is published by the Apparel Manufacturing Technology Center of the Georgia Tech Research Institute, Atlanta GA. and covers the full spectrum of activities being carried out under the sponsorship of the U.S. Defense Logistics Agency.

Chapter 7. QR Macroeconomics.

This chapter contains a great deal of information. It is concerned with estimating the quantitative benefits that accrue from the adoption of QR, both by sector and for the system as a whole. Order lead times, their effect on the accuracy of the buyer's merchandise plans and thus the extent of retail stockouts and markdowns are examined first. This is followed by the introduction of the concept of reorder while the selling season is underway and the original estimate of consumer preferences can be modified. The power of reorder is clearly dependent on the seasonality of the merchandise and this effect is also quantified.

The second part of the chapter pulls together all the factors affecting pipeline performance under QR; the higher costs of diversity and rapid distribution, and the off-setting reductions in inventory, stockouts and markdowns. Department Stores and Mass Merchants are treated separately and the impact of different mixes of basic, seasonal and fashion goods is taken into consideration. The assumptions used in this 'model' are spelled out in considerable detail and extensive use is made of Appendices. The intention is to supply enough detail to allow the reader the opportunity of evaluating the effect of different assumptions.

To make the calculations more pointed, the two representative garments used in previous chapters, the seasonal poplin slack and the fashion pongee blouse, are used as examples, but the intent was to be as "macro" as possible while recognising that the hundreds of types of merchandise in the system each has its own cost characteristics.

Unlike the more recent, product specific, cost/benefit study described in Chapter 10, the costs associated with adding specific technologies is absent. As an off-set to this, however, the increases in business volume that stem from the adoption of QR are also ignored. Neither of these factors is large enough to affect the main thrusts of the chapter; to obtain an estimate of the overall QR benefit to the pipeline and to provide a basis for assessing the improvements in the industry's international competitive position, the subject of Chapter 8.

Order Lead Times

The work of the Boston Consulting Group on the "hidden" costs of importing was discussed earlier. As part of this effort, their analyses aimed at quantifying the merchandise planning errors made by retail buyers because their purchases are made so far ahead of the actual selling season.

The placing of orders for apparel is referred to as the open-to-buy (OTB) period and usually, in the case of imported apparel, manufacture of the planned merchandise is booked 7-8 months ahead of the opening of the selling season. For domestically sourced goods, the OTB is 4-6 months ahead of the season and there is greater latitude in freezing the complete order. The BCG interviews attempted to identify the relationship between the order lead time and how well the merchandise plan correlates with actual consumer purchases. Each of the six garments investigated had its own distinctive relationship, but, in general, the longer the lead time, the greater the error; men's wear lead times produced smaller errors than did women's wear and the greater the fashion component of the apparel, the greater the error.

These early findings were confirmed and extended by KSA who developed the generalized relationship shown in Figure 7.1. The important part of the curve, and that which is central to QR methodology, is the lower right hand sector. If the pipeline can be compacted sufficiently, the possibility of reorder becomes feasible. The term 'reorder' is defined as follows. It is the elapsed time between the confirmation of an order at the SKU level of detail by a retail buyer to a manufacturer whose fabric supplier has guaranteed greige fabric and the arrival of the garments at the store. In this sense, very little reordering is done as part of the traditional buying procedure.

The central tenet of QR is that reductions in inventory and WIP allow the OTB lead time to be shortened significantly. The application of the reorder principle means that only part of the order need be SKU specific at that time, with the balance of the order being specified after the opening of the season, when the consumer has indicated style and color preferences. In this way, the merchandise plan becomes more of a real time document, forecast errors are reduced and stockouts and markdowns are minimized. Easily said, but difficult to achieve.

Figure 7.1
Order Lead Time vs. Forecast Error
Fashion Product

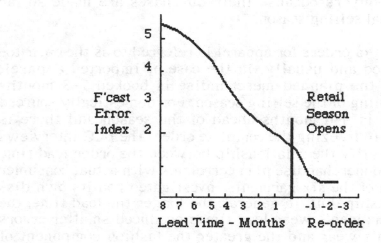

Seasonality & Reorder Potential.

The shelf life of the garment and the reorder response time together determine the extent to which reorder is possible. Consumer preferences can be estimated weekly following the start of a new season and the plan adjusted accordingly. The greater the number of such estimates, the better the fit between shelf availability and consumer demand.

Table 7.1 shows the interaction between shelf life, reorder response time and the proportion of the goods that can be reordered. Clearly, the complement of the reorder percentage is the amount of the initial order.

In Table 2.3, the proportion of all apparel falling into the 2-3 seasons category was estimated at close to 50%, with another 28-30% being 4-6 season goods. Thus, the concept of reorder is applicable to around 70-75% of all apparel, with the higher estimate applying to department stores and the lower to mass merchants.

Table 7.1
Potential Retail Reorder
(% Total Requirements)

Shelf Life	Reorder Response Time (Weeks)				
	1	2	4	6	12
20 Weeks	75%	70%	60%	50%	20%
10 Weeks	50%	40%	20%	--	--
7 Weeks	45%	30%	--	--	--

In the case of basic goods, the idea of reorder has little obvious relevance as, by definition, the needs of the consumer should be know with considerable accuracy. However, the practices of inventory minimization and frequent, smaller, drop shipments do apply, as does the concept of replenishment. Replenishment means that the stocks held by a store are continually monitored by the vendor, who replenishes them as necessary. It is at present an expensive service, but with the installation of point-of-sale tracking systems and greater electronic interchange of information, replenishment can become an automatic procedure with a significant impact on the pipeline inventories of basic goods.

High fashion merchandise can be affected only marginally by the reorder procedure. Alternative strategies involving the greater use of CAD and Style Testing were, however, discussed in Chapter 4 and these offer promise.

In the last couple of years much progress has been made in demonstrating that very short reorder times are possible. One program now in place is that described by Milliken and Company at the Bobbin Show of 1987. It applies to well integrated textile, apparel, retail partnerships and requires that agreed upon greige fabric stocks are available. Table 7.2 shows the levels of change that are now considered feasible. It should be noted that the total traditional response of 14 weeks is very conservative - 20-25 weeks has been in wider practice.

The shorter response times involve greater costs, some of which have already been discussed, e.g., the costs of diversity. Daily shipping of fabric, cut parts and garments can add approximately $0.10, $0.02 and $0.02 per garment, respectively, to the traditional distribution costs. Drop shipping of garments at the store, instead of going through the retail distribution center adds $0.07-$0.10 per garment, using a carrier such as United Parcel Service. Off-setting such direct shipping charges, however, is a cost saving to the system of $0.35-$0.65 per garment which comes from price ticketing and other procedures during manufacture.

Table 7.2
Order Response Times
(Weeks)

	Trad.	Phase I	Phase II	Phase III
Fabric Order Process.	1.0	0.5	0.0	0.0
Dye & Finish Fabric	4.0	2.0	2.0	1.0
Ship Fabric	0.5	0.5	0.2	0.2
Receive Fabric	0.5	0.1	0.1	0.1
Quality Check	1.0	0.0	0.0	0.0
Garment Order Process.	1.0	0.5	0.1	0.1
Cut & Sew Garment	5.0	2.0	1.0	1.0
Ship Garment	0.5	0.5	0.5	0.5
Receive Garment	0.5	0.5	0.1	0.1
TOTAL	14.0	6.6	4.0	3.0

The retailer is well aware of the benefits of short response times. In 1984, Emanuel Weintraub Associates surveyed buyers with 50 of the country's leading retailers, whose gross sales together exceeded $30 billion, and who represented products carried in over 2,000 stores. Two out of three of the buyers supported the proposition that cutting the order response time from 8 to 5 weeks is worth a 10-15% purchase price premium. Those buyers not willing to pay a premium almost all said they would give order preference to the manufacturer with the faster turn-around time. Their reasons included the following:

• Allows shopping the market longer, thus spotting or confirming trends.

• Increases the length of the selling season on merchandise that is checking out.

• Permits greater inventory turns.

• Increases sales by up to 15%.

Table 7.3
Weighted Wholesale $/Unit
Men's Slack
Department Stores

Product Life & Response Time	Initial Order	Re-Order	% Re-Order	Wtd. Ave. Cost	% Trad.
50 Week Basic					
Traditional	$8.25				
6 Week	$8.25	$7.98	75%	$8.05	98%
3 Week	$8.25	$8.78	85%	$8.70	105%
20 Week Seasonal					
Traditional	$8.74				
6 Week	$8.74	$8.54	50%	$8.64	99%
3 Week	$8.74	$9.81	65%	$9.44	108%
10 Week Fashion					
Traditional	$9.16				
3 Week	$9.16	$9.81	30%	$9.36	102%
5 Week Fashion					
Traditional	$9.37				

Putting The Pieces Together – The Costs.

With most of the pieces of QR available, it is now possible to start putting them together. The added costs of diversity, which are the penalty to be paid for shorter response times at both the fabric and garment manufacturing stages are integrated with the logistics costs in Appendices F1-F2. These Appendices give the Department Store wholesale cost structures for Unit Production System manufacturing, for both the slack and the blouse for each of the seasonalities and a range of response times. The weighted average of the traditional and reorder costs for each situation are also shown. For convenience, the weighting calculations of the wholesale cost of the slack produced using UPS and sold through a Department Store are shown in Table 7.3.

The Benefits.

The above are the additional incurred costs of manufacturing and distribution. The complete picture requires that the advantages of QR, i.e., the reductions in inventories, forecast errors, stockouts and markdowns be worked into the calculations. The assumptions made in calculating the effects of these positive factors are given in detail in Appendices G1-15 for Department Stores and Mass Merchants, for each classification of seasonality and for the different response times. Tables 7.4 and 7.5 summarize these assumptions and give the gross values of QR.

The quantity of data being presented in this section may appear excessive but without it, the reader has little feeling for the way in which QR benefits are estimated; in particular, the weighted average benefits for the mixes of seasonalities involved.

Table 7.4
QR Simulation Assumptions
Department & Specialty Stores

Seasonality	5 Wk.	10 Wk.	20 Wk.	50 Wk.	Total
% Business	11%	32%	38%	19%	100%
Forced M.D. (% Net Retail)					
Present	23.3	26.3	20.3	5.9	19.8
6 Wk. Reorder	14.6	13.6	7.8	2.6	9.5
3 Wk. Reorder	14.6	11.9	6.7	2.6	8.5
Inventory - Wks.					
Present	55.5	62.2	66.6	62.1	64.7
6 Wk. Reorder	44.0	47.1	45.7	47.7	46.4
3 Wk. Reorder	41.6	41.2	40.6	42.6	41.4
Inventory Costs. (% Net Retail)					
Present	4.41	5.76	6.72	7.50	6.31
6 Wk. Reorder	3.61	4.52	4.71	5.44	4.66
3 Wk. Reorder	3.29	3.63	3.92	4.62	3.89
Margin Loss On Stock-Outs. (% Net Retail)					
Present	5.76	6.36	4.39	0.81	4.50
6 Wk. Reorder	3.70	3.33	1.73	0.38	2.20
3 Wk. Reorder	3.70	2.93	1.46	0.38	1.97
% Reorder					
Present			20	64	19.8
6 Wk. Reorder			50	75	33.2
3 Wk. Reorder		30	65	82	49.9
Forecast Error % Initial + Reorder					
Present	45	50	52	16	43.8
6 Wk. Reorder	31	29	22	9	22.8
3 Wk. Reorder	31	25	19	8	20.2

Table 7.5
QR Simulation Results
Mass Merchants

Seasonality	5 Wk.	10 Wk.	20 Wk.	50 Wk.	Total
% Business	3%	20%	52%	25%	100%
Forced M.D. (% Net Retail)					
Present	16.5	19.3	19.4	5.1	15.7
6 Wk. Reorder	10.7	10.5	9.3	2.7	8.0
3 Wk. Reorder	10.7	7.9	7.8	2.4	6.5
Inventory – Wks.					
Present	55.0	61.5	64.0	68.2	64.3
6 Wk. Reorder	43.2	45.5	43.6	43.7	44.1
3 Wk. Reorder	40.9	39.4	38.5	38.7	38.9
Inventory Costs. (% Net Retail)					
Present	4.36	5.65	6.27	6.98	6.26
6 Wk. Reorder	3.50	4.30	4.41	4.80	4.46
3 Wk. Reorder	3.21	3.40	3.48	4.01	3.59
Margin Loss On Stock-Outs. (% Net Retail)					
Present	3.41	3.99	3.90	0.60	3.08
6 Wk. Reorder	2.20	2.17	1.87	0.31	1.55
3 Wk. Reorder	2.20	1.64	1.58	0.28	1.28
% Reorder					
Present			20	64	26.4
6 Wk. Reorder			50	75	44.7
3 Wk. Reorder		30	65	82	60.3
Forecast Error % Initial + Reorder					
Present	45	50	35	13	32.8
6 Wk. Reorder	31	29	18	7	17.8
3 Wk. Reorder	31	23	15	6	14.8

By subtracting the appropriate reorder percentage values from the traditional figures in Tables 7.4 and 7.5, i.e. the improvements in markdowns, inventory costs and stockout losses, and summing them, the gross margin impacts of QR are obtained. These are summarized below in Table 7.6 as improvements over the traditional system, and are expressed as % of net retail sales. The gains are impressive.

Table 7.6
Total Gross Value Of QR
(% Net Retail Sales)

Department & Specialty Stores

Seasonality % Business	5 Wk. 11%	10 Wk. 32%	20 Wk. 38%	50 Wk. 19%	Total 100%
6 Wk. Reorder	11.6	16.9	17.2	5.8	14.3
3 Wk. Reorder	11.9	19.9	19.3	6.6	16.2
Mass Merchants	3%	20%	52%	25%	100%
6 Wk. Reorder	7.9	12.0	14.0	4.9	11.0
3 Wk. Reorder	8.2	16.1	16.7	6.0	13.7

Net Value of QR.

Subtracting the cost of QR systems, determined earlier and detailed in Appendix F, from the gross values obtained above, yields the net value of QR - how much the entire system benefits. The results are shown graphically in Figures 7.2 and 7.3.

Mass Merchants have less to gain from QR than do the Department and Specialty Stores, but the benefit patterns are very similar. The clear winner is the 20 week, seasonal goods category. Here, the net value amounts to 9-13% of net retail sales with little variation from response times in the range 6 to 2 weeks. Ten week merchandise shows a strong pick up in value as response times decrease to 4 and 2 weeks. As might be expected, the high fashion goods require very short reorder times before the benefits become significant.

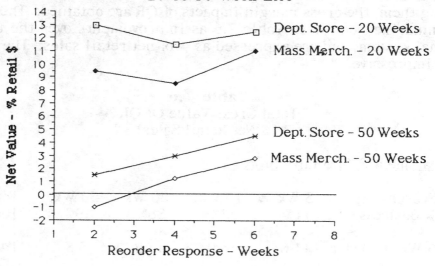

Figure 7.2
Net Value Of QR
20 To 50 Week Life

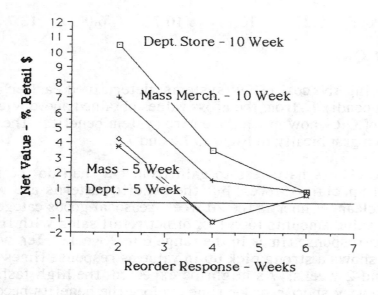

Figure 7.3
Net Value Of QR
5 To 10 Week Life

The basics category is best served by response times of 6-12 weeks; for shorter times the higher cost of the goods fails to off-set the benefits from lower inventories and markdowns.

It is important to recognise that the savings that accrue from QR should benefit everyone in the pipeline, including the consumer, if the domestic industry is to be more competitive with imports. Increased competitiveness is a prime objective of QR and the subject of the next chapter, but it is appropriate at this point, to give some indication of pipeline benefits. Table 7.7 summarizes the achievable financial improvements for the manufacturer, the retailer and the consumer.

Table 7.7
Estimated Financial Improvements
From Quick Response
(% Change)

	Seasonal	Fashion
Reduction Wholesale Price	7	15
Reduction 1st. Retail Price	9	13
Reduction Ave. Retail Price	2	6
Increase Pre-Tax Profit		
• Manufacturer	40	40
• Retailer	80	80
Reduction In Assets		
• Manufacturer	0	0
• Retailer	18	18
Increase % Return On Assets		
• Manufacturer	40	40
• Retailer	120	120
Net Cost Improvement	8	12
(% Ave. Retail)		

More concrete, dollars and cents, examples of these improvements in costs and prices is provided in Table 7.8, again using the slack and blouse considered in this chapter. That they are achievable at retail prices competitive with those of imports is the most important point made by the data.

Table 7.8
Potential QR Savings
Private Label - Mass Merchant
($/Unit)

	Seasonal Slack			Fashion Blouse		
	Trad.	QR	Gain	Trad.	QR	Gain
Apparel Mfg.						
Operating Profit	0.39	0.53	0.14	0.35	0.48	0.13
Retailer						
Operating Profit	0.54	1.19	0.65	0.74	1.04	0.30
Consumer						
Net Price	13.48	13.10*	0.38	11.48	10.41*	1.07
Total Improvement			1.17			1.50
% Improvement vs. Typical Retail Price			8.7%			13.1%

  * Based on same initial price as garment imported directly by retailer.

Potential System Savings.

Earlier, the total cost of operating a $100 billion traditional apparel supply system was estimated to be $25 billion (see Table 2.4). Using the results obtained above, it is now possible to come up with the reduction in that figure as a result of applying QR. The broad, system wide results are summarized in Table 7.9 and show a 50% reduction in the cost of operation, or a saving of $12-13 billion.

The data in Table 7.9, however, draw attention to a potential problem that was hinted at earlier; the very heavy weighting of the benefits in favor of the retailer and the apparel manufacturer. These amount to $3.5 billion for the manufacturer and $8.2 billion for the retailer - a total of $11.7, or 94% of the total benefit.

90

Expressed as a percent of sales, the two savings levels are roughly equal at 6-8% and far exceed those of the fiber and textile manufacturers at 2-3%. And yet the primary producers assume many of the burdens of inventory risk, JIT shipping and diversification cost. The solution is simple; fiber and fabric pricing should reflect these risks. As a minimum, the down-stream customer should assume an earlier and larger ownership stake in the suppliers products. However, achieving such equitable pricing or committment levels, will not be easy, despite the fact that there is plenty to go around. It will test the strength of the partnerships necessary for the QR system to work.

Table 7.9
Potential System Savings
($ Billion)

	Forced Mark-Downs	Stock-Outs	Invent.	Total
Fiber & Textile	0.3	–	0.5	0.8
Apparel Manuf.	2.0	0.2	1.3	3.5
Retailer	5.0	1.7	1.5	8.2
Total System	7.3	1.9	3.3	12.5

It should be remembered that the analyses covered above were carried out in 1985. At that time, there had been none of the confirmatory trials involving retailers and their suppliers that showed surprisingly large increases in both the volume and the profitability of business carried out in a QR mode. Neither was the cost of implementing QR well understood in terms of hard and software requirements throughout the pipeline. Analyses of these off-setting factors, which are covered in Chapters 10 and 11, would have to wait until 1988-89. However, the earlier results have proved to be quite durable and they provided much of the methodology used in subsequent work.

Notes – Chapter 7.

The contents of the chapter are based on the KSA and duPont studies undertaken on behalf of CWP.

Chapter 8. QR Competitiveness.

The make-up of the costs of garments produced in the developing or newly developed nations for sale in the U.S. differs sharply from that for domestic producers. The differences in labor rates predominate, affecting both fabric and apparel economics, but there are also large logistics differences and other importing costs, such as duties, have no domestic equivalent. Costs also vary from source to source as productivity differences make an impact and the ways in which costs are allocated change, supplier to supplier. Thus, although the cost of a particular garment may be known with precision in the U.S., it is difficult to be specific about the identical garment produced "off-shore" or in the "Far East".

Despite these difficulties, this chapter attempts to compare the financial attractiveness of imports in comparison to U.S. goods manufactured in the traditional and QR modes. Merchandise is imported both by the retailer, direct, and for the retailer by the manufacturer and the economics of the two routes are very different. Also, the cost structures of branded and private label goods differ. These will be taken into account as the analysis proceeds.

Factors Affecting Sourcing.

The major factors influencing decisions as to where to source may be grouped as follows:

Favoring The U.S.

- The garment has one of the following attributes:
    - A low labor content.
    - The fabric cost represents a high proportion of the total garment cost.
    - The fabric used is produced in large, low cost volume in the U.S.

- The garment is basic in style and is produced in long runs.

• A brand is important to the retailer and the manufacturer wants to control production closely.

• The retailer or the manufacturer is backward integrated.

• There is a level of style or fashion risk which favors short lead times, fast initial deliveries and rapid reorder responses.

Favoring Off-Shore Manufacture.

• The garment has either,
    - A high absolute labor content, or
    - A high labor-to-fabric ratio.

• There are short runs of limited volume, fashion merchandise.

• Garment lines require a wide variety of lightweight fabrics.

• Basic products tolerant of long lead times and where price is the major criterion and quality is not important.

• Fabrics are not made in the U.S., e.g. silk.

• The garments are designed off-shore.

Sourcing Costs.

The major factors affecting the manufacturer's and retailer's sourcing decisions can be portrayed simply using a format developed by duPont The following sequence of Figures shows the impact of fabric weight and cost, labor intensity, and duty rate, as determined by the fiber content, on U.S. competitiveness when operating in traditional, best and QR modes.

The labor rate impact is shown on the horizontal axis as a percentage of the garment cost and examples of typical garments falling into the low, medium and high ranges are appended. The ordinate shows the cost of Far East sourced garments at the retail distribution center as a percentage of the domestic cost. The ordinate legend also shows the chief value fiber, a determinant of the import duty.

Figure 8.1
Manufacturers Sourcing Cost Comparison
U.S. versus F. East
Labor Content Sensitivity Analysis

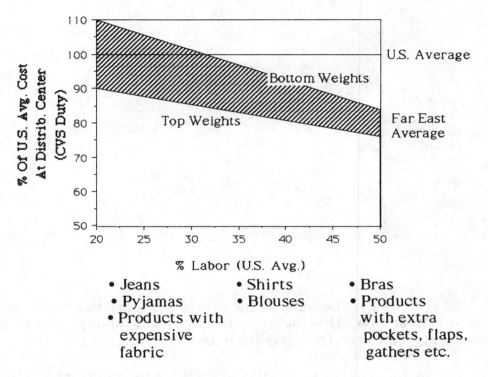

- Jeans
- Pyjamas
- Products with expensive fabric

- Shirts
- Blouses

- Bras
- Products with extra pockets, flaps, gathers etc.

The following notes should make clearer the meaning of the graph:

• The average U.S. manufacturing cost is shown as 100%.

• 20%-50% of the cost of U.S. made apparel is labor.

• Far East fabric prices range from 65% to 85% of U.S. prices, with top weights generally having the greater advantage. This difference is depicted by the two lines labelled with the weight class in Figure 8.1.

• The landed cost of apparel made in the Far East is represented by the shaded area in the graph. It improves as labor content increases with top weights having the greatest advantage because of their labor intensity.

Figure 8.2

Manufacturers Sourcing Cost Comparison
Improved Manufacturing
Labor Content & Manufacturing Style Sensitivity

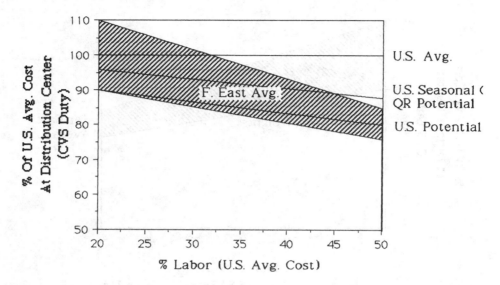

Figure 8.2 is the same as the previous Figure but with additional information. This includes the impacts of raising plant manufacturing standards from average to best and the impact of QR.

• The U.S. has the capability to reduce apparel manufacturing costs through engineering and technology, as shown by the line labelled U.S. Potential. These investments have a rapid payback - one year or less - and, as shown, lead to costs competitive with most Far East imports.

• When engineered plants provide Quick Response on seasonal products, costs increase approximately 7% over U.S. Potential because of shorter runs and more frequent style changes. These effects were explored in the previous chapter.

• Not shown in the Figure is that QR leads to better financial performance even though manufacturing costs are higher.

• Figure 8.2 relates to Chief Value Synthetic (CVS) goods. Garments made from cotton (CVC), carry a lower import duty and are lower in delivered cost by 7-10%, depending on the type of garment.

The sourcing cost picture for retailers who import private label goods directly is shown in Figure 8.3 which has the same basic format as the previous two Figures. Retailers can buy from the Far East on the same terms as the manufacturer, thus getting round the usual manufacturer markup. This gives them wholesale costs 10% to 40% below those for U.S. made apparel and substantial markups compared with the usual 25%, or so, for domestic private label. The penalties are, of course, lack of flexibility and the risk of heavy markdowns.

Figure 8.3
Retailers Sourcing Cost Comparison
Labor Content Sensitivity Analysis

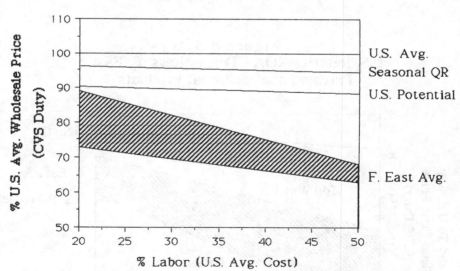

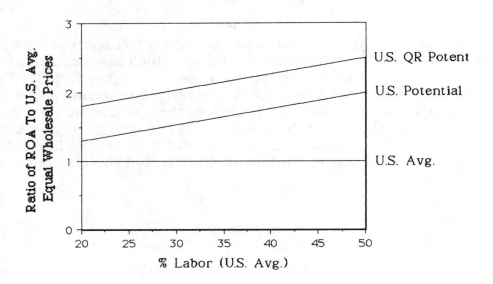

Figure 8.4
Manufacturer Return On Assets
Private Label Seasonal Products

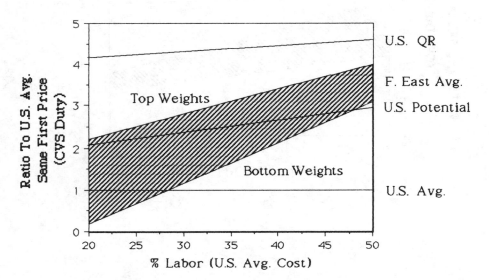

Figure 8.5
U.S. Retailer ROA - Domestic vs. F. East
Private Label Seasonal Products

Sourcing & Return On Assets.

Figures 8.4 and 8.5 examine the impact of QR strategies on the financial consequences of sourcing off-shore. Figure 8.4 shows the potential for improvement in ROA for the apparel manufacturer who either engineers his plant and upgrades his technology or adopts QR fully. As before, the ROA's are shown for a wide range of garment types. The data are for CVS; the ROA's are even higher for CVC. Figure 8.5 gives the equivalent information for the retailer and shows the dramatic improvement in financial performance possible with QR, despite the large cost gap.

There is a great deal of information packed into Figure 8.5 and again a few notes are in order:

• Although direct imports offer the retailer 10-40% lower wholesale costs than the domestically produced equivalent, the "hidden" costs of importing reduce this substantially for the average retailing operation. Du Pont studies have identified working capital of 19 weeks vs. 15 for the U.S. and supported the findings of Katz and the BCG with the following costs of importing expressed as % of retail sales:

– Markdowns	5.0%
– Buyer Travel	1.5
– Storage & Distribution	1.5
– Communications	1.2
– Management Control	0.5
	10.0%

• The average retailer's return on assets for domestically sourced private label products, shown above with an index of 1.0, is only competitive with low labor content garments made from bottomweight fabric.

• QR applied to seasonal goods can improve significantly the retailer's financial performance as is shown by the line marked "U.S. QR".

• U.S. QR requires less working capital - 10 weeks vs. 19 weeks for imports - and improves turns from 2.7 to 5+.

99

• The higher cost of imports, itemized above, also increases when QR is employed:

- Markdowns	11.0%
- Storage and Distribution	3.5
- Reduced Stockouts	2.0
- Communications	1.2
- Buying and Travel	1.5
- Management Control	0.5
	20.0%
- Freight and Systems	(2.0)
	18.0%

• Figure 8.5 holds true for goods paying CVS duties. CVC duties increase the competitiveness of imports by moving the shaded area vertically by 1 to 1.5 units on the ordinate. Even with this shift, however, QR is competitive for all but the most labor intensive topweights.

Competitive Economics.

Now that the framework has been built it is possible to consider in more detail the economics of specific garment types, produced domestically and in the Far East.

First, a broad brush look at the make-up of the ROA's from the point of view of a mass merchant sourcing private label slacks and blouses, both CVS and CVC. In Tables 8.1 and 8.2, the first retail prices are held constant; $20/unit for the slack and $15/unit for the blouse.

The Tables show the greatly strengthened competitive position that QR can confer on the domestic producer. The constancy of the pricing used in these examples may be questioned; in an industry as competitive as apparel, a part of the increased profitability due to QR should be passed on to the consumer as lower prices. At the time these analyses were carried out, this was believed to be the case, but the subsequent QR trials and cost/benefit studies find that this need not hold. The more detailed analyses of the costs of meeting short re-order times, and installing EDI equipment require higher fabric prices and maintenance of the domestic garment wholesale price structure. However, the retailer's improved financial performance more than off-sets the need for matching domestic to import prices.

Table 8.1
Men's Seasonal Slacks
By Mass Merchants
($/Unit)

| | Direct Import | | | |
	CVS	CVC	U.S. Avg.	U.S. QR
1st. Price	20.00	20.00	20.00	20.00
% Markup	54.6	58.1	41.5	44.8
Costs $/unit				
Whole. Price	9.09	8.39	11.70	11.04
Other	9.40	9.40	7.40	5.80
	18.49	17.79	19.10	16.84
Operating Profit	1.51	2.21	0.90	3.16
Assets $/unit				
Fixed	4.00	4.00	4.00	3.64
Inventory	3.32	3.07	3.37	2.12
	7.32	7.07	7.37	5.76
ROA	20.6%	31.1%	12.2%	54.9%

Note: The data include Far East fabric prices that are 85% and 65% of U.S. prices for the slack and the blouse respectively. The U.S. Average manufacturing costs include 36% and 41% labor for the slack and blouse respectively.

101

Table 8.2
Ladies' Seasonal Private Label Blouse
Mass Merchants
($/Unit)

| | Direct Import | | | |
	CVS	CVC	U.S. Avg.	U.S. QR
1st. Price	15.00	15.00	15.00	15.00
% Markup	62.1	65.9	41.5	45.1
Costs $/unit				
Whole. Price	5.68	5.12	8.78	8.24
Other	7.05	7.05	5.55	4.35
	12.73	12.17	14.33	12.59
Operating Profit	2.27	2.83	0.67	2.41
Assets $/unit				
Fixed	3.00	3.00	3.00	2.73
Inventory	2.08	1.87	2.53	1.58
	5.08	4.87	5.53	4.31
ROA	44.7%	58.1%	12.2%	55.9%

The final set of examples, shown in Table 8.3 demonstrates the impact of a lower price structure for domestic goods, using the same types of garment and similar financial analyses.

Table 8.3 gives the pricing structure and profitability for both the manufacturer and the retailer selling a slack and a blouse. Markdowns and discounts are included in the data.

The Table shows clearly the enormous benefits of the QR system; higher returns at lower prices, full competitiveness in the case of slacks and greatly increased competitiveness in the case of blouses, one of the most import-prone garment types. However, the Table is just a summary. The complete data on which it is based are to be found in Appendix H. Further, a series of semi-detailed graphic displays of the economics of QR is given at the end of the chapter, together with an explanation of how they should be read.

These data and graphics are what this book is all about and deserve careful study.

Table 8.3
Sourcing Summary – Mass Merchant Private Label
($/Unit)

| | U.S. Manufacturer | | | | | Direct Import | |
| | Domestic | | | F. E. Imp. | | | |
	Avg.	QR	QR	Avg.	QR	Avg.	Best
Slack-20 Wk.							
Manufacturer							
1st. Price	9.52	9.52	8.88	9.52	8.88		
Avg. Price	8.66	8.76	8.16	8.30	8.09	6.50	6.50
ROA %	8.2	22.1	11.2	15.8	13.1		
Retailer							
1st. Price	15.98	15.98	14.49	15.98	14.49	14.49	14.49
Avg. Price	13.48	14.45	13.10	13.48	12.57	11.80	12.30
ROA %	9.6	40.1	25.9	9.6	13.0	24.8	38.8
Blouse-10 Wk.							
Manufacturer							
1st. Price	7.94	7.94	6.79	7.94	6.79		
Avg. Price	6.96	7.08	6.05	6.53	5.95	4.63	4.82
ROA %	10.5	39.1	14.1	27.6	4.3		
Retailer							
1st. Price	14.00	14.00	12.00	14.00	12.00	12.00	12.00
Avg. Price	11.48	12.14	10.41	11.48	10.13	9.45	9.91
ROA %	15.9	40.2	26.9	15.9	18.6	36.4	46.5

Note: 1st. Price is either the original wholesale or the original retail price. The Average Price is either the realized wholesale price or the net price paid by the consumer.

Manufacturer Summary.

As indicated above, the amount of detail available in Appendix H is difficult to digest. For this reason, the following summary of its contents is included.

• With present wholesale prices, domestic manufacturers can dramatically improve their profitability, expressed as ROA, by using engineered Quick Response.

• QR permits wholesale price reductions at substantially better ROAs than are presently the norm for the manufacturing industry.

• Thus, QR eliminates the economic justification for the present manufacturers' imports from the Far East on most products produced there with traditional methods.

• Were the Far East manufacturer to go to engineered QR, he could match the domestic manufacturers' ROA on Private Label, but not on Branded goods.

• For Private Label, the retailers' ROA would be higher with domestic QR, at the same retail price points.

• Domestic engineered QR can eliminate the economic justification for about half of apparel manufacturers' imports, even if the Far East adopts QR.

Retailer Summary.

• Retail price points can be reduced on domestic Private Label by means of QR.

• Far East QR will not reduce the the wholesale cost of Private Label to the retailer.

• Thus, retailers will not need to import to hit a low Private Label price point on many classes of merchandise.

• Domestic QR can double retail profitability on domestic Branded and Private Label products, in addition to reducing retail price points.

• Private Label direct imports yield an equal or higher return to the retailer - depending on the product type - despite QR. Far East QR can widen the gap significantly.

• To compete fully with Private Label direct imports, very quick response, techniques such as Style Testing, direct stock replenishment or 807 manufacture will be required.

Notes – Chapter 8.

Most of the material presented in this chapter is unpublished. It was developed jointly by duPont and KSA on behalf of CWP. There have been summaries of the results in the trade journals, the most complete of which are to be found in Apparel Industry Magazine.

Figures 8.6 through 8.11 are included in order to present, in as compact a form as possible, much of the information contained in Appendix H. They are price/profitability charts at wholesale and retail for seasonal and fashion garments using both traditional and QR systems.

There are two sets of Figures; one set for seasonal slacks, the other for fashion blouses. For each garment type, the Figures compare typical and QR systems for traditional and lower (import matching) price points. Each set contains three Figures. The first gives wholesale information, i.e. importing by the manufacturer; the second set refers to domestic and indirectly imported goods from the retailer's perspective; the third set relates to domestic sourcing vs. direct importing, again from the point of view of the retailer.

For each set of circumstances, there are two bars; one marked "Price" and the other "Assets". They are coded to show their components. The percentage values alongside the Price bars are the appropriate pre-tax ROA values. The Wholesale Figures show one set of ROA values; the Retail Figures show two sets. The Retail ROA's closer to the abscissae are the same as the corresponding Wholesale values; they are carried over for reasons of clarity.

The Wholesale and Retail Direct Import charts include 807 data. As mentioned earlier, these are garments assembled off-shore from fabrics made and cut in the U.S. They are assessed for duty on the basis of the added value only. Most 807 garments are made in the Caribbean because of the combination of low labor rates and proximity to the U.S. market. 807 can offer an extremely low cost counter to the Far East.

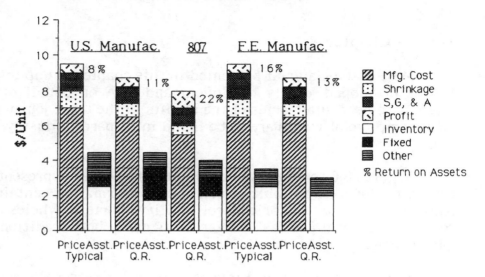

Figure 8.6
Wholesale Price/Profitability Comparison
Private Label Seasonal Slack

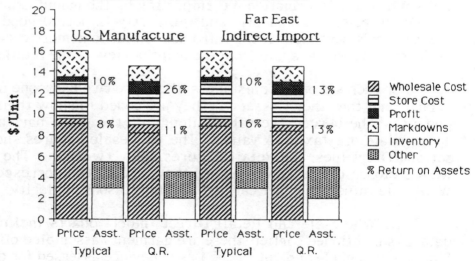

Figure 8.7
Retail Price/Profitability Comparison
Seasonal Private Label Slacks

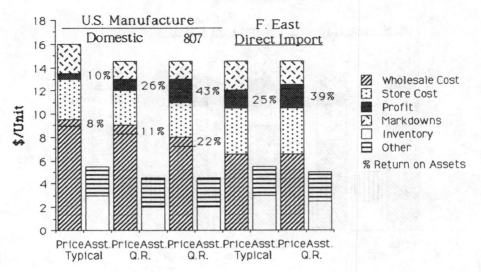

Figure 8.8
Retail Price/Profitability Comparison
Slacks - Direct Import

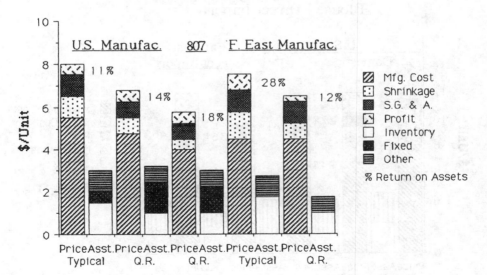

Figure 8.9
Wholesale Price/Profitability Comparison
Fashion Private Label Blouse

Figure 8.10
Retail Price/Profitability Comparison
Private Label Fashion Blouse

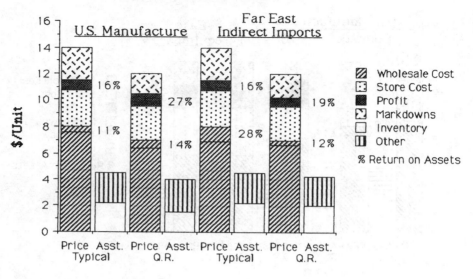

Figure 8.11
Retail Price/Profitability Comparison
Blouse - Direct Import

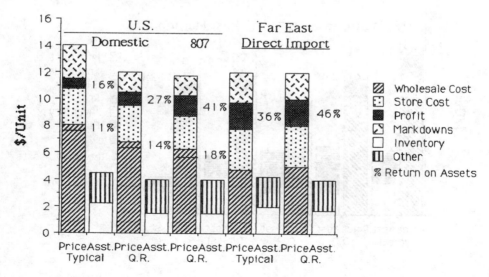

PART III
IMPLEMENTING QUICK RESPONSE

Chapter 9.   QR Trials.

Early in the program to develop QR methodology, the importance of carrying out practical demonstrations of its feasibility and value was well understood. Accordingly, in the summer of 1985, CWP retained KSA to set up and manage four trials. Each of the trials would be based on a partnership between a textile producer, a garment manufacturer and a retailer and each would involve a single garment in a full range of colors and sizes.

Fall 1986 was the earliest selling season that could be targetted because of the time needed to reach agreement on the ground rules for the trials, the work involved in setting up systems and controls that would allow operational and financial comparisons between the existing and QR procedures, and because of the lead times for supply of the merchandise. Three of the trials were carried to completion.

Participant Requirements.

The first step was to develop check lists of the requirements that would be placed on the participants. It must be remembered that many of the items listed below were new in concept and required substantial changes to be made to existing systems and procedures - in effect, the setting up of mini-businesses.

Retailer Requirements:

- Careful selection of category and vendor.

- Stores segregated into Test and Control.

- For selected categories and stores:

    - Merchandise information systems at the SKU level.
    - Agreement to delay Open-To-Buy.
    - New and faster distribution systems.
    - New planning and order systems, involving:

* Time-phased commitments.
* Assortment planning.
* Receipt and inventory management procedures.
* Fast reorder system.

Apparel and Textile Requirements:

• All aspects of quality control.

• Time-phased block scheduling and delivery.

• Direct order entry.

• Participation in the development of a forecasting system.

• New fabric forecast, order and receipt systems.

• Short cycle/small lot fabric finishing.

• Short cycle cut planning and smaller cuts.

• Short cycle sewing with frequent style changes:

    – Small bundle with block schedule and control, or
    – Unit Production Systems.

• Price ticketing and direct distribution.

• Back-up finished goods inventory to protect retail testing.

In other words, every effort was made to have the trials be as close to real QR as possible.

Trial Results.

Three partnerships were put together. The members of each and the broad results of the trials are given below.

<u>Wal-Mart/Seminole/Milliken</u> – Basic Men's Slacks

- 900 stores were involved.

- Unit sales increased 31% on a same store basis.

- Turns increased 30%, from 3.7 to 4.8.

- Average SKU's in stock at retail from 71% to 83% with target of 90%.

- The GMROI (Gross Margin Return On Inventory) increased 30%.

- Based on the trial results, Wal-Mart planned to expand the QR operation to 7 major vendors.

The principal contributors to these improvements were:

- Bi-weekly store counts instead of monthly.

- Count to ship of 11 days rather than 22 days.

- A 10 day manufacturing cycle.

- 10 day fabric replenishment.

<u>Dillards/Lady Arrow/Milliken</u> – Seasonal Bow Blouse

- 20 test stores were compared to plan.

- Unit sales increased 47%.

- Turns increased 36%, from 6.2 to 8.5.

- GMROI increased 37%.

- A plan to expand the program to 3 to 5 additional vendors/product categories.

Contributing to the results were:

- Desk-top computer based plans by SKU.

- POS data capture.

- Weekly re-order.

- 10 day replenishment cycle.

- Monthly plan adjustment.

- Engineered distribution.

J.C. Penney/Lanier/Burlington - Tailored Clothing.
(Basic/Seasonal - 60%, Fancy - 40%)

- 4 pilot vs. 4 control stores.

- 59% increase in unit sales.

- Turns increased 90% - from 1.1 to 2.1.

- Inventory reduction of 20%.

- Gross margin ($) increased 82%.

- Plans to adopt QR for tailored clothing and to add other categories.

The following changes contributed to these results:

- Automatic weekly re-orders by SKU.

    - 2 week replenishment cycle for basics and seasonal goods.
    - 6 week cycle for fancies that were made to order.

- Training at region and store levels.

- Monthly rotation of fancy fabrics within style groups.

The results obtained in the trials were almost unbelievably good. There is no doubt that the extra attention called for, and given, the special merchandise did much to increase performance. However, the greatest part of the improvements were real. Stockouts and markdowns both dropped sharply as the frequently updated merchandise plans ensured the correct mix of colors and styles on the shelves. The greatly reduced cycle times also guaranteed higher inventory turns. These were fundamental improvements that came as results of system changes.

The retailers involved in the partnerships all expressed their desire to roll out the QR program to other categories. Such an expansion is, however difficult to accomplish. It is one thing to set up a pilot program with new planning, point-of-sale tracking and inventory control equipment and software to handle a single line on a one time basis, and another thing to effect a complete, company-wide change. That takes time and money. It also requires that a very broad group of vendors and their suppliers be equipped to participate and to have adopted the bar code standards and procedures only now being set up.

Notes - Chapter 9.

The results of the first QR trials were widely reported in the trade press and journals and can be obtained from the CWP organization.

Southern Textile News July 24, 1989 reported the results of a very successful QR children's wear trial involving the Baby Superstore chain, a specialty retailer, the Warren Featherbone Company and Springs Industries. In a four month trial, 10 units of the 25 store chain adopted QR procedures and 11 stores were selected as the control group. Weekly POS data were transmitted to the manufacturer vs. the normal 30 day count and reorders were filled within five days. The major results included a 31% increase in retail sales, profits increased over 50% for the selected lines and there was an immediate reduction of 25% in the manufacturer's fabric inventory.

Chapter 10. QR Cost/Benefit Analyses.

The QR trials sponsored by Crafted With Pride and discussed in the preceding chapter were extremely successful and attracted a great deal of attention in the trade. The companies that participated in the trials and learned how the QR process works moved without delay to expand their Value Adding Partnerships (VAPs) with suppliers and to roll out the programs to include additional product lines. Certainly, both the participating retailers and the more progressive of their competitors were quick to realise that QR methodology was capable of increasing sharply both their share of market and financial performance at the expense of companies employing traditional supply methodologies.

The trials did, however, raise a number of questions, including, "What is the investment pay-off for Basic, Seasonal and Fashion merchandise?" and "What are the QR economics for specific garment categories?". To provide information to the industry on these issues, KSA and du Pont undertook a series of cost/benefit studies on behalf of CWP. These analyses are the subject of the present chapter.

Scope Of The Analyses.

To avoid confusion with the earlier competitiveness studies, it is helpful to remember that the two are compatible in most ways but differ in level of detail and in time frame. The earlier analyses were macro in approach, made no attempt to be truly product specific and were carried out before the trials had revealed the extent to which, for example, stockout levels would actually decrease and sales would increase. The assumptions made in the earlier QR models proved to be soundly based, but restricted by the lack of actual experience. The later cost/benefit analyses also took into account the real costs of implementing QR at the textile, apparel and retail levels based on the newly available studies of VICS, TALC and the other linkage associations that specified the required level of involvement in POS, bar coding, etc.

Actual products sold by a major retailer were the basis of the analyses and reflected real sourcing costs. Selected expenses, working capital requirements and fixed investment data were also based on actual industry experience. Two Basic, two Seasonal and three Fashion products were studied in detail, fabric through retail, and cost bases were developed for additional fabrics and garments. In addition, comparisons were made between domestic and imported garments, with and without QR. Increases in sales levels resulting from the adoption of QR procedures were based on the QR trials using values of 20%, 30% and 35% for Basic, Seasonal and Fashion merchandise, respectively.

The sequence of analyses was to model the retail scene and then to examine the implications of retail actions, first on the apparel and then on the textile supply operations.

An important aspect of the cost/benefit analyses was the recognition that full implementation of QR is expensive and time consuming. Accordingly, the impacts of both full and partial involvement in QR were examined.

Retail Analyses.

Before getting into the details of the various products, it is instructive to examine the broad operating performance results of the analyses. The values for the Return on Sales, Return on Assets and the Gross Margin Return on Inventory are shown in Table 10.1, together with the Inventory Turns under both the Traditional and the QR systems. All the indicators show strong gains. It will be remembered that the early work on QR had been directed toward Seasonal goods as offering the greatest opportunity for operating improvement. Table 10.1 shows, however, that there is a substantial benefit for Basic goods and that Fashion merchandise stands to benefit the most from the application of QR.

Common to the retail analyses were the following direct operating cost assumptions:

• Freight. The garments were assumed to weigh an average of 0.75 pounds. The freight for imported goods was based on current ocean transit charges but the charges for QR domestic goods were assumed to be 25% greater than for garments shipped in the traditional manner because of the increased frequency of shipping and the smaller lot sizes.

• Merchandise Processing. This category covers the direct labor involved in the receiving and marking of garments and industry average data were used. The cost of direct labor is lower under QR because of the reduction in double handling, the pre-ticketing of products and cases by the vendor and the more even flow of shipments.

• Purchase Order Processing. Again based on industry averages, such costs increase under QR because of the increase in the number and frequency of orders. However, the higher costs do not reflect the savings associated with EDI order transmission which lead to an overall reduction in P.O. processing costs.

• Communications. Assumed to be unchanged for domestic QR products.

• Selling and Sales Support. As with communications, assumed to be unchanged in dollar terms but lower as a percent of sales because of the higher volume.

• Buying Cost. Costs associated with travel are assumed to remain unchanged. Time costs, which are based on base salary and fringe benefits, are assumed to be lower under QR where automation allows a given buyer to handle a broader product range. However, it is recognised that a buyer's time commitment could well increase in the initial stages of QR implementation until the new techniques have been learned.

• Space Costs. These costs decrease under QR because of lower inventory requirements, though the relationship is not linear.

Table 10.1
Summary of Retail Results
QR vs. Traditional

	ROS		Invent.		ROA		GMROI	
	Trad.	QR	Trad.	QR	Trad.	QR	Trad.	QR
Basic								
Men's Dress Shirt	7.3	10.1	2.8	4.5	10.7	17.9	3.9	6.3
W. Oxford Blouse	4.9	8.5	4.0	5.0	7.5	14.4	4.9	6.3
Seasonal								
Men's Casual Slack	5.6	10.2	3.5	5.9	8.5	17.9	4.5	7.3
W. Tailored Slack	3.2	8.2	4.0	6.0	5.0	14.5	4.6	7.2
Fashion								
Men's Knit Shirt	4.1	9.8	4.0	8.0	6.4	18.2	4.8	10.0
Women's Blouse	2.5	8.9	4.5	8.0	4.0	16.3	5.1	9.6
Women's Skirt	(0.5)	5.9	4.0	8.0	(0.8)	10.8	3.7	8.0
Average	3.9	8.8	3.8	6.4	5.9	15.7	4.5	7.8
Improvement								
Basic QR vs. Trad.		3.2		1.3		7.0		1.9
Seasonal QR vs. Trad.		1.8		2.2		9.5		2.7
Fashion QR vs. Trad.		5.2		3.8		11.9		4.6

Table 10.2 summarizes the cost elements for each of the merchandise groups. The values shown relate to $100.00 of net sales under the traditional system (see Tables 10.3 - 10.5).

In addition to the general assumptions listed above, the following were assumed for the three classes of product.

• Sales increase 20%, 30% and 35% over traditional levels for the Basic, Seasonal and Fashion items, respectively, because of the improved in-stock position that leads to fewer lost sales.

• Clearance markdowns are halved as a result of lower inventory levels and stock replenishment based on POS data by SKU.

• Inventory turnover increases because of lower inventory levels. It should be noted here that the increase is very much dependent on the level of service adopted by the retailer and the number of SKUs required for a product, including the "fringe" SKUs. Inventory turns for Basic products is generally lower than for Seasonal or Fashion goods.

Table 10.2
Components of Direct Retail Cost
($ per Unit)

	Basic		Seasonal		Fashion	
	Trad.	QR	Trad.	QR	Trad.	QR
Sourcing/Systems/ Selling	<u>10.40</u>	<u>10.90</u>	<u>10.40</u>	<u>11.30</u>	<u>10.40</u>	<u>11.49</u>
Freight	0.80	1.20	0.80	1.30	0.80	1.35
Merch. Processing	1.70	1.44	1.70	1.56	1.70	1.62
P.O. Processing	0.60	1.08	0.60	1.17	0.60	1.21
Communications	0.40	0.40	0.40	0.40	0.40	0.40
Sales Support	5.50	5.50	5.50	5.50	5.50	5.50
Buying Cost						
Time	1.20	1.08	1.20	1.17	1.20	1.21
Travel	0.20	0.20	0.20	0.20	0.20	0.20
Space Cost	10.00	9.24	10.00	9.00	10.00	7.90
TOTAL	20.40	20.14	20.40	20.30	20.40	19.39

The comparative QR vs. Traditional economics for the three lines of merchandise are shown in more detail in Tables 10.3, 10.4 and 10.5 below. Rather than using the actual value per garment, or its equivalent, the data relate to $100 of net sales under the traditional system for each garment, i.e., the fourth line of each table is the base line. Markdowns appear above this line and information on markups below it. The cost data follow and include the cost of markdowns as well as the direct costs from Table 10.2. The reductions in inventories under QR are also identified. In addition to the usual measures of performance, the Contribution Margin Return on Inventory (CMROI) is calculated. As POS information becomes more readily available, the CMROI should emerge as a more common measure of buyer performance.

One other analysis remains to be discussed; the comparative economics of QR domestic and traditional imported garments. These are shown in Table 10.6 for the men's knit shirt, the women's blouse and the skirt. They are characterized by the higher freight costs and greater markdown levels for imports because of the retailer's inability to respond to true consumer demand. Also, the inventory turns for imports are lower, in line with the longer shipping times and the inventory commitment associated with the letter of credit being cashed at the time of production.

The improvement in performance made possible by switching from imports to domestic QR for Fashion goods can only be described as dramatic, particularly in the cases of the knit shirt and blouse import categories.

Table 10.3
QR vs. Traditional Economics
Basic Products

	Men's Dress Shirt		Women's Blouse	
	Trad.	QR	Trad.	QR
Potential Sales $	112.00	132.00	116.00	135.60
Clearance Markdown $	4.00	2.40	6.0	3.60
Promotional Markdown $	8.00	9.60	10.00	12.00
Net Sales $	100.00	120.00	100.00	120.00
Initial Mark-up %	60.0	60.0	58.0	58.0
Mark-up $	60.00	72.00	58.00	69.60
Cost of Markdowns $	4.80	4.80	6.72	6.55
Gross Margin $	55.20	67.20	51.28	63.05
Direct Prod.Op. Cost $	20.40	20.14	20.40	20.14
Contribution Margin $	34.80	47.06	30.88	42.91
All other costs $	23.00	26.40	23.00	26.40
Pre-tax Profit $	11.80	20.66	7.88	16.51
Net Profit $	7.31	12.81	4.89	10.23
Turnover	2.8	4.5	4.0	5.0
Inventory (Retail)	35.71	26.66	25.00	24.00
Inventory (Cost)	14.28	10.66	10.50	10.08
Other Working Capital	35.00	42.00	35.00	42.00
Fixed Investment	19.00	19.00	19.00	19.00
Total Investment $	68.28	71.66	64.50	71.08
Return on Sales %	7.3	10.7	4.9	8.5
Return on Assets %	10.7	17.9	7.6	14.4
GMROI	3.9	6.3	4.9	6.3
CMROI	2.4	4.4	2.9	4.3

Table 10.4
QR vs. Traditional Economics
Seasonal Products

	Men's Slack Trad.	Men's Slack QR	Women's Slack Trad.	Women's Slack QR
Potential Sales $	116.00	145.60	121.00	150.15
Clearance Markdown $	8.00	5.20	11.00	7.15
Promotional Markdowns $	8.00	10.40	10.00	13.00
Net Sales $	100.00	130.00	100.00	130.00
Initial Mark-up %	59.0	59.0	57.5	57.5
Mark-up $	59.00	76.70	57.50	74.75
Cost of Markdowns $	6.56	6.40	8.93	8.56
Gross Margin $	52.44	70.30	48.57	66.19
Direct Prod. Op. Cost $	20.40	20.30	20.40	19.30
Contribution Margin $	32.05	50.00	28.17	45.89
All other costs $	23.00	28.60	23.00	28.60
Pre-tax Profit $	9.04	21.40	5.17	17.29
Net Profit $	5.60	13.27	3.21	10.72
Turnover	3.5	5.5	4.0	6.0
Inventory (Retail)	28.57	23.67	25.00	21.67
Inventory (Cost) $	11.71	9.70	10.63	9.21
Other Working Capital $	35.00	45.50	35.00	45.50
Fixed Investment $	19.00	19.00	19.00	19.00
Total Investment $	65.71	74.20	64.63	73.71
Return on Sales %	5.6	10.2	3.2	8.2
Return on Assets %	8.5	17.9	5.0	14.5
GMROI	4.5	7.3	4.6	7.2
CMROI	2.7	5.2	2.7	5.0

Table 10.5
QR vs. Traditional Economics
Fashion Products

	M. Knit Shirt		W. Blouse		W. Skirt	
	Trad.	QR	Trad.	QR	Trad.	QR
Potential Sales$	119.00	153.23	125.00	158.63	125.00	158.63
Clear. Markdowns$	11.0	7.43	15.00	10.13	15.00	10.13
Promo. Markdowns$	8.00	10.80	10.00	13.50	10.00	13.50
Net Sales $	100.00	135.00	100.00	135.00	100.00	135.00
Initial Mark-up %	58.0	58.0	58.0	58.0	54.0	54.0
Mark-up $	58.00	78.30	58.00	78.30	54.00	72.90
Cost of Markdowns$	7.98	7.66	10.50	9.92	11.50	10.87
Gross Margin $	50.02	70.64	47.50	68.38	42.50	62.03
Dir. Prod. Op. Cost	20.40	20.39	20.40	19.39	20.40	19.39
Contrib. Margin $	29.62	51.25	27.10	48.99	22.10	42.64
All other costs $	23.00	29.70	23.00	29.70	23.00	29.70
Pre-tax Profit $	4.10	13.36	2.54	11.96	(.56)	8.02
Net Profit $	6.62	21.55	4.10	19.29	(.90)	12.94
Turnover	4.0	8.0	4.5	8.0	4.0	8.0
Inventory (Retail) $	25.00	16.88	22.22	16.88	25.00	16.88
Inventory (Cost) $	10.50	7.09	9.33	7.09	11.50	7.76
Other W. C. $	35.00	47.25	35.00	47.25	35.00	47.25
Fixed Investment $	19.00	19.00	19.00	19.00	19.00	19.00
Total Investment $	64.50	73.34	63.33	73.34	65.50	74.01
Return on Sales %	4.1	9.8	2.5	8.9	(0.6)	5.9
Return on Assets %	6.4	18.2	4.0	16.3	(0.8)	10.8
GMROI	4.8	10.0	5.1	9.6	3.7	8.0
CMROI	2.8	7.2	2.9	6.9	1.9	5.5

Table 10.6
Domestic QR vs. Traditional Import Economics
Fashion Products

	M. Knit Shirt		W. Blouse		W. Skirt	
	Trad.	QR	Trad.	QR	Trad.	QR
Potential Sales $	122.00	153.23	128.00	158.63	128.00	158.63
Clear. Markdowns $	14.00	7.43	18.00	10.13	18.00	10.13
Promo. Markdowns $	8.00	10.80	10.00	13.50	10.00	13.50
Net Sales $	100.00	135.00	100.00	135.00	100.00	135.00
Initial Mark-up %	60.0	58.0	60.0	58.0	65.0	54.0
Mark-up $	60.00	78.30	60.00	78.30	65.00	72.90
Cost of Markdowns $	8.80	7.66	11.20	9.92	9.80	10.87
Gross Margin $	51.20	70.64	48.80	68.38	55.20	62.03
Dir. Prod. Op. Cost	22.90	19.39	22.90	19.39	22.90	19.39
Contrib. Margin $	28.30	51.25	25.90	48.99	32.30	42.64
All other costs $	23.00	29.70	23.00	29.70	23.00	29.70
Pre-tax Profit $	5.30	21.55	2.90	19.29	9.30	12.94
Net Profit $	3.18	13.36	1.74	11.96	5.58	8.02
Turnover	2.9	8.0	3.1	8.0	2.9	8.0
Inventory (Retail) $	34.48	16.88	32.25	16.88	34.48	16.88
Inventory (Cost) $	13.79	7.09	12.90	7.09	12.07	7.76
Other W. C. $	35.00	47.25	35.00	47.25	35.00	47.25
Fixed Investment $	19.00	19.00	19.00	19.00	19.00	19.00
Total Investment $	67.79	73.34	66.90	73.34	66.07	74.01
Return on Sales %	3.2	9.8	1.7	8.9	5.6	5.9
Return on Assets %	4.7	18.2	2.6	16.3	8.5	10.8
GMROI	3.7	10.0	3.8	9.6	4.6	8.0
CMROI	2.1	7.2	2.0	6.9	2.3	5.5

The economic comparison of domestic QR vs. import sourcing shown in Table 10.6 will have an important effect on the attitude of the retailer toward import pricing. Traditionally, imports must be landed 10-15% below domestic costs because of the higher risk and expense. QR will increase that permissible discount by a factor of two to three. Table 10.7 shows, for a typical fashion product, the kind of calculation required to quantify this equivalence discount.

Table 10.7
Purchase Price Comparison
QR, Traditional Domestic and Imported

	QR Dom.	% Net Sales	Trad. Dom.	% Net Sales	Trad. Imp.	% Net Sales
Unit Cost $	14		14		12	
Mark On $	16		16		18	
First Selling Price $	30		30		30	
Turns	7.5		4.5		3.8	
Units Sold	125		100		100	
Clearance MD $	224	7.0	295	12.0	360	15.0
Promo. MD $	321	10.0	246	10.0	240	10.0
Net Retail Sales $	3205		2459		2400	
COGS $ *	1750		1400		1200	
Gross Margin $	1455	45.4	1059	43.1	1200	50.0
Source./Syst./Sell. $	263	8.2	255	10.4	278	11.6
Space	192	6.0	246	10.0	264	11.0
Inventory @ 10%	10	0.3	17	0.7	46	1.9
Allocated Costs	465	14.5	518	21.1	588	24.5
Contrib. Margin $	990	30.9	541	22.0	612	25.5
Lost Contrib. $			449		378	
Lost Contrib./Unit $			4.49		3.78	
Discount Required To Equal QR			32%		32%	

* Cost Of Goods Sold

Apparel Manufacturing Analyses

The analyses of the apparel manufacturing operations required to supply the retailer with the specific products described in the previous section were carried out in considerable detail. Models of typical PBU plants were constructed, with all the necessary assumptions as to floor space, investment, staffing etc. These were then modified to reflect two levels of QR involvement.

It is not possible in the body of the text to list all of the model assumptions - these are given in Appendix J - or the detailed results of the simulations, which are provided in Appendix K. However, the principal factors governing the analyses together with the major findings are summarized below.

The plant was modelled as opening in 1979 with 255 sewing and finishing operators and maintained in good operating condition. In 1986, conversions to QR manufacturing were initiated and carried to completion over the next two years in one of two modes:

• Quick Response I is the term used to describe partial involvement. The TALC and VICS standards described earlier, including direct electronic linkage systems with both textile suppliers and retail customers, are assumed to have been implemented. Raw material inventories are at a minimum.

• Quick Response II indicates full participation in QR. In addition to the procedures listed above, short cycle, flexible manufacturing is in place to minimize WIP inventories and superior forecasting, planning and scheduling techniques are used to reduce finished goods inventories.

QR I and QR II were applied to both Basic and Seasonal goods. In the case of Fashion merchandise, only QR II was compared to traditional performance as QR I is believed to confer no benefit on the supply of short season goods.

On an aggregate level, the improvements brought about by QR are shown in Table 10.8. It must be remembered that the QR data reflect volume increases of 20%, 30% and 35% over traditional levels for Basic, Seasonal and Fashion goods respectively. As was the case at retail, QR improves operating performance dramatically.

Table 10.8
Business Performance Summary
QR vs. Traditional

	Basic		Seasonal		Fashion
	QR I	QR II	QR I	QR II	QR II
Gross Margin %	24.1	25.9	33.1	37.7	42.1
Pts. Improvement	0.7	2.5	0.7	5.3	4.1
After Tax ROS %	3.6	4.8	8.0	11.0	10.5
Pts. Improvement	0.6	1.8	0.6	3.6	2.9
After Tax ROI %	6.5	9.8	15.2	24.6	24.7
Pts. Improvement	1.3	4.6	2.6	12.0	11.7
After Tax ROE %	8.2	13.2	18.4	31.5	30.6
Pts. Improvement	1.5	6.5	2.9	16.0	14.9

The investment levels required to implement QR are substantial, and especially so in the case of QR II. Table 10.9 shows the average investments required and the paybacks achieved for the three product classes.

Table 10.9
QR Investment and Payback

	Basic		Seasonal		Fashion
Proj. Lost Benefits	QR I	QR II	QR I	QR II	QR II
Δ Pre tax profits/ annual SAH *	$0.29	$0.92	$0.43	$2.34	$2.43
Δ Released WC/ annual SAH	0.06	0.46	0.09	0.54	0.63
	$0.35	$1.38	$0.52	$2.88	3.06
Cost/Annual SAH					
Capital Invest.	$1.06	$2.18	$0.76	$1.61	$1.48
Expense	0.18	1.32	0.17	1.26	1.32
	$1.24	$3.50	$0.93	$2.87	$2.80
Payback (Simple)					
No. Years	3.4	2.4	1.8	1.0	0.9

* Standard Allowed Hours.

The data in Tables 10.8 and 10.9 are averages for the three classes of garments. In order to give some idea of the variability within a class and also to provide specific examples of product performance improvements, business performance, plant performance and QR implementation cost/benefit information are provided in Tables 10.10 and 10.11 for each of the three fashion garments analysed in the study.

Table 10.10
Plant & Business Performance
QR vs. Traditional Manufacturing
Fashion Garments

	M. Knit Shirt		W. Blouse		W.Skirt	
	Trad.	QR II	Trad.	QR II	Trad	QR II
Standard Cost						
Sew/Fin. SAH/Doz.	2.14	1.92	2.12	1.94	2.48	2.29
Productivity						
Ann. SAH/Employee.	1108	1427	1076	1455	1076	1386
Ann. SAH/Sq. Ft.	12.20	18.20	9.70	16.80	10.10	15.90
Overhead						
% of Stand. D.L.*	135.30	108.60	145.10	111.80	146.40	114.40
Tot. Mill Cost/Doz. $	26.84	21.85	27.41	22.00	31.68	25.66
Gross Margin %	37.30	41.20	38.40	45.50	38.40	39.60
After Tax Returns %						
On Sales	6.90	9.90	7.60	12.70	7.60	8.90
On Investment	12.80	24.70	12.90	28.50	13.20	20.90
On Equity	15.10	29.70	15.90	36.30	16.10	25.90

* Direct Labor.

The extent to which QR improves operational performance differs from garment to garment, but in each case there is a substantial improvement. The underlying cause of the variability is not always obvious. In the case of skirts, for example, the high cost of providing short fabric runs lowers the level of QR improvement, whereas many other categories are less sensitive to fabric supply costs.

Table 10.11 gives estimates of the investment required to implement QR. This is a very new field of study and depends not only on the type of product being made, but also on the state of readiness of the firm making the change and the equipment at its disposal. Another factor is the extent to which consulting and training costs must be factored into the payback calculations. One thing is sure; for fashion, more than for less seasonal goods, the paybacks are excellent.

Table 10.11
QR Implementation Costs and Paybacks
Fashion Goods

	M. Knit Shirt		W. Blouse		W. Skirt	
	Trad.	QR II	Trad.	QR II	Trad.	QR II
Investment in QR						
Annual Sales/SAH $	–	54.50	–	38.78	–	43.36
% Investment (Capital)						
in QR (% of Sales)	–	1.60	–	2.50	–	1.90
in Expansion	–	1.00	–	1.70	–	1.30
Total		2.60		4.20		3.20
Pre-Tax Profit						
$/Annual SAH	5.73	8.61	4.51	7.80	5.04	6.15
Δ vs. Trad. $	–	2.88	–	3.29	–	1.11
Value of Working Capital Release						
W. C./Ann. SAH $	20.23	14.38	14.14	9.34	16.17	11.19
Value @ 12%	–	0.70	–	0.58	–	0.60
Tot. Ben./Ann. SAH $		3.58		3.87		1.71
Implementation Expense $						
Cap./Annual SAH		1.44		1.63		1.37
Expense/Ann. SAH		1.32		1.32		1.32
Total		2.76		2.95		2.69
Simple Payback (years)		0.8		0.8		1.6

The more detailed data contained in Appendix K are based on a number of assumptions about modular manufacturing efficiencies. Again, this is a relatively new area for the plant engineer and there remains a great deal to be learned. Industry experience to-date shows that modular manufacturing is not a panacea for all products and that a great deal of thought must be given to its implementation. Properly handled, however, it can provide tremendous flexibility of the kind needed to minimize finished goods inventories while providing the retailer with the all important capability for re-order.

Although mentioned in several other parts of the book, it must again be stressed that the key to implementing QR is more than just systems and technology; it is the mind set summed up by the phrase "Value Adding Management". QR simply will not work, no matter what the investment, unless all the parts, technology, modular layouts, engineering, total quality management and employee involvement are combined into a way of life.

Textile Analyses

The most complicated part of the KSA/du Pont study is the analysis of the application of QR to textile operations. As with the apparel analyses, much new ground had to be covered, particularly in the areas of short run weaving and short cycle dyeing and finishing. Further complications arose from the need to define very carefully the fabric commitment and shipping schedules associated with the three classes of fabrics and to attempt to represent the very wide range of fabric types used in apparel manufacture. In carrying out the work, extensive use was made of the very detailed textile cost models built up over many years by du Pont.

Because of the complexity of the analyses, it is important to spell out the model structure and assumptions in rather more detail than was given for retail and apparel manufacturing.

I. Capacity Commitment.

• For Basic products, there is a continuing commitment for greige fabric that is updated on a monthly or quarterly basis. Color projections are updated more frequently, e.g., each week, depending on the customer's sales patterns.

• In the case of Seasonal goods, an initial commitment is made at the greige level for 75% of the fabric selection with the balance being reserved in weeks 7-8. 50-60% of the color assortment is made at the beginning of the season with the balance being specified following week four of the season on a weekly basis.

• All fabrics for Fashion products are contracted.

II. Dyeing Schedule.

	Traditional	With QR
• Basic	Dye ahead plus color rotation, light to dark, on 1-2 week cycle.	All colors weekly.
• Seasonal	As above.	As above.
• Fashion	As above.	As requested.

III. Fabric Delivery Schedule.

	Traditional	With QR
• Basic	Bi-weekly	Weekly
• Seasonal	50% of order in 16th. week after P.O., 40% in 20th. week and 10% in 24th. week.	45% in 10th. week, 55% in weeks 13-28 on weekly basis.
• Fashion – Spuns	90% of order in week 20, 10% in week 24.	40-60% of order in week after receipt of P.O.; balance as needed.
– Textured	As above.	40-60% in week 7, balance as needed.
– Spun Knits	90% in week 14, 10% in week 17.	40-60% of order in week 7 with the balance as requ'd.

	- Textured	As above.	40-60% in week 5 with balance as needed.

IV. Linkage.

• In the QR cases, TALC and FASLINC standards are adhered to and EDI for P.O.s, shipping notices, invoices, etc. is practiced.

V. Study Fabrics.

• Basic
   - 50/50 Polyester/Cotton Broadcloth - 60" finished width; 2.82 yards/pound.
   - 40/60 P/C Oxford - 60"; 2.59 yards/pound.

• Seasonal
   - All Cotton Twill - 60"; 1.10 yards/pound.
   - 65/35 P/C Twill - 60"; 1.55 yards/pound.

• Fashion
   - All Cotton Yarn Dyed Madras - 45"; 5.12 yards/pound.
   - 100% Polyester Pongee - 60"; 6.00 yards/pound.
   - 50/50 P/C Jersey Knit - 60"; 2.91 yards/pound; white with printed stripe.

VI. Operations - Traditional Cases.

• A separate model is set up for each of the fabrics considered. The textile mill complexity and product diversity characteristics used were those common in today's operations.

• Mill operating schedules are based on 5 days for both greige and dyeing and finishing plants.

• Production levels used are in the range of:
   - 0.4-0.6 million yards per week for individual greige mills,
   - 1.0-2.0 million yards per week for dyeing and finishing plants.

• Traditional forecasting, production planning and scheduling techniques are used and staffing is in accordance with industry practice.

• The overall production planning goals of minimizing greige style changes and maximizing D&F lot sizes are assumed.

• The product information provided to the customer is limited to nominal fabric width and quality, with a small number of shades being shipped to each customer.

VII. Operations - QR Cases - Basic.

• Technology is up-dated to handle TALC and FASLINC standards and investments are made both to improve finished fabric inspection and packaging and to allow EDI with suppliers and customers.

• Mill operating schedules increase to 6 days to handle increased demand for fabrics. This raises production levels to 0.5-0.7 million yards per week for greige mills and 1.2-1.4 million yards per week for D&F plants.

• Textile mill complexity and product diversity levels are unchanged but more looms are scheduled on shorter runs and the dyeing and finishing operations produce color assortments with a two week lead time on 100% cotton and blends and a one week lead time on 100% polyester fabrics.

• Additional staffing reflects effort to improve quality, production planning and customer service.

VIII. Operations - QR Cases - Seasonal.

• Mill schedules increase to seven days for greige operations with D&F held to six. Production levels become 0.52-0.78 million yards per week for greige and 1.3-2.6 million for D&F.

• Mill complexity and product diversity increase for warping, slashing, drawing-in, tieing, weaving and wet processing.

• Greige and finished inventories are reduced.

• Investment are made to improve fabric sampling capability.

• Two QR cases are developed:

- QR I represents limited implementation and involves D&F only.
- QR II is the full approach.

IX. Operations - QR - Fashion.

• As for the cases above, plus the following:

• Mill production levels become 0.54-0.81 million yards and 1.35-2.70 million yards per week, respectively, for greige and wet processing operations.

• There are substantial increases in D&F complexity and product diversity, more warps drawn and beams are smaller.

• Further investment is made in fabric sampling capability.

Making use of all the assumptions outlined above, each of the case fabrics was modelled for the appropriate set of conditions, both traditional and QR. However, in order to explore the consequences of each case on a common basis, a 50/50 P/C poplin was first modelled under the full set of conditions. Also, different annual poplin production levels were used to reflect the increased sales volumes resulting from QR. These were:

Traditional - 60 million yards   Seasonal - 78 million yards

Basic - 72 million yards   Fashion - 81 million yards.

Table 10.12 shows the overall economics of QR.

The investment required to implement QR is summarized in Table 10.13 which is consistent with Table 10.12. Following Table 10.13 is a second tabulation (Table 10.14) that looks at the investment required if no additional yardage is gained by going to QR i.e. if the yardage remains at 60 million per year. In both cases the paybacks are excellent.

Table 10.12
Summary Economics For Poplin

	Basic		Seasonal		Fashion
	Trad.	QR II	QR I	QR II	QR II
Net Sales (Mill $)	101.8	123.3	137.1	141.3	154.6
Annual Yards	60	72	78	78	81
AT Profit/Yd. $	0.085	0.103	0.102	0.105	0.119
ROS %	5.0	6.0	5.8	5.8	6.2
ROA %	9.1	12.2	12.7	12.8	13.4

Table 10.13
QR Investment At Higher Volumes

	Basic	Seasonal		Fashion
	QR II	QR I	QR II	QR II
Investments ($000's)				
Systems (TALC etc.)	576	1,040	1,040	1,620
Inspect, pack, ship	336	423	423	486
Greater flexibility etc.	–	283	1,843	6,510
Consulting/VAM culture	340	525	525	690
Total	1,252	2,271	3,831	9,306
Returns – $				
Increased profit/yard	0.018	0.017	0.020	0.034
Inc. profit/yr. ($000)	2,316	2,856	3,090	4,539
Payback (months)	7	10	15	25

In studying the impact of QR on the textile operation it was assumed that the greige mills could expand capacity to meet the additional demand. The question of adding new capacity has not been addressed here as it is a very complicated subject. However, expansion of wet processing capacity is more tractable and Table 10.15 shows the levels of investment required and the approximate returns on those investments.

Tables 10.12 through 10.15 are concerned with the economics of a poplin fabric. This was done to provide a common thread for the investment/return story. Details of the economics of the poplin and the case fabrics are given in Appendix L. When examining these data one aspect of the transition to QR will be noted; the sharp increase in direct labor at both the greige and wet processing stages. These increases reflect the present lack of short cycle, flexible manufacturing capability in the textile industry. As discussed earlier, the textile industry has for many years concentrated on the long runs that are compatible with basic apparel. The shift to flexible operations with only a nominal increase in cost is a very difficult task that calls for a fundamental re-thinking of the whole manufacturing process. The more progressive mills have already embarked on such programs.

The magnitude of this task and of the attendant rewards are indicated in Table 10.16 which shows the percentage increase in process labor for each of the case fabrics on going from traditional manufacture to QR.

Table 10.14
QR Investment At Constant Volume

	Basic QR II	Seasonal QR I	QR II	Fashion QR II
Investments ($000's)				
Systems	480	800	800	1200
Inspect etc.	280	325	325	360
Consulting etc.	340	525	525	690
TOTAL	1,100	1,650	1,650	2,250
Returns - $				
Increased profit/year	1,080	1,020	1,200	2,040
Payback (months)	12	19	16	13

Table 10.15
Investment For QR And Additional Capacity
Dyeing And Finishing

	Basic QR II	Seasonal QR I	QR II	Fashion QR II
Net Sales ($ millions)	123	137	141	155
Annual Yards (millions)	72	78	78	81
Investments ($000's)				
Additional capacity	-	3,007	3,007	5,520
QR Investment	-	1,746	3,306	8,616
Training, consulting etc.	-	525	525	690
TOTAL	-	5,278	6,838	14,826
Returns ($000's)				
Increased profit/year		2,544	2,700	3,891
Payback (months)		25	30	46

137

Table 10.16
% Increase Process Labor Costs
QR Over Traditional

	Greige		D&F	
	QR I	QR II	QR I	QR II
Basic Products				
Broadcloth		7.3		13.6
Yarn Dyed Oxford		6.5		14.3
Seasonal Products				
Cotton Twill	17.2	34.4	29.4	34.4
P/C Twill	17.3	37.5	34.4	37.5
Fashion Products				
Madras		45.5		50.0
Pongee		43.0		37.5
Jersey		9.0		9.0

Summary.

It is impossible to overstate the importance of the KSA/du Pont Cost/Benefit Study discussed in this chapter. The results show clearly the feasibility of QR, the acceptability of the paybacks on investment and the greatly enhanced financial performance for the apparel supply pipeline as a whole and for its parts.

In practical terms, the conversion to Basics QR is now well on its way. Rolling out to Seasonal and Fashion goods is the next challenge. Here the initiative will most likely be taken by the retailer who has the most to gain. When the leading retailers experience the full range of QR benefits, the apparel and textile industries will have no choice but to follow if they wish to remain suppliers.

But much remains to be done. Fully working out the complications of modular, flexible manufacturing and developing flexible textile manufacturing methodologies have been mentioned. The problem lies in the fact that no two plants are alike, each has its own peculiarities and unique requirements. Each company must, therefore, undertake its own cost/benefit studies; those provided here are only a guide.

One further point should be mentioned. The sales gains used in the study are, in one sense, opportunistic. Once the majority of retailers have converted to QR, and this will not happen over-night, the volume increases will be much smaller. When QR is the norm and full competitiveness reestablishes itself, growth will come in two areas; the replacement of imports and any increases in the share of the general public's discretionary spending resulting from lower price inflation and improved in-store service. These effects are not well understood but a back-of-the-envelope analysis suggests that they may well amount to 3-7%/year versus the one time 20-35% used in the study.

Notes – Chapter 10.

Most of the material in this chapter is to be found in the Kurt Salmon Associates 1988 publication, "Quick Response Implementation - Action Steps For Retailers, Manufacturers & Suppliers" and its Detailed Data Supplement, September 1988. This study was carried out with the duPont Company and on behalf of the Crafted With Pride Council. It can be obtained by contacting any of these organizations.

Chapter 11.   VICS Implementation Studies.

The previous chapter gave the results of QR cost/benefit studies of specific fabrics and garments. While this work was underway, two other analyses were being performed under the sponsorship of VICS, the organization developing linkage standards at the manufacturer/retailer interface. VICS commissioned the consulting firms of Arthur Andersen & Co. and KSA to examine the costs and benefits of implementing QR for retailers and manufacturers, respectively. These studies complemented those sponsored by du Pont in that they were based on in-depth interviews with major companies experienced in the implementation of QR and VICS technologies and the results were aggregated to give an industry wide picture.

The results of the VICS studies were released at a meeting in Dallas in March 1989. It was attended by over 1200 industry representatives. The reception given the study findings gave clear signals that the period of asking if QR would work was over and that the future focus would be on how and when QR will be implemented.

The VICS Retail Study.

The Andersen Study was based on interviews, work sampling and operational reviews of 75 companies representing each major retail segment and with sales that ranged from tens of millions to tens of billions of dollars. The costs and benefits were broken into two major categories; those associated with the VICS endorsed technologies and those resulting from QR business strategies, with the former being a pre-requisite to the latter. Results were expressed in terms of both dollars, industry wide, and percent of sales, thus allowing individual companies to estimate their own performance measures.

The results are summarized in Table 11.1 below. Full implementation of the VICS technologies and QR strategies themselves were estimated to yield $9.6 billion per year in improved performance for the apparel retailing industry as a whole. This would involve an initial investment of some $3.6 billion and recurring costs of approximately $520 million per year. Table 11.1 also shows that these results are quite uniform; they vary little by type of outlet.

Table 11.1
Retail Cost/Benefit
Full QR Implementation
(% Sales)

	Initial Invest.	Annual Cost	Annual Benefits
Department Stores	2.2%	0.2%	4.9%
Mass Merchants	1.7%	0.2%	5.3%
Speciality Stores	1.8%	0.6%	5.0%
TOTAL RETAIL	1.9%	0.3%	5.1%
Amounting to:	$3,600M	$520M	$9,600M

A breakdown of the costs and benefits of both applying VICS technologies and adopting QR strategies are shown in Table 11.2. There, the technologies are grouped under three headings:

• Universal Product Code (UPC) & Point Of Sale Scanning. As discussed elsewhere, these allow companies to discontinue all but a few store counting procedures, to remove pricing and ringing-up errors, to reduce significantly the practices of distribution center ticketing and promotional re-ticketing and to increase check-out productivity.

• Electronic Data Interchange (EDI).

• Shipping Container Marking (SCM). This practice speeds goods through the Distribution Centre and automatically records additions to inventory.

141

When compared with the benefits they yield, the initial and recurring costs of technologies are small. Once implemented, QR strategies are possible with their highly significant impact on company performance.

Table 11.2
Retail Cost/Benefit By Component
(% Sales)

	Initial Invest.	Annual Cost	Annual Benefit
UPC + Scanning	0.88%	0.23%	1.41%
EDI	0.01%	0.03%	0.14%
SCM	0.02%	0.01%	0.25%
QR	1.00%	–	3.30%
TOTAL	1.9%	0.3%	5.1%

Table 11.3
Retail Benefits By Store Type.
(% Sales)

	Dept. Stores	Mass Merchants	Spec. Stores
Reduced Markdowns	3.0%	2.1%	2.7%
Administration	0.1%	0.1%	0.1%
Distribution	0.5%	0.4%	1.0%
Merchandising	0.6%	1.0%	0.5%
Inventory Costs	0.7%	0.7%	0.7%
TOTAL	4.9%	5.3%	5.0%

A breakdown of the benefits of the VICS technologies and QR itself, by type of store and major function are shown in Table 11.3. They are consistent with the previous data and are self-explanatory.

The VICS Manufacturer Study.

While the Andersen study concentrated on the retail operations themselves, the analyses undertaken by KSA included, specifically, the impact of cooperation at the manufacturer/retailer interface, i.e., the partnership aspect of QR.

The study considered implementation of QR in two stages:

Stage 1.

• VICS Technologies - Product Marking (UPC-A), EDI (ANSI X12) & Shipping Container Marking (Code 128).

• QR Partnerships.

Stage 2.

• Stage 1 plus Integrated Merchandising and Manufacturing (real time merchandising and short cycle flexible manufacturing).

The results are given in Table 11.4. They are extremely impressive and show both the low cost of getting started in QR - applying VICS technologies and starting to form QR or Value Adding Partnerships - as well as the excellent returns resulting from a full commitment to integrated manufacturing and merchandising.

More detailed analyses of the components of cost and their paybacks are given in the schedules, one for each of the steps in the QR process, that follow Table 11.4.

Table 11.4
Manufacturer Costs/Benefits.
(% Sales)

	Ave. Investment	Ave. Return
VICS Technologies	0.1%	0.3%
VICS + QR Partnerships	1.5	2.0
Stage 2.	7.1	11.3
Financials. (%)	ROS	ROA
Traditional	4.0	6.0
VICS + QR Partnerships	5.7	13.2
Stage 2.	6.9	22.2

VICS Technologies.

• One time investment of 0.11% of sales.

- Product marking; 0.07%. Of this, 60% is for bar code printing, scanning and label application equipment; the rest is for software, catalog and training.

- EDI; 0.02%. Software and installation.

- Shipping container marking; 0.02%. Labels, software and scanning.

• Recurring expenses of 0.15% of sales.

- Product marking; 0.10%. Ticket printing and label at taching.

- EDI; 0.02%. Third party EDI, maintenance, adding partners.

- Shipping container marking; 0.03%. Printing and la belling labor.

• Recurring benefits average 0.26% of sales.

- 0.09% from EDI savings on clerical and forms.

- 0.07% from reduced inventory control and distribution labor and time. In effect, QR systems merge the manufacturer and retailer distribution functions. KSA found the average time from order to shelf under traditional procedures to be 16-17 days; with QR this time is shortened to 9-10 days. Further, the average manhours per 1000 units drops from an estimated 30 to under 20.

- 0.06% from faster order receipt and turns.

- 0.04% from reduced chargebacks due to container marking.

QR Partnerships.

• One time investment of 1.4% of sales.

- 0.3% for data processing systems.

- 0.4% for partnership development.

- 0.7% for improved distribution.

• Recurring expenses of 0.2% of sales for added shipping, maintenance.

• Recurring benefits average 1.1% of sales.

- 0.15% from reduced fabric inventories.

- 0.25% from reduced markdowns.

- 0.70% from increased sales.

145

Integrated Merchandising/Manufacturing.

- One time investment of 5% of sales.

    - 2% for training

    - 2% for plant layout, equipment and expansion.

    - 1% for merchandising, CAD/CAM.

- Recurring expenses of 1.2% of sales.

    - 0.6-0.7% due to lower material utilization.

    - 0.5-0.6% for Style Testing, equipment operators.

- Recurring benefits amount to 6.2% of sales.

    - 2.0% higher sales. This number is, in one sense, contro-
    vertial. The basis for it is that manufacturers who en
    ter into QR partnerships with retailers will inevitably in-
    crease their share of business. While this is undoubtedly
    true in the short term, over time there will be a return to
    a more competitive environment. Thus, the advantage
    should be viewed as "one shot".

    - 1.2% from reduced inventory and WIP.

    - 0.9% from reduced labor.

    - 0.9% from reduced markdowns.

    - 0.7% from reduced seconds.

    - 0.5% due to space reductions.

Despite the overwhelming evidence for the profitability of QR,
it must not be assumed that the industry will adopt it universally or
quickly. At present, the major focus is on Basic goods where QR really means very rapid replenishment of low stock items - in other
words, a form of JIT. The transition to Seasonal and Fashion goods
will take longer to implement, although the benefits are considerably greater. The types of partnerships required, the sophistica-

tion of the systems and the basic changes in manufacturing practices will be developed only slowly. However, the retailing community now has a clear vision of where it can go and that is the most important prerequisite for full QR implementation.

Notes - Chapter 11.

The results of the VICS sponsored studies are to be found in two reports:

"Quick Response - A Study of Costs and Benefits to Retailers of Implementing Quick Response and Supporting Technologies", by Anderson Consulting, Arthur Andersen & Co.

"Implementing VICS Technology & Quick Response - Making QR Work in Consumer Products", by Kurt Salmon Associates.

The studies were widely reported in the U.S. trade press during March and April of 1989.

Chapter 12. Technology.

The earlier chapters made frequent reference to the importance of technology in the QR scheme of things and the purpose of
this part of the book is to pull together the major elements of the
various technologies now available to the industry. EDI and the
work of the Linkage Councils has been dealt with earlier. Future
technologies, including those now being worked on, as well as the
wish list, are the subject of Chapter 13.

Every year, at one or more of the major exhibitions, the
world's equipment manufacturers and systems development companies show literally hundreds of new or modified products. Keeping
current is a full time endeavor and much of the work of the trade
journals is devoted to this end. The best that can be done here is to
outline the scope of the principal groups of technologies, both hard
and soft. The Chapter Notes contain references to significant publications covering technology.

The Importance Of Technology.

One major impact of recent technical developments on the
textile and apparel industries is that they reduce the effect of differences in labor rates between the emerging nations and the developed countries of the world. They provide a way to substitute capital intensity for labor intensity, increase productivity and make the
competitive playing field more level. The labor gap is only partly
closed by today's products, but it is sufficient to make the domestic
industry competitive against fully half of the apparel now being imported. However, nothing is static. Continued invention is needed
to off-set the steady decrease in tariffs which will occur over the
next ten to twenty years.

Consumer responsiveness is the second of the major impacts
and a leading concern of QR methodology. Hard and soft technologies enable the pipeline industries to be more focussed and efficient
by compressing the time taken to design and manufacture the goods

the consumer actually wants, at attractive prices. To this should be added, "and at the required quality levels". One benefit of automation sometimes overlooked is its ability to produce goods of any quality level with vastly improved consistency through reduction of human error or variability. A second benefit is that of flexibility, the ability to shorten runs and increase the range of product offerings with minimal increases in cost.

It is often stated that the use of technology de-skills the manufacturing operation by reducing dependence on the abilities of the practiced operator. This is true and of great importance in an industry with a tradition of high labor turn-over and a constant need to train new operators. There is, however another side to the coin. Technology also demands new skills. Programming the new generations of equipment now capable of handling every aspect of manufacturing, fully utilizing computers and computer systems and maintaining the new machines calls for new skills. At a different level in the organization, the ability to manage technology, and the cultural changes it brings with it, is fast being recognised as an important attribute of those who would lead the company. The traditional ways of looking at investments and the criteria used in decision making are often invalid or inadequate because they are tactical rather than strategic in nature and capital intensity calls for different rules.

It is important to remember that the major exporting countries, Hong Kong. Taiwan and South Korea are learning these new rules and are also investing in apparel technology. They are doing so both to free up labor for other, growing industries such as electronics, with higher pay scales and to provide greater responsivenes to U.S. and European customers. The belief that Far Eastern cannot justify high technology because of their low labor rates is simply not true. Their investment policies are at least as strategically oriented as those of industrial nations.

It is no exaggeration to make the following statement. At the macro, or industry level, technology offers an alternative to replacement by off-shore producers; at the level of the firm, the choice becomes one of technology versus oblivion through declining competitiveness. Forty or so years ago, Henry Ford put the situation very compactly; "If you don't invest in new technology, you will pay for it without ever owning it."

The emphasis in this chapter is on apparel manufacturing technology, because there the need is greatest, the rewards are large and a high level of sophistication is required in the replacement of human operations. Many of the major, apparel-related advances in fiber and textile technologies have already occurred and are well understood, though there remains a steady pattern of adoptions of new technologies as they become available.

As a broad generalization, it can be claimed that technology intensity has moved down-stream in the apparel pipeline over time. The 1950's saw many of the fiber innovations in both process and product. These were followed by developments in very high speed filament yarn texturing and multi-feed circular knitting. In the 1970's it was the turn of the spinner and weaver. Opening rooms were automated, carding speeds were increased, drawing became semi-automated, open-end spinning systems were developed and new breeds of high speed weaving machines became available. The 1980's have seen the same types of break-through for apparel - CAD/CAM, UPS, programmable sewing equipment, etc. In the 1990's the focus is likely to be at retail with the main emphasis on soft technology. POS tracking and allied merchandise control systems will be adopted, video marketing will grow in importance as cable networks change to high resolution TV and CAD, style tracking and Style Testing will become parts of the buyers' box of tricks.

As the focus of technology has moved down-stream, it has placed increasing demands on the up-stream supplier. Very high speed looms required superior yarns, which in turn placed greater demands on the fiber producer and spinner. This has led to today's emphasis on process control and quality assurance which encourage employment of voice recognition and imageing technologies and these, in turn permit greater use of robotics for package doffing, handling and distribution. QR's insistence on short response times and greater product diversity is already beginning to have a similar effect on the up-stream industries. The traditional fabric defect and shade variability levels are at odds with inventory reduction and highly automated spreading and cutting equipment and short runs demand reduced fabric forming and wet processing down-times.

This model of technology movement is useful for both pulling together what has happened in the past and providing insight into the ways things are likely to develop in the future. The pipeline is not only a marketing and manufacturing pipeline, it is also a technological pipeline - the sectors are connected in all respects.

Computer Assisted Design.

CAD is one of the few technology developments concerning which nothing bad can be said; everything about it makes sense.

The use of computers for design purposes started in the 1960's, with its first applications in the aerospace and automobile industries. Architectural and general engineering design followed and by the beginning of this decade, textiles and then apparel applications were under development.

CAD for textiles is, by now, a highly developed technology. The leading equipment suppliers can simulate fibers of different thicknesses and color blends at different twist levels in the fabric. Surface effects such as brushing or nubs are also faithfully simulated. Colors, patterns and constructions can be changed rapidly, on screen, and printed out with extreme accuracy. Fabric costing or cost change algorithms, linkages to allow automatic drawing and entering of warp yarns and driving of weaving and knitting patterning mechanisms are becoming available.

An early reservation about CAD was that the colors on the screen could not be related to the colors as seen on dyed fabric - one system is color additive and the other is color subtractive. Also, fabric color varies with angle of view, type of lighting, etc. These reservations still hold but they have decreasing importance as the correlations between systems are better understood and as companies develop their own translation expertise.

CAD for garments is an order of magnitude harder to develop than any other application. There are still limitations on what CAD can do vis-a-vis a pattern maker, but the gap is narrowing steadily.

There are three garment making processes in which CAD is involved. These are the actual design of the garment, with its silhouette, color and fabric texture, the actualization of the design, i.e. its translation into the traditional two dimensional pattern pieces and, thirdly, the interface with the first of the manufacturing processes, viz. marker making and cutting.

There is a growing number of CAD systems that can handle the pure design function, with varying degrees of sophistication and for a wide range of prices. Designs can be started from scratch, using a tablet and stylus with colors and textures flooded in from large libraries. Previous designs can be recalled and modified to suit the new season's requirements. Designs can be copied from photographs, etc., digitized and modified. Different fabric drapes and garment lighting can be simulated and the finished design printed out in high resolution color prints. And it can all be done in minutes or hours instead of the days or weeks required before CAD.

The actualization of the design is what separates the men from the boys. The major CAD suppliers are all working toward true 3-D systems that can subsequently break down the design into the 2-D blocks that comprise the traditional pattern. A leader in this field is Computer Design Inc., whose system builds a 3-D frame on which the fabric can be laid in the preferred design. The model can be rotated or a split screen used to view it from different angles simultaneously. Lighting, drape etc. are adjustable. Pieces of the garment can be removed and their shape modified before returning to the on-screen model. Once the designer is satisfied, the system prints out a pattern for a sample to be made or for the pattern maker to adjust. In the case of simple garments, it goes straight to the marker. Grading, the process of making patterns for different sizes of garment, is automatic. Powerful algorithms are now available for laying out the pieces in the marker to keep fabric waste to a minimum, but there is still a need for further improvement if waste is to be truly minimized.

For most conventional designs, the best CAD systems can simulate true 3-D very well. More or less standard blocks can be modified to give different silhouettes with only minor input from the pattern maker, if any. Also, a great deal of progress has been made in coping with patterned fabrics, to ensure that the edges of the pieces match at the seams.

The biggest problem arises when radical design changes occur, such as tulip skirts or extreme raglan sleeves, and the system has no basis on which to build the blocks. However, as experience is developed and broader ranging libraries of patterns are accumulated, the problem will fade. The ultimate actualization program will probably incorporate an Artificial Intelligence shell that can build into the pattern such intangibles as comfort and fit and incorporate fabric parameters such as those of Kawabata to portray drape more accurately.

Cutting.

Development of an interface between CAD and the manufacturing process has made remarkable progress. Shaped pieces are assembled into a marker and instructions given to the computerized fabric laying and cutting equipment. Cutting itself can be done with knives, laser beams, water jets and plasma gas - each process has its advantages and disadvantages. Investronica, a leader in cutting technology, offers an attachment which scans plaid fabrics to ensure matching seams.

Of particular importance for QR is the development of efficient low-ply cutting equipment such as that developed by Gerber. Significant reductions in planning and cutting times, with improved material utilization, can be achieved while holding cutting costs for the much reduced cutting heights needed for frequent style changes. Such integrated processing can reduce operating times by as much as 1-2 weeks.

The economic justification for the purchase of CAD or CAD/CAM systems is usually straight forward. Pattern makers can cost a company $50,000/year; designers, say, $25-$45,000/year. CAM can get a job done in a fraction of the traditional time or do much more in the same time. A company with 20 sample makers can accomplish the job with half that number and pay for a sophisticated, $250-$300,000 computer driven system in the first year.

Flexible Sewing & Finishing.

Virtually all new sewing and pressing machines are equipped with microprocessors that permit some degree of operations programming. These allow rapid handling of different styles without loss of worker productivity, sequences of operations without operator intervention, multiple operations carried out simultaneously, e.g, the sergeing of two pieces while simultaneously seaming them, and edge controlled sewing to name just a few. The implications for shop floor flexibility are obvious. Other, more dedicated equipment will carry out a complex series of operations such as collar sub-assembly, demanding only that the operator makes the initial positioning of the parts accurately and keeps feed stocks available. Re-

153

cently, robotic equipment that assumes even this role has appeared on the market and more can be expected.

As noted earlier, the big change in such systems is the type and skills of the operators - programming skills replace manual dexterity to a large degree - and the different training that is required. The other problem encountered with automated sewing is that of justification. The machines are expensive and actual sewing needle operating times must be maximized to off-set the investment. In the traditional Progressive Bundle System, the needle is operating only 20 - 25% of the time and that is not good enough, unless performed on a multi-shift basis. Bundle handling and clerical work have to be removed from the operator whose job is to keep the machine operating. Two good ways of achieving high machine utilization are Unit Production Systems - a hard technology - and Modular Manufacturing, which employs industrial engineering concepts.

Unit Production Systems.

Over 40 years ago, many apparel plants used the "straight line" production system which processed individual garments rather than bundles. Sewing machines were linked by chutes and table extensions. This type of production set-up was a non-mechanical version of today's UPS. It was largely succeeded by the PBU system which demonstrated lower costs and higher productivity and was not as sensitive to absenteeism and labor turnover. Straight Line, although fast, relied heavily on operator cooperation and was more conducive to group than to individual incentives. Some companies stayed with Straight Line, however, and those that did have shown it to be extremely efficient in terms of today's QR requirement.

The first mechanical "straight line" system was developed over 20 years ago in Sweden by Eton. The first U.S. installation was in 1978. Though widely used in Europe and in Canada, the equipment was considered controvertial for most of its life and, even today, its utility is widely debated. In the last 3-4 years, however, computerization of UPS has allowed its full potential to be recognised as the inclusion of control and reporting functions became possible and UPS became compatible with individual incentive pay schemes.

There are probably 20 or so UPS brands on the market. They vary in the number of bells and whistles they carry, but they all have similar mechanical functions. A UPS is an overhead rail conveyor that moves carriers holding parts or partly sewn garments from one work station to the next one at which the part is needed. The fabric pieces, labels, trim, etc., are individually loaded into carrier "clips" in accordance with a computer prepared master plan. The computer then ensures that the sewing machine operators are fed with the correct parts as needed. Each sewing step completed, the operator reloads the clip and it moves off to the next position. The main lines and work station entrance and exit lines can also be used as parking or holding areas that buffer hitches in the system until things are running smoothly.

The benefits of UPS include the following:

• Reductions in direct and indirect labor, increased productivity and improved overhead absorption. These come from reductions in the handling of garments which are presented to the operator optimally; no bundles, tickets, etc. Also the continuous flow of work improves both momentum and morale. Claims of productivity gains of the order of 40% have been made but it is generelly true that at least half of such improvements are a result of the engineering of the shop that must take place for the UPS system to operate. A 20% gain will go far, however, toward paying for the equipment.

• Reductions in WIP inventory and through-put time. These are the most noteworthy of the UPS benefits and allow more of manufacturing to be to customer order and less to stock.

• Improvements in quality. Garments are clearly visible at all stages in processing and are never buried in bundles. In this way, mistakes are discovered quickly and corrected before downgraded goods accumulate.

• Ability to handle style and product changes. Changing routing patterns or changing machines at specific stations can be carried out with a minimum of cost or lost time. Most UPS systems have built-in flexibility features.

• Improvements in worker safety. Tidier work areas, less lifting and no bending over bins, have contributed to lower insurance premiums.

• Reductions in training time as operators have only to learn the sewing techniques.

• Reduced turnover. Most systems today provide the supervisor and operators with a great deal of real time information about performance against standard, quantity produced and earnings. The INA system allows the operator to see exactly what the pay status is at all times. Further, the loss of earnings due to malfunctions or running out of parts is minimized by the station monitoring features of the UPS and the electronic communications between supervisor and operator. These features have had a significant effect on job satisfaction.

There are drawbacks to UPS. The first is that they cost money - a simple one, around $4,500 per work station. More time must be spent on pre-planning and changes to the program must be made quickly. More is demanded of the supervisor who must be more highly trained than previously. Surplus equipment must be available to slide into the line when a breakdown occurs or maintenance is required. Also, installation of a UPS disrupts the shop, more floor space is required, initial operator retraining costs money and the service lines will in all likelihood have to be re-installed. When up and running, however, the benefits are in most cases clear to see.

Disappointments with UPS, particularly in the days before computer controls were available, tended to be environmental rather than functional. Often insufficient attention was paid to the type of operation and the quality and reliability of the work force. Absenteeism can play havoc with UPS. A highly pre-line engineered, basic, long-run operation may find that UPS has little to offer. The trade experience generated to date indicates that as seasonality of goods increases and run lengths and response times decrease, UPS becomes more valuable.

Modular Manufacturing.

Modular, or Flexible manufacturing is an old idea which, in Japan and then in the U.S. auto and allied industries, has resurfaced as a tool of JIT, Quality Management and, most recently QR. Leaders of the apparel industry are now viewing its application to sewn products as a possible solution to many of their problems.

A modular plant is easily recognised from its floor plan. Instead of lines of skill centers with work progressing in bundles, the modular plant is made up of many product centers in each of which the complete garment is made by small groups of workers responsible for all operations. Each product center contains the equipment needed for all the manufacturing operations and this is laid out in a circular or horseshoe configuration. The group is usually highly cross-trained to allow real-time balancing of the work loads. Further, the pay and incentives systems are geared to the group and not the individual. The management of a modular plant is also very different. There is heavy reliance on employee participation in overcoming operational difficulties, quality is stressed and peer pressures is the primary tool for solving productivity problems. Modular manufacturing, then, combines the best of straight line manufacturing with the mental attitudes of employee involvement groups such as quality circles.

The benefits of modular manufacturing can be grouped under six headings. They are compared with the typical PBU attributes below.

Modular	PBU
• Faster response time.	• Long cycle time and limited responsiveness to customers' needs
• Worker motivation enhanced.	• Labor motivation comes primarily from piece rate.
• High quality.	• Quality variable and uncertain.
• Lower total costs.	• High costs for indirect labor, quality maintenance and rework.
• Freed up capital.	• High inventory levels

• System conducive to change and improvement.	• System is frozen – hard to change

There is a another important aspect of modular manufacturing. It offers many of the advantages of UPS without the capital outlay and this capital avoidance aspect is attracting increasing attention. That is not to say UPS and modular are mutually exclusive, clearly they can coexist very successfully under certain circumstances. However, many apparel companies have a phobia about fixed assets while being progressive in their operational thinking.

A recent ARC Research Notes gave an excellent example of the improvements that are possible with modular manufacturing. A tee-shirt has an SAM of about 3 minutes. With a typical cycle time of 4 days, the work-to-wait ratio is 1:800. One manufacturer converted two plants to modular manufacturing and in the space of one year saw the following improvements:

• Manufacturing cycle time down to 1 day

• Productivity up 10-15%

• Floor space reductions allowed 24% more direct labor to be added

• Labor turnover at 10% and 5% for the two plants

• Absenteeism of 2 1/2 - 3%

• Workmanship seconds at 0.2%

A second example was that of a men's tailored clothing company that modularized its cutting room. Cycle time was reduced 75% and costs by one third or more in the second week of operation.

A du Pont study of the comparative economics of PBU, UPS and modular manufacturing for a new plant has shown how attractive the modular system can be. These findings are summarized in Table 12.1. The complete data and basic assumptions are given in Appendix I. New plant economics were chosen, at least in part, because they give the best comparison. Consideration of existing fa-

158

cilities requires endless assumptions about the pre-conversion plant condition, layout, etc.

Table 12.1
Economic Summary For QR Manufacturing Venture

	Seasonal			Fashion		
	PBU	UPS	Mod.	PBU	UPS	Mod.
Women's Slacks						
Ann. Doz. (M)	83.8	89.9	89.1	72.3	77.1	74.8
SAH	4.4	4.1	4.0	4.8	4.5	4.4
C. of S. ($/Doz.)	176.7	173.9	169.4	192.4	189.5	183.6
Pre-Tax Profit *	30.0	32.8	40.5	35.8	38.7	48.1
After-Tax ROI %	28.4	30.5	43.3	29.1	30.6	43.9
Net ROE %	34.4	38.6	52.9	35.8	39.3	54.4
Int. Rate of Rtn. %	23.4	26.9	38.8	25.2	28.4	41.2
Women's Blouses						
Ann. Doz. (M)	73.7	77.4	76.7	63.1	66.5	64.4
SAH	5.0	4.8	4.7	5.5	5.2	5.1
C. of S. ($/Doz.)	130.0	128.2	122.7	147.8	145.5	138.5
Pre-Tax Profit *	18.2	20.0	27.8	22.8	25.2	34.8
After-Tax ROI %	19.6	20.0	33.2	20.5	20.7	30.3
Net ROE %	25.5	27.2	43.7	27.0	28.6	45.4
Int. Rate of Rtn. %	13.5	15.4	27.2	15.4	17.5	29.7

* 98% 1st. quality for Modular vs. 95% for PBU and UPS.

Computer Process Control.

The establishment of industry linkage standards and their electronic and bar code formats were discussed in an earlier Chapter, as was the need for Computer Integrated Manufacturing (CIM) protocols. These are recent developments and tend to obscure the

159

extent to which the computer has penetrated the textile and apparel industries.

KSA's 1986 survey of vendors of computer software applications for apparel management listed 91 companies representing over 4,000 installations. These figures had increased by 12 companies and more than 1,000 installations from a year earlier. The applications surveyed included:

Order Processing	Finished Goods Inventories
Allocation	Production
Raw Material Inventories	Accounts Receivable
Incentive Payroll	Planning
Shop Floor Control	General Accounts
Forecasting	Standard Costs
Imports	Merchandise Planning
Standards Data	Order Entry

Clearly there is no shortage of internal information and control applications. The problem is more likely to come from trying to exchange information in languages that are mutually unintelligible and the construction of overall Management Information Systems remains a formidable task.

Technology Demonstration Sites & (TC)^2.

The Defence Logistics Agency, as part of its program to broaden and modernize the military apparel manufacturing base, recently funded three manufacturing technology sites; one each at F.I.T. in New York, Georgia Tech./Southern Tech. and Clemson University. The contracts were let in 1987 and the Centers became operational late in 1988. Each has installed fully functional operating lines producing complete garments using state-of-the-art equipment, and is open to the trade.

In a separate initiative, (TC)^2 founded its own demonstration center in Raleigh in 1987. The Center opened in the Spring of 1988 as a combination of manufacturing operation demonstration, laboratory and classroom. The site was chosen partly because of its proximity to NCSU's Colleges of Textiles and Engineering, thus allowing university research programs to be carried out using advanced equipment. An example of this is the exploration, now in progress, of shop floor simulation models to improve plant lay-out, scheduling and balancing.

The Center houses over 60 pieces of equipment and 30 employees and chose as its first demonstration the manufacture of men's slacks. These are made for three days each week in a "best" production mode, and are supplied on contract to a retailer. Only by operating in a semi-commercial atmosphere, does $(TC)^2$ believe that the demonstrations can be realistic. For the other two days of the week, the Center is open to member companies which can study the machines at their leisure and conduct their own experiments. In time, the Center will also house the commercial versions of the machines developed at Draper Laboratories. These are robot controlled using advanced vision systems and feed fully automated sewing equipment. For more detail, see Chapter 13.

Products other than slacks will eventually be made at the Center and, as it becomes available, new equipment will be added.

Non-Traditional Methods Of Assessing Capital Expenditures.

Non-traditional methods of assessing capital expenditures are of increasing importance as the technology content of equipment increases. Such equipment is usually much more expensive than the machinery it replaces. And so it should be; it does more. But its purchase can be difficult to justify if traditional financial techniques are used.

A 1982 Harvard Business Review article crystallized the problem when it identified the new CAM equipment as offering value in a "systematic", rather than the usual "point" sense. CAM's ability to tie together other processes, to turn isolated pieces of equipment into an operating unit, requires that it be evaluated in new ways.

Since that time, engineering and acedemic journals have explored the matter very fully. Books have been written on the subject and it has taken root as an Industrial Engineering discipline, though one that is relatively unknown to industry, and certainly to those in industry who assess capital appropriation requests or who sign the cheques. The Defense Logistics Agency, when it funded the three advanced apparel manufacturing demonstration sites, included in its Statement of Work an objective requiring research into the justification of equipment and systems.

The criteria usually employed when assessing new capital expenditures are heavily quantitative and are limited to a handfull of well understood concepts; Payback, ROI, LTROI, DCFROI, Net Present Worth, and the like. Frequently, leading-edge equipment, when evaluated in these ways, fails to pass today's high financial hurdle rates.

There are really two groups of concerns. The first, referred to in the HBR article cited above, is that individual pieces of equipment should not be viewed individually, but as part of the total manufacturing capability. In order to optimize a manufacturing facility, matching sets of the new machinery, plus the attendant systems and software are needed. Until they are all in place and linked together in the way they were designed to be linked, their full potential is not realized; to look at each piece separately is meaningless. Further, it is only when the complete system is operational that management sees improvements in the intangibles - moral, absenteeism, competitiveness - which are rarely worked into classic analyses.

The second concern is more fundamental. It is the place of capital in the company's strategic plans. Most apparel companies either ignore long-term strategy or assign it a time horizon which is very short compared with industries that are traditionally capital intensive. The substitution of capital for labor is a painful process and only to be undertaken when the long-term objectives of the enterprise are clearly seen - usually as the result of a great deal of effort. Analysis is part of the process, but only part; the rest is mostly qualitative judgement involving the need for such market-oriented factors as quality, flexibility and speed of response. Risk considerations also play a more important role. Greater benefits are usually accompanied by greater risk or uncertainty and it is notoriously difficult to be objective about such matters, because they tend to be qualitative in nature.

Non-Traditional Decision Analysis methods allow these "soft" attributes to be worked into analyses of capital expenditure proposals alongside the usual financial measures by giving them rankings or weights on numerical scales.

There is a variety of techniques available. Some are very simple and directed at helping the analyst to be logical and objective; others are more rigorous and are designed to handle complex series of alternative investment options. While no attempt is made to go into detail about any one of them, a partial listing of their names is given below and reference sources to extensive listings are to be found in the Chapter Notes. The methods fall into three groups:

Graphical Techniques

    Scorecards
    Profile charts
    Polar graphs

Multi-Attribute Methodologies

    Multi-attribute weighted evaluation analysis
    Analytic Hierarchy Process
    Multi-attribute utility analysis
    Goal/multi-objective programming analysis

Risk/Uncertainty Techniques

    Sensitivity analysis
    Decision trees
    Monte Carlo simulation

Software developers have made the techniques more accessible in the last few years. There are now at least thirty programs for microcomputers, each under $1,000, that facilitate the organization and analysis of data for most of the important methods.

Notes - Chapter 12.

"Automation and Robotics in the Textile and Apparel Industries", G. A. Berkstresser and D. R. Buchanan, Noyes, 1986, provides a good overview of the technology finding its way into the industry.

A particularly rich source of information is the papers of the International Apparel Research Conferences sponsored by AAMA. The Conferences held in 1985-8 all featured papers on a wide range of technologies. The Apparel Research Committee of AAMA periodically publishes Notes and three of these are of particular interest; Volume 4, No. 3 on cutting, sewing and other equipment, including UPS, Volume 7, No.1 on Modular Manufacturing and Volume 8, No. 5, also on Modular Manufacturing. The Technical Advisory Committee of AAMA also issues a series of reports. The 1988 report on Flexible Manufacturing Systems is particularly good.

Bobbin Magazine is a fine source of articles on the application of technology to apparel manufacture. Typical of these is the 1984 "World Technology Update" by Manuel Gaetan. Since then there have been literally dozens of analyses of specific technologies.

Apparel Industry Magazine is a strong proponent of QR and, as part of its service to its readers, has focussed on "success stories". Starting in December,1984, the magazine has named the annual AIM All-Stars - the leaders in manufacturing modernization - chosen primarily by polls of their peers. Each featured company is written up in some detail and these profiles provide good examples of what the application of technology can achieve.

Material on textile technology is also available in the trade journals and one paper worth study is "The Changing Face of Competitiveness", presented by Raoul Verret of Werner Management Consultants at the 1988 Annual Meeting of ATMI.

An extremely good introduction to non-traditional financial analysis is "Economic and Mutiattribute Evaluation of Advanced Manufacturing Systems", John R. Canada and W.G. Sullivan; Prntice Hall, 1989.

PART IV
THE FUTURE

Chapter 13. Research Directions.

The discussion of technology has so far been restricted to commercially available equipment or systems. The research efforts being devoted to expanding this base are equally important. Much that goes on is, of course, proprietary and this is more the case with the large fiber and textile houses and machinery manufacturers than for the apparel community where many of those involved are small and cannot support "custom" research. Four major research programs and their affiliated projects will be discussed here; $(TC)^2$, Japan's MITI project, the EC's BRITE program and the Swedish IN-TER-LINK project. In addition, some of the other work either under way or deserving of attention will be listed.

$(TC)^2$.

This organization was created as a non-profit coalition of management, labor and government in 1980, following studies by John Dunlop of Lamont University and Fred Abernathy of Harvard of the possible impact of automation on the cost structure of apparel.

The focus of the first research program to be sponsored by the coalition was on the handling of fabric parts. Only 25% of a typical operator's time is spent sewing; much of the rest is devoted to opening and closing bundles of parts and to positioning fabric for the sewing operation. The objective was to build a transfer line type assembly operation encompassing a sequence of automated fabric handling and transfer stations interspersed with automated sewing positions. Draper Laboratories was commissioned to carry out this research and, in order to focus the effort, a man's tailored coat sleeve was chosen as the vehicle. Making a sleeve involves many of the most demanding steps in garment construction; sewing the inseam with fullness, folding and refolding the cuff, tacking the vents, precision alignment of the inseams and outseams and adjustment of the sleeve parts to ensure a good mating at the top of the sleeve where it joins the jacket.

By 1985, all the elements of the required machine had been developed on a modular basis. The Draper staff had approached the problem of sleeve manufacture without any preconceived ideas and several of their inventions reflect this fresh approach. The modular units were:

• An automatic loader to insert cut fabric parts into the transfer line.

• A viewing table that allows an automatic vision system to recognise the parts and their alignment relative to the line and the sewing head.

• A hinged transfer door equipped with a series of parallel, foam coated belts that comes down and slides the parts to and from the sewing station.

• A sewing unit with feed belts and sewing head controlled by computer. Rather than move the fabric under a stationary sewing head, the fabric edge, as registered by the vision system determines the movement of the sewing machine. Thus, the need for precise positioning of the fabric part when loading is eliminated. Continuous, interlocking belts, above and below the fabric, hold it firm, part for the sewing head as needed, and, when driven at different speeds, allow "easing", i.e., the movement of one fabric piece relative to the other to impart fullness to the seam.

• A robot to fold the fabric and align the edges accurately. In this module, the fabric lies on a perforated surface and is held in place by suction. Its position and alignment are determined by the vision system which feeds the information to a robot. The robot arm holds a specially developed end-effector which consists of an adjustable spline carrying small pickers. These can be activated individually to grasp and hold a single ply of fabric while it is moved into alignment with the edge to which it is to be sewn. The spline adjusts first to the shape of the edge to be picked up and then the curve is modified to match the second edge. The information for the setting of the spline curves is supplied by the vision system. With the edges aligned and held, first under partial vacuum, and then by the transfer door, the piece is returned to the sewing module for joining.

167

At this point, the Singer Company entered into an agreement with $(TC)^2$ to commercialize the technology. After extensive studies of the potential for machine cost reduction and the operations most likely to benefit from the Draper technology, Singer identified its first project as the the development of a transfer line for sequentially forming trouser leg side seams, waistband seams and inseams. Other projects included back and sleeve machines. Unfortunately, in the Spring of 1989, Singer closed its robotics division, the relationship with $(TC)^2$ was terminated and the work will be transferred to the Technology Center in Raleigh N.C.

A second sponsored project at Draper Labs. was the development of an automated sweatpant sewing system. The work was carried out with the assistance of Russell Corporation which will install thefirst production unit in 1990. Full commercialization of the system has been assigned to Jet Sew, a division of WestPoint Pepperell.

The Raleigh Technology Center is rapidly expanding its research capabilities. A skipped stitch detector, an automatic felled seamer and a shop floor computer simulator have been developed and other projects are in work.

AAMA - Apparel Research Committee.

The AAMA is highly structured in terms of committees, but it has no functional research capability and no budget for the funding of research by other agencies. $(TC)^2$ on the other hand has only a small number of members from the apparel, as opposed to the tailored clothing, industry and has lacked input from the majority of garment producers on the most beneficial research fields or the priorities to be attached to them. Accordingly, in 1987 the two organizations agreed to an alliance which recognised $(TC)^2$ as the research agency of AAMA. AAMA acquired representation on the committees of $(TC)^2$ and a channel for recommending research projects. In return, AAMA urges its membership to support $(TC)^2$ financially by becoming members. The partnership has win-win potential; all that is needed is to extract the greatest good from it.

The MITI Project.

In 1982 the Japanese textile and apparel industries undertook a 10 billion yen, long-range program to rationalize the manufacture of garments through the development of fully automated systems. The program called for a demonstration plant to be operational in 1990.

The research program takes place under the Large Scale Project System of MITI, the Ministry of International Trade and Industry. The government contributes through its Research Centers for High Polymer Fabric, Machine Technology and Manufactured Products Science; industry by means of the Union for the Research of Automated Sewing Technology, a consortium of 28 enterprises including sewing, textile, machinery, dyeing, chemical and utilities.

The program, since its inception has been highly structured. The first 2-3 years were devoted mainly to planning for both the overall project and its constituent parts. The task was broken down into technology development projects and the companies involved undertook research within clearly defined parameters. 1987 was a watershed year in which progress was measured and plans were developed for the final detailed work program. The 1988 annual review indicated that the schedule is holding, particularly as it apples to fabric handling and sewing preparation technology. The development of automated three dimensional sewing systems is clearly the most difficult part of the exercise.

The scheme of work is outlined below:

I. Sewing Preparation Technology.

- Techniques for evaluation of fabrics in terms of distortion, drape, etc.

- Automation of characteristic data collection, together with its use for control purposes.

- Systems for the temporary stiffening of fabrics, including ways to correct distortions.

- Automatic fabric inspection.

169

• Knife mesh and laser cutting technologies.

II.   Sewing and Assembly Technology.

• Development of glueing methods as an adjunct to, or replacement for, conventional sewing.

• Three dimensional sewing using a miniature sewing head on a robot arm.

• "Super-Sewing" technology using single thread loop sewing together with glue.

• High performance pressing techniques, possibly including stereo finish-pressing with a flexible dummy.

III. Cloth Handling Techniques.

• Development of vertical and parallel holding systems to allow uninterrupted sewing.

• Sewing handlers for positioning fabric, software to operate two handlers in cooperation and jigs for joint seam sewing.

• Development of fabric conveying devices; mating and stock modules.

IV.   Systems Management and Control Technology.

• General management techniques, including production planning models, production process controls, etc.

• Software for inspection of shapes and colors of partly finished products.

• Systems to diagnose malfunctions.

• Control information provision and recognition techniques and the required software.

The individual developments have high performance standards. For example, the fabric inspection system has been designed to meet the following specs:

- Inspection speed of 50m/min.

- Width control of ± 3 mm.

- Length control of ± 0.3%

- Dirt spots > 2 sq. mm.

- Holes > 1 sq. mm.

- Slubs > 1mm. thick and 5mm. long

The locations of the faults are mapped and fed to the automatic marker maker and cutting system for defect avoidance control.

An associated research project is concerned with correcting distortions in the fabric and stabilizing it. Woolen fabrics can shrink in finished garment pressing and light weight woven and knit fabrics are readily distorted in handling. To prevent such deformations carrying through to the finished garment, the fabric is treated with resins on the underside, distortions are removed using bow and skew rollers and the resin is cured in a steam press operation.

The project places considerable emphasis on the mechanical properties of the fabric and how they relate to handling and sewing. To this end there is heavy reliance on the Kawabata Evaluation System (KES) which attempts to relate the subjective properties of fabrics (stiffness, smoothness, fullness, crispness, etc.) to such mechanical properties as bending modulus, shear, compression, etc. Tables 12.1 and 12.2 below outline the connections between the various parameters.

The reason for the interest in KES is that a skilled sewing operator can compensate for different fabric properties while handling the fabric on the sewing table and as it enters the needle. Without the operator, ways of doing the same thing mechanically, while preserving stitch uniformity and seam pucker standards, are required. To achieve this level of mechanical handling sophistication, the characteristics of the fabric must be known with precision. In recent years the Japanese tailored clothing industry has gained a great

171

deal of experience in understanding how the various fabric mechanical properties relate to in-shop garment manufacture.

Table 13.1
Fabric Mechanical Properties And
Fabric And Garment Characteristics

Fabric Mechanical Properties	Quality & Mechanical Performance.
Uniaxial and biaxial tension	Fabric handle and drape
Fabric shear under tension	Fabric formability and tailoring properties
Pure bending	Garment appearence and seam puckering
Lateral compression	Mechanical stability and shape retention
Longitudinal compression and buckling	Relaxation shrinkage, dimensional stability, wrinkle recovery and crease retention
Surface roughness and friction	Abrasion and pilling resistance and comfort

In another program related to the difficulties associated with fully automated sewing, research has been carried out on the shape and mating of garment patterns. The objectives are to redesign and/or combine patterns to allow decreases in handling time, length of cut, length of sewing seam, difficulty in pressing and number of operations. The research so far has led to a computer expert system program with more than 60 rules. If two adjoining pieces satisfy one or more of the rules, the computer redraws the pattern, combining the pieces and reidentifying darts, notches, etc. Working on a woman's blazer, the researchers have achieved the following:

- Reduction in total process time of 17%.

- Reduction in garment parts from 17 to 13.

- Reduction in process steps of 5.

Table 13.2
Kawabata Evaluation System Parameters

Property	#/Symbol		Parameter
I. Tensile	1.	LT	Linearity of load-extension curve
	2.	WT	Tensile energy
	3.	RT	Tensile resistance
II. Shear	4.	G	Shear rigidity
	5.	2HG	Hysteresis of shear force @ 0.5 degrees.
	6.	2HG5	Hysteresis of shear force @ 5 deg.
III. Bending	7.	B	Bending rigidity
	8.	2HB	Hysteresis of bending moment
IV. Compression	9.	LC	Linearity of compression-thickness curve
	10.	WC	Compressional Energy
	11.	RC	Compressional resilience
V. Surface	12.	MIU	Coefficient of friction
	13.	MMD	Mean deviation of MIU
	14.	SMD	Geometrical roughness
VI. Construction	15.	W	Weight per unit area
	16.	T	Fabric thickness

A novel system of pattern cutting has also been developed for use on mutiple plies of small parts or difficult fabrics. Rather than have a blade move around, often in tightly constrained paths, a mesh or grid of small knives is used. The mesh moves over the fabric, the computer selects the knives to be lowered to give the shape of the part and the mesh itself is then lowered, cutting the piece. For single ply cutting, a new laser cutter has been developed.

Although the original stated objective of the MITI project was that of "rationalizing the textile/apparel industry, through transfor-

173

mation of its labor intensive nature and increasing productivity", the real purpose is to gain a strong number one position in the apparel machinery business. Very few apparel companies in Japan are large enough to afford the kind of capital expenditure that will be needed for the comprehensive system being developed. If modularized, however, the U.S. and European markets could put pieces of it to full use. The whole thing has characteristics similar to those of the U.S. space program - needed doing, great for national pride, etc., but the real benefit is the technology spin-off.

The BRITE Program.

The Basic Research in Industrial Technologies for Europe, or BRITE program was adopted by the European Community in March 1985 with a funding of 125 million Eurodollars over four years. Industry supplies matching funds. Early in 1986, the first 95 projects were funded and of these, 13 were apparel related, 3 for work on polymers, 4 for textiles, 1 for fiber and 5 for composites. The funding applies to cooperative research projects in manufacturing between companies or groups in different member countries and has the objective of increasing the cohesiveness of R&D in the European Community. BRITE covers "pre-competitive" research, i.e., an intermediate stage between fundamental research and development work immediately preceding commercialization. To allow this form of cooperative research, there has been a significant relaxation in the anti-trust climate.

A partial listing of the project titles is instructive as it shows the commonality of the research interests of the U.S.A., Japan and the E.C., though the three approaches to attacking the problems are widely different, reflecting, as they do, different political and social bases. The list below contains only projects that are apparel related. There is considerable overlapping. In one sense this is wasteful, but it allows a greater number of participants and more possible solutions to complex problems can be tabled.

• Advanced technology for the melt spinning of continuous synthetic filament yarn to improve the competitiveness of the European textile industry.

• Development and application of modular and flexible systems for computer aided management of discontinuous production processes.

174

• Folding devices and sensors to automate sewing machines for mixed production.

• Highly flexible programmable modular sewing center capable of performing the full range of operations foreseen to produce an article of clothing.

• Research for automatic sewing and ironing unit with heads coupled to simultaneously work the two opposite sides of an article of clothing.

• Developing a real time integrated operator communication system affordable by clothing manufacturers.

• Computer Aided Design of clothing.

• A continuous cutting system with automatic inspection and dynamic pattern layout as applied to the garment industry.

• A flexible manufacturing system for automated assembly of apparel.

• Fit-optimized pattern design on the interactive graphics screen.

• 2D and 3D garment modelling.

• Automation of the processing and cutting of patterned materials.

• Planning, development and demonstration of a pilot flexible cell for diversified manufacturing of clothing.

• Planning and development of an information and communication system for CIM in the apparel industry.

• Development of a standardised material transport device for the sequential automation of the processing of flexible materials.

INTER-LINK.

With Chalmers Tekniska Hogskola, Gothenburg, Sweden as its center and Nilas Nilsson as its inspiration, very long term research into the philosophy as well as the technology content of apparel research has made rapid progress. Sweden has the highest apparel import penetration level of any developed nation - of the order of 90% - in part because of a firm belief in free trade. But, being outside the E.C., Sweden can only participate in BRITE indirectly. These circumstances have led some Swedes to adopt a unique approach to solving the problem of apparel manufacturing viabilty.

Basically, they have opted out of detailed short and medium term research and concentrated, instead, on defining the kind of systems and equipment that should be in place 10 or more years in the future. The level and quality of the conceptual thinking that characterizes their work is of a very high order indeed.

The overall approach is to ask, "What is the ultimate in consumer responsiveness?", and then to conceptualize systems that will match this defined need. At this level there is no hesitation in defining in-put and out-put of black boxes without trying to explain the workings of the box itself. At lower levels of analysis, the system requirements are specified where possible, but always within the framework of the major premises. Implicit in the Swedish approach is the belief that there will be no shortage of appropriate technology as needed.

INTER-LINK is defined as the fully integrated linkage of consumer-pulled informatics for the creation, manufacture and distribution of customized goods in the apparel trade. It centers on the EGO SYSTEM which is driven by consumer body measurements taken with an EGO-METER together with fabric color and garment design preferences. This information is generated at PROCAMS, an electronic shop. With the want defined, the system then uses every information, design and manufacturing integration technique available (FIGARMA) to deliver the unique product to the customer in the very shortest possible time. The extra cost of such a system is to be off-set by massive reductions in the traditional inventories of finished goods waiting for someone to buy them and by the removal of markdowns. Each of the functional modules of INTER-LINK and its sub-systems is the focus of research groups at the university or

176

in industry, e.g., INTRA-CUT, a continuous marking, cutting and coding machine designed to feed automatated sewing machines.

In the period 1987-88, a number of innovations were added to the system. The EGO-CARD was introduced. This "credit card" carries up to 4 megabytes of information about its owner, including a digitized photo and full body measurements as well as banking, medical, etc., information. PROCAMS was equipped with a "Magic Mirror". On inserting the card, the face and body outline of the consumer appear on a screen. Fabric colors, designs and textures as well as garment designs can be examined electronically or in sample books and transferred to the screen in the form of a garment that fits the consumer precisely. Orders can then be placed as before.

In the Spring of 1988, the PROTEKO textile/clothing center opened in Boras, the traditional Swedish textile region. Funded by the government, other funding agencies and industry, the center is equipped with the latest in technical facilities and has as its purpose, the dissemination of knowledge about new apparel technology. The educational and R&D facilities at Chalmers have been transferred to Boras, which is now the center for the industry.

Also taking place in 1988 were the first discussions of the proposed Landala Experiments. Although there have been delays in implementing this work, there is no question of its potential importance to the long-term future of retailing. The objective of the experiments were:

"To register and analyse the shopping habits of consumers and scientifically and systematically to study the impact of new image based and interactive information technologies in the form of network based consumer-pulled informatics as compared to the present, conventional system of producer-pushed production and distribution."

Initially the intention was to concentrate on consumer goods that are bought daily, e.g., groceries. The product line and service offerings would be increased gradually and, ultimately, would include apparel manufactured and distributed using the systems outlined above.

As originally conceived, the Experiments would involve several consumer panels selected from the 3,000 or so households in Landala, who would use interactive, image based teleshopping and telebanking facilities in the home. The ICA group (retailers), SE-BANKEN (banking), the state owned Telephone Company, the NOKIA/Ericsson Group (terminals) and the BULL Corporation (memory cards) all participated in the preliminary studies of this work.

Other Research Programs.

Outside of the structured or centralized research programs outlined above, there is a great deal of work either under way or identified and awaiting funding.

The Apparel Research Committee of AAMA has identified 12 areas of research its members consider important. Several of these have been mentioned in connection with the MITI and BRITE progams - algorithms for translation of 3D CAD to 2D patterns, material stiffening for automated sewing, protocol for CIM, relationships between fabric properties (KES) and the type of instructions to be given automated sewing machines, and automatic marker generation that, for optimum fabric usage, still needs the input of a skilled operator. In addition to these, the following deserve mention:

• Auto separation of fabrics. To-date, over 35 U.S. patents for separation systems have issued, but none of these have universal application. The Clue Picker, which is the most widely used, is best at handling shirtings or materials with a smooth, slick finish that can be cut without fraying or interlocking of fibers. The Walton Picker used in the Draper Labs. project may lead to a more universally applicable system.

• Injection sewing. Given today's ink jet technology, with its precision and color capability, it should be possible to replace sewing thread with a liquid jet that polymerizes in the interstices of the fabric parts being joined. Such an invention would encourage the development of very light weight, robot controlled sewing heads. Chalmers University has such an R&D program, but the work could be broadened with advantage.

178

• Physiometric measurements. The last fully published study of the shapes of U.S. consumers is close to 50 years old and, even then, it was confined to women entering the armed forces. A more recent armed forces study has been carried out but the results are not yet available.

There are few standard size 10 women and yet this shape decides the other grades/sizes. Alterations, disappointments, poor fit, the uncertainty over any ticketed size having meaning are some of the results. Mass merchants have good control of size standards, inadequate though they may be, but among the leading designer houses, the problem is far worse. One major retailer of high price apparel recently sampled dresses from over a dozen different such houses. Ticketed sizes 8, 12 and 16 were measured at the bust, waist and hips. The largest of the "8"s had the same dimensions as the smallest "16" and for any size, there was a 4" spread in each dimension measured.

Some jeans designers have used the present sizeing chaos to advantage. They have targetted certain shapes of men and women and thus gained a large measure of customer loyalty.

• Invisible piece and garment identification. Such a development would have a variety of applications. Work tracing and work credit under incentive pay schemes involves a great deal of effort on the part of the manufacturer. In manufacturing, 1% to 4% of the standard cost is attributable to the reporting of production. At retail, the problem of theft by employees and customers is a major operating cost. Chalmers has also pointed out that in a fully automated manufacturing cell, such built-in encoding of parts would allow the part to direct sequences of mechanical operations instead of the machines being programmed.

There is another aspect of self identification that has not yet received attention. Despite the benefits of bar coded receipt/inventory/POS tracking, the present "shrinkage' or theft levels at retail are not only costly, but are large enough to give misleading information about potential stockouts and could affect reorder procedures.

• Computer modeling of manufacturing schedules and line balancing. Much is going on in this area in other industries, but work is needed specifically for the textile/apparel industries. McDonald Douglas, GM, Litton Industries and others are working on the modeling of manufacturing processes and GE makes extensive use of its own modeling program in the analysis of new plant capital expenditure proposals. ASAE Corp. in Sweden is installing a modeling system (HOCUS) for its Volvo cut and sew upholstery plant. Manchester Polytechnic is making good progress with a model called POCUS that is being used to balance sewing lines under conditions of change and to identify the key factors preventing the operators reaching standard speeds in shorter times. Clemson University also has a similar program under development.

A list similar to that of the ARC is needed for the textile industry. Perhaps now is the time for ATMI to organize functional committees to provide guidance in the areas of research, education, systems, standards, etc., along the lines of AAMA. Several of the needed research directions have already been discussed. Further reductions in fault levels and shade variation, fabric alignment and stabilization, reducing down-times at spinning, weaving, knitting and, very important for rapid re-order, dyeing and finishing.

The last of the ARC projects discussed above is soft technology and it is toward this area that a great deal of future research must be directed. As fashion goods take a greater share of the market, there must be optimal usage of the capital intensive equipment needed to handle very short WIP times and run lengths. Management decision support systems will become increasingly important and they must be capable of handling the interlocked activities of the entire operation.

As the pipeline contracts, problems not yet identified will surely surface. The development of QR methodology was carried out at speed and several aspects of the system's behavior were either ignored or glossed over. Programs of research into several of these aspects of QR are either under way at NCSU or have been identified as being worthy of research efforts. They include:

• The dynamic modelling of the entire pipeline to allow better understanding of the impacts of different technologies on operating and financial performance. Such understanding is important to working up the cost/benefit profiles of major capital items in a non-traditional manner.

•The impact of QR on pipeline cyclicality under conditions of changing consumer demand must be understood if the limits to inventory reduction are to be defined properly.

•Thorough modelling of retail stock-outs and markdowns and the way they are affected by re-order procedures is needed, again for cost/benefit analysis.

• MRP, MRP II and other Industrial Engineering methodologies must be made specific to textile and apparel operations. Many companies are too small or have inadequate staffing to undertake such studies themselves

• The lack of QR analysis of the knitting industry has already been mentioned. Apart from a U.K. study, little is available and yet this is an area particularly hard hit by imports.

• Other parts of the textile industry, including domestics and upholstery would also benefit from a systematic investigation of the beneficial impact of new technology on their pipeline characteristics.

• Point-of-sale tracking by SKU at retail will make possible the analysis of trends in garment styles, should they in exist. There is a feeling that fashion shifts have become so rapid that they are essentially chaotic in the dynamical sense. However, if there are trends, no matter how poorly defined, the industry will benefit from understanding them as they will form a useful adjunct to Style Testing.

• When, under computer control, the CAD designed pattern has been prepared, the marker laid out and the fabric cut, for the first and only time, the precise location and orientation of each piece is known. The next step is traditional; a human being destroys this information by bundling or loading into an overhead rail carrier. Eton, with its new automatic loader, takes the place of the human, but still destroys the information which could be used to present the pieces to the sewing head robotically.

There remains a great deal to be done.

Notes – Chapter 13.

The material in this chapter was obtained from a variety of sources. Papers presented at the Apparel Research Conference over the past few years provided much of the material. (TC)^2 publishes periodically reviews of the progress being made in Japan with the MITI project. Information on the European ventures is available in their journals and research workers frequently visit American Universities. Other information was obtained from private correspondence.

Early in 1989 the BRITE program was extended. BRITE II is now underway with funding approximately 30% greater than the original program. Under new rules, nine priority areas have been defined. These include: laser technology as a production tool; mathematical modelling for small and medium firms, and new material joining techniques.

Chapter 14.   Is QR Enough?

QR methodology is believed to be soundly based, though much remains to be done before it is fully understood. However, just having it available is a long way from putting it into practice or applying its philosophy to the total business culture. Also, there are business aspects that require attention if the full benefits of QR are to be achieved. These include such topics as design, aggressive import substitution, who invests in the technology, education and training and the management of change.

Design.

NEXT is a rapidly growing fashion and home furnishings chain in the U.K. Several years ago in a taped interview its chairman spelled out the reasons for the success of NEXT in some detail. They centered around his view of the role of design in both his organization and its suppliers. He placed the design function at Board level along with Marketing, Finance and other functions normally to be found at the top.   Design was seen as the principal connection with suppliers; not only manufacturers, but spinners, weavers and knitters. Further, design was a continuous activity; not one that is broken down into seasonal efforts.

NEXT's vision of a flow of well designed merchandise, continually refreshing the retail shelves is neither new nor unique. El Corte Ingles in Spain is well on its way to achieving it through its common ownership with Induyco, its principal supplier and Investronica, a leading developer of apparel manufacturing technology and equipment. Their target is 50 seasons per year. Every senior merchandising executive in the business has had the same dream at one time or another. And yet much of the thinking in the pipeline is constricted by basic or seasonal merchandise practices - cold weather clothing still appears on the shelves early in Summer and it is difficult to find a swim suit after May.

The U.S. has many good designers, most of whom go off-shore for manufacturing. They do this for reasons of cost, fabric availability, quality and reliability. A strong base of reliable, responsive contractors could go far toward bringing these houses back on-shore, thus providing the leadership for a more design oriented industry. The private label concept could have the same effect, but buyers need design conscious vendors to work with and the design function has limited scope and stature in this country.

That there is plenty of opportunity for the manufacturer or retailer oriented toward continuous design updating is clearly demonstrated by the rapid growth of the specialty chains and boutiques. The Benettons, Esprits and Limiteds have shown that the customer subscribes to the idea and their host of imitators underline their success. It can be argued that the majority of Americans are fundamentally "seasonal" and conservative in their dressing habits and there is much truth to this. However, such preferences do not exclude good design or the frequent updating of it; there is little that is flashy or shallow or badly designed about the leading design houses such as Claiborne or Klein with their multiplicity of seasons.

The U.K. knitting industry found itself facing the same problems and in 1985 took an innovative approach to their solution. To encourage the large number of smaller companies with no formal design capability to take advantage of the large number of students emerging from the design schools each year, a designer "employment" service was inaugurated. In this, both newly graduated designers and those with industrial experience can register in a computer based file. The file contains details of their design background and training, interests and experience. The registration fee is small for new graduates and slightly larger for those with work experience. Textile and apparel companies pay a fee to enter the files to find suitable employees, be it for a permanent position or a particular project for someone interested in freelance work. No details of the success of this initiative are yet available, but the idea is sound and could well work in the U.S. where CAD will encourage the dispersal of the design function from the large metropolitan areas, closer to the manufacturing operations.

Import Substitution.

The present U.S. import situation can be looked at in two ways; as a disaster or as an opportunity. U.S., and most European consumption, is growing only a little faster than population and each time the import penetration increases, there is the temptation to scale down production capacity to match the new domestic market share. This "ratcheting down" is essentially defeatist and, ultimately, destructive. The alternative is to "ratchet up". Every time there is an upswing in business, the new high can be viewed as the base or floor level of capability. To sustain the new floor and to improve upon it, there must be a source of new business and this can be either the gradually increasing domestic consumption or something with greater growth potential – going after import programs, or import substitution. A third alternative, exporting, is not explored here as it is a subject to itself. However, the formation of American Export Textile Company (AMTEC) in 1988 has set an important precedent for other trade groups. AMTEC was organized by 36 members of the American Yarn Spinners Association as a vehicle for increasing yarn exports.

With over half the market going to imported garments or imported apparel fabric, there is no shortage of opportunity for growth. The problem, then, becomes one of getting the business and two approaches have been shown to work.

The first is the Import Fair which has been practiced in the U.K. for a number of years and which is now taking off, in a modified form, in the U.S. The concept is simple: retailers display their imported lines and domestic producers are given the opportunity of going after the business.

The U.K. versions are organized by a quasi-government body, the National Economic Development Office, on behalf of and with the help of industry groups. Retailer buyers take space in an exhibition hall and display their lines, which are fully marked as to specifications, including materials, price and delivery. In place of the general public, interested manufacturers and textile companies register to attend and are encouraged to discuss substitution of their own products. Ample facilities are provided for relaxed and private discussions The success of the Fairs is only partly the immediate or short term transfer of specific business, which in any case is usually under contract with the off-shore supplier; the real benefit comes from vendors and buyers establishing contacts and, over time, relationships. The medium to small vendor has most to gain from broadening his contact base and exchanging ideas on how he can best interact with the retail community.

Auburn University led the U.S. approach. In 1986, it organized and managed a Fair at Auburn, inviting retailers and the Alabama manufacturing and textile industries. The Governor gave strong personal support to the initiative, thus helping ensure its success. Keeping registration at the State level was a second important feature of the event. Other Fairs of one type or another have followed and in 1988, the first national effort was undertaken alongside the Bobbin Show in Atlanta.

In a more traditional initiative, the National Knitwear and Sportswear Association has sponsored a new trade show called SOURCEAmerica. Started in 1988, the show will allow the retail buyer to shop the products of over 100 major U.S. knitwear manufacturers in one place.

America For Kids, an association of childrens wear manufacturers formed in 1986 by Pat Valentino, has as one of its objectives increased dialogue with retail buyers. The aim is import substitution achieved by discussing import programs prior to and immediately following off-shore buying trips.

The second method of import substitution does not require industry effort or organization. It simply involves a company asking for the business directly after identifying a retail import program of interest to it. A prime source of information about what is being imported is the mail order catalog.

The U.S. Textile Fiber Products Identification Act of 1958, which came into force in 1960, required that imported garments be labelled with the country of origin. It did not require that domestically made goods be suitably labelled and made no provisions for the prominence of the label. The result was that few items of U.S. made clothing were identified as such and it was frequently difficult to find the country of origin label of imports; difficult because they were attached in hard-to-find places unless they conferred prestige.

In preparation for its Crafted With Pride program of asking the consumer to buy American made clothes, the industry asked for and got amendments to the Act that entailed stricter labelling requirements. The Amended Act became law in 1985. Garments are now clearly and prominently labelled as to country of origin - including the U.S. - and, if they are manufactured from imported fabric, the label says so. A further provision was that apparel mail order catalogs must prominently display the country of origin.

There is a large number of apparel catalogs and among these, 70-75 are substantial, non-specialist, outerwear catalogs for the general public. To give some idea of the content of the catalogs, 50-55 display 100 items or more, and of these, 15-20 show over 200 items on a regular basis. Analysis has shown that the import penetration of catalogs overall is in reasonable agreement with national data.

The percentage of items that are imported varies widely among catalog houses, but the number stays relatively constant between successive issues of any given catalog and each catalog has a characteristic profile. For Spring 1986, 12 catalogs contained 20% or less of imported merchandise and 10 catalogs contained 70% imports or more. These figures include garments made from imported fabric which were given a 1/2 point rating. In addition, several houses made heavy use of imported fabrics, $\approx 40\%$, without relying on garment imports.

There is a marked correlation between a catalog's import penetration level and its price points. Figure 14.1 shows this for women's blouses (excluding silk). Each of the twenty points represents a major Fall 1985 catalog with its % imports and its average blouse price. The number of blouses in a catalog ranged from 8 to 58, the low and high prices, overall, were $18 and $128 respectively. The import penetration level ranged from 0% to 100% and for the majority of the catalogs, the average price of the imported garments exceeded the domestic average. These findings are in agreement with the trend over the past few years of off-shore producers concentrating on higher price point merchandise. Clearly, price is not a problem when going after a selected program.

For the most part, the fabric and garment descriptions together with the photographs of catalog imports allow potential import replacements by domestic goods to be identified; especially when the items are carried season to season. From among the Spring 1986 catalogs, a dozen or so stood out as prime candidates, this was in addition to those using a high level of imported fabrics.

187

Figure 14.1
Import Penetration vs. Average Price
Women's Blouses

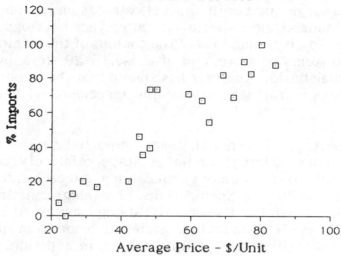

It might be argued that by the time the catalog is published, it is too late to get the business. This is true, but misses the point. The consistency of catalog house importing patterns suggests strongly that certain types of garments or fabrics will be imported in subsequent years and the aggressive domestic producer will start to form a relationship with the buyers concerned to get a piece of the future business.

Investment In QR.

The next topic to be covered is somewhat controvertial and has to do with import substitution in its broadest sense.

If the growth of imports is to be first slowed and then reversed, the prime way to do it is by adopting QR, not only for the main stream of basic and seasonal manufactures, but as a replacement for the more fashion oriented goods now imported by the designer community and the jobber and for the buyer specified private label merchandise made by off-shore contractors. These three groups of customers will insist on quality and delivery assurance as well as responsiveness to order and reorder. But there is, at the present time, a shortage of modern, engineered plants operating the most modern equipment. Who, then, will add such capacity? And for which types of apparel?

Analysis of U.S. import data shows that the biggest import sector is that of women's sportswear, which was traditionally U.S. made and supplied by branded manufacturers or jobbers. These vendors are now heavily involved in importing this class of merchandise, concentrating domestic manufacture on men's, boy's and childrenwear. It is estimated that of women's sportswear sold by the major companies and representing one-third of the U.S. market, 65% is imported in contrast with a 20% figure for other categories.

The first potential source of new QR capacity is the branded manufacturer intent on regaining domestic market share. As an alternative to this route, the manufacturer could turn to the QR contractor if, in fact, such a manufacturer were freely available. Similarly, the design house and the jobber now sourcing off-shore could make use of the services of this kind of contrator. The problem is that though there are several outstanding exceptions, the contractors who survived the import surge generally lack the capital resources or the management mentality or skills to develop QR programs. This suggests that there is a window of opportunity for the establishment of modern QR plants for the women's wear market by investors from outside the traditional complex.

The economics of new QR plants was introduced in Chapter 12 in the context of comparing PBU, UPS and Modular manufacturing systems. Table 12.1 gave estimates of the kinds of financial returns that can be expected from investment in such operations, producing typical garment types. The data base used for the Table was provided in Appendix I and it is worth reexamination, this time in terms of an investment opportunity by a single entity or a consortium of investors from inside or outside the industry.

Table 14.1 is intended as a rough guide to such an investor putting together a significant apparel producing company of about 20 normal sized plants serving 10 major retailers with women's sportswear in QR partnerships. The returns are attractive and are not overstated. Should a strong emphasis on design be included in the company's strategy, the returns could improve significantly.

The feasibility of this type of investment is demonstrated by the growing number of Far Eastern companies concerned over quotas, the uncertain future of Hong Kong or the weaker dollar, that have opted to shift part of their of their manufacturing base to the U.S.

Table 14.1
QR Manufacturing Venture
Financial Summary
($Million)

Sales	$300
Pre-Tax Profit	35
After-Tax Profit	18
Investment:	
Permanent	35
Working Capital	40
Total	$75
After-Tax ROI	24%
Fifth Year Summary:	
Net Cash Flow	Even
Net Return on Equity	29%
Internal Rate of Return	18%

A large new investment is probably the best approach to the problem being discussed here, but there are partial or alternate solutions. For example, modern, computer linked and driven, marker making, spreading and cutting equipment is expensive by traditional contractor standards. One reason for this is low utilization - one or possibly two shifts. If it is operated around the clock, however, the returns are very attractive. Such an operation would exist if a textile producer were to supply cut parts to his customer, the markers being transmitted electronically. Alternatively, a large, multi-customer contract cutting operation in or near a large garment center would offer good returns.

One of the strongest arguments in favor of QR is that the proper application of technology, inventory and WIP reduction and QR management precepts pays back the technology investment; it is not only a survival strategy. J. J. Ulman of KSA, in an elegant paper delivered to the 1985 International Apparel Research Conference, examined the productivity increases experienced since 1960 by aggressive manufacturers who made full use of existing technological developments as they became available. He found that productivity had doubled over the past 25-30 year period, and in some applications, at a better rate. He then speculated that with the present rate of technology growth, productivity could well double again in the next 10-15 years.

Ullman then coupled this assumption with another; that in line with QR analyses, over one-third of traditional inventory and WIP stocks can be taken out of the system. The KSA Financial Profiles of Public Apparel Firms for 1984, had shown that for the major companies, 37% of assets were tied up in inventories and 21% in net fixed assets. Inventory represented 21 cents per dollar of sales and net fixed only 12 cents. QR teaches that 7 cents can be moved out of inventory and into fixed assets. Ullman illustrated the impact of such a conversion using a hypothetical manufacturer who behaves in an optimal manner over the next 10-15 years.

The manufacturer now employs 1,000 direct labor operators in four plants that are quite well engineered. Based on existing technology, there is available a productivity increase of somewhere around 25%, but, assuming a steady flow of innovation, it should be possible to increase productivity by 5-6%/year for the foreseeable future, or a doubling in 13 or 14 years. The manufacturer will also develop QR programs with his customers.

At the end of the 14 year period, he will be able to operate with 500 workers in two plants. Having invested in a capital intensive operating environment, the manufacturer will go to two shifts per day to get a good return on his investment i.e., one factory with two, 250 worker, shifts.

Using the industry averages given above, he has, currently, $10.5 million in inventories and $6 million in fixed assets. Down the road he will convert 7 cents per constant dollar of sales, or $3.5 million to fixed assets, bringing the total to $9.5 million. This higher level of assets will be applied to a single plant running two shifts, for a depreciating fixed asset investment of $30,000 per work station, allowing for surplus equipment. This is eight times the current investment level and it has all been paid for internally.

This kind of creative, back-of-the-envelope, analysis is crucial to the implementation of QR by management teams intent on increasing profitability and remaining competitive over the long haul.

One final point on investment. It is fatally easy to put off the purchase of new equipment on the grounds that the cost will decrease over time, that "the bugs need to be worked out" or that "it needs a few more bells and whistles before we can take full advantage of it". It can be demonstrated that getting onto the experience curve now gives far greater benefits than starting to accumulate experience at a later date. The manager who consciously decides not to invest in technology has made a perfectly valid strategic decision; he has opted to be out of the business within the next ten years.

Education & Training.

The transition to technology intensive textile and apparel manufacturing will call for very different human skills at all levels of the organization. Manual dexterity will be replaced in large measure by programming skills. Maintenance of computer driven equipment is very different from traditional mechanically oriented maintenance. Also, the office and managerial environments will rely on the rapid provision, analysis and despatch of information. The types of persons required for these new operations will not walk in off the street; provision must be made for training them or the industry will continue to lag other manufacturing fields in terms of technology transfer.

The U.S. fiber and textile industries have long had strong ties to the universities which provide the core of their textile trained future managers, and shifts in educational emphasis are accomplished with little difficulty. The apparel industry is far less structured with regard to its supervisory trainees and educational requirements are not well stipulated. Further, the industry has a poor public image and a tradition of paying poorly in the early years of a person's career - making it difficult to compete for the kind of strategically necessary new graduate.

At the technologist level, for all sectors, there is little in the way of formal, industry specified, training available in the U.S. The new entry must pick up the business as he/she goes along and the frustration and disappointment levels experienced by supervisor and trainee alike can be costly and time wasting.

As fewer, larger firms come to dominate the industry in the next decade or two, it is hoped that the U.S. will adopt some of the approaches taken by most European countries toward structuring the learning process of the new technician. There, courses are set up in the vocational schools in the regions where textile and apparel manufacturing is concentrated, and these can be taken either full time prior to employment or as part of a "time off for training" program administered by the firm. The curricula are, in general, set up and administered by the "social partnership" of government, labor and business and there is a well developed diploma accreditation.

The European training systems have little chance of evolving, as is, in the U.S. Progress will best be made by the industries themselves setting entry standards, working with the vocational schools to supply equipment and part time training help and then offering the graduating students well paying jobs. Time off for study by promising juniors would complement this appoach. There is some evidence that the more serious and far-sighted of the industry leaders have seen the need for formal training and are ready to begin the structuring process.

Managing Change.

The extent to which change is taking place in the textile related industries and the importance of actively adopting change in order to survive and prosper, has been covered ad nauseam throughout this book. The reason for bringing it up one more time is to stress that none of the benefits of QR implementation, technology adoption, import substitution or export agressiveness can occur until the CEO firmly, publicly and irrevocably commits his organization to change.

With that as the first step, the chances of achieving change will remain small until a top-down change program is developed and implemented; until each person in the company has a clear view of the objectives of the company, together with the time-table for achieving them and a personal feeling of involvement. And, built into the program, there must be the recognition that the implementation of change in an organization takes a long time.

Most companies will benefit from the advice and assistance of a consulting company with experience in implementing change. There is no shortage of these, both industry related and those with a general management background.

Notes - Chapter 14.

The combination of "small" and "design" is discussed in an interesting account of industry structure in the Prato region of Italy contained in "Beyond Vertical Integration - the Rise of the Value-Adding Partnership". Johnston and Lawrence, HBR, July-August 1988.

The relationship between import penetration and catalog price comes from a study on behalf of CWP by the author.

The economics of new QR capacity was based on an unpublished du Pont study.

An excellent review of the training programs used in Europe was given by K. Pye of the U.K. Clothing and Allied Products Training Board (CAPITB) at the 1987 International Apparel Research Conference. Since that time, the AAMA has embarked on an investigation of the industry's training needs.

Another source of information on comparative industrial training methods is "Competence and Competition - Training and Education in the Federal Republic of Germany, the United States and Japan", published by the U.K. National Economic Development Council.

	Dept. Stores			Chains			Total		
	%Tot.	%MD	Turns	%Tot.	%MD	Turns	%Tot.	%MD	Turns
Womenswear									
Dresses	10	25.5	3.6	7	18.1	4.1	8.5	21.8	3.8
Coats, Suits	5	22.0	3.9	3	17.3	4.0	4.0	19.9	3.9
Sportswear	33	21.7	4.0	24	15.0	5.1	28.5	18.4	4.5
Sub-Total	48	22.5	3.9	34	16.0	4.9	41.0	20.1	4.4
Intimate Apparel	7	12.4	3.6	5	10.8	3.6	6.0	11.6	3.6
Hosiery	3	7.6	3.3	5	6.1	4.3	4.0	6.8	3.8
Bras & Corsets	4	6.3	2.5	4	5.8	3.1	4.0	6.0	2.8
Sub-Total	14	9.6	3.2	14	7.6	3.7	14.0	8.6	3.4
Tot. Womenswear	62	19.3	3.8	48	13.3	4.4	55.0	17.2	4.1
Menswear									
Clothing & OW	9	20.4	2.6	12	13.5	4.0	10.5	17.0	3.3
Sportswear	4	16.5	3.4	3	11.0	4.1	3.5	13.8	3.8
Shirts & Sweaters	9	16.2	3.1	6	9.0	3.7	7.5	12.7	3.4
Sub Total	22	18.3	3.0	21	11.7	4.0	21.5	15.0	3.5
Underwear, Hose	3	7.3	3.4	4	5.0	3.3	3.5	6.1	3.5
Tot. Menswear	25	15.5	3.0	25	10.5	3.9	25.0	13.0	3.4
Childrenswear									
Girls	6	20.3	3.2	10	13.1	4.3	8.0	16.4	3.7
Boys	4	17.7	3.2	12	11.0	3.5	8.0	12.7	3.4
Infants, Toddlers	3	15.3	3.2	5	8.0	4.2	4.0	11.6	3.7
Total CW	13	17.6	3.2	27	11.2	3.9	20.0	13.9	3.6
Total Apparel	100	20.1	3.6	100	12.1	4.1	100	16.1	3.8
Women's OW	48	22.5	3.9	34	16.0	4.9	41.0	20.1	4.4
Mens & C's OW	35	17.8	3.1	48	11.4	3.9	41.5	14.5	3.5
Underwear & Hose	17	9.1	3.2	18	7.0	3.8	17.5	8.0	3.4
	100	20.1	3.6	100	12.1	4.1	100	16.1	3.8

APPENDIX B
Fiber & Fabric Inventories – Basic Fabrics
Working Days & Weeks

Man Made Fiber	PE Staple Present	Potential		PE Textured Filament Present	Potential
Raw Material	11.0	9.0		11.0	9.0
W.I.P.	6.0	4.0		9.0	7.0
Fin. Goods Inventories	22.0	9.0		24.0	9.0
Total Fiber Days	39.0	22.0		44.0	25.0
Weeks @ 6 days/wk	6.5	3.5		7.3	4.1

Basic Fabric	Poplin			Pongee	
Fiber	7.4	5.7		5.0	3.0
Spin	8.3	4.2	Tex.	5.0	3.0
			Inv.	5.0	3.0
Warp & Weave	9.8	7.8		12.5	10.0
Greige	10.0	8.0		10.0	8.0
WIP Finish	7.5	5.0		6.5	4.0
Sub-total	43.0	30.7		42.0	31.0
Finished Inv.	37.5	10.0		37.5	10.0
Total Fabric: Days	80.5	40.7		79.5	41.0
Weeks @ 5 days/wk	16.1	8.1		15.9	8.2
Total Fiber & Fabric, Days:	119.5	62.7		123.5	66.0
Total Weeks:	22.6	11.6		23.2	12.3

APPENDIX C
Logistics Times & Costs
(Days & $/Units)

	Trad. Days	$	Quick Days	$	V. Quick Days	$
Fab. Finishing Mill						
• Rec. Order, Pull Pieces	5.0	0.007	1.0	0.009	1.0	0.009
• Ship To Central Cutting	2.0	0.034	2.0	0.096*	2.0	0.096*
Central Cutting Plant						
• Receive & Process	2.5	0.020	2.0	0.030	2.0	0.030
• Spread, Cut & Clear	3.0	--	3.0	--	1.0	--
• Ship To Sewing	2.0	0.019	1.0	0.042*	1.0	0.042*
Distribution In	14.0	0.080	9.0	0.177	7.0	0.177
Sewing Plant						
• Sew & Finish	20.0	--	12.5	--	3.5	--
• Vendor Pack						
- For Vendor's D.C. **						
& Ship	4.0	0.065				
- Price Tag & Pack						
For Store			1.5	0.036	1.5	0.036
Ship To Store						
• Via Vendor's D.C.						
- Pack & Ship To						
Consolidation	5.0	0.341				
- Ship To Retail D.C.	3.0	0.048				
- Process & Price Tag	5.5	0.266				
- Transfer To Stores	1.0	0.064				
• Via Retail D.C.						
- Ship To Regional D.C.			5.0	0.130		
- Cross Dock Transfer			1.0	0.020		
- Transfer To Stores			1.0	0.064		
• Ship Direct To Stores						
Via U.P.S.					3.0	0.217
Distribution Out	38.5	0.784	21.0	0.250	8.0	0.253
Total Time & Cost	51.5	0.864	30.0	0.427	15.0	0.430

* More frequent shipments of smaller lots
** Distribution Center

Fabric Inventory and Cost Summary
Pongee
(Working Days & $)

	Diversity Level			
	1	2	3	4
Grey Fabric				
Raw Material				
Polyester Feed Yarn	5.0	8.0	11.0	16.0
Semi-Finished				
Texturing	3.0	3.0	3.0	3.0
Lag @ Weaving (inc. ship)	5.0	6.0	7.0	10.0
Weaving – Warp Base	5.55	6.90	8.50	10.60
Weaving-2oz/sq.yd.	16.80	16.63	16.67	16.60
Fill	1.05	1.20	1.45	1.80
Cloth Room	1.00	1.15	1.35	1.60
Total @ 51% Warp	<u>20.89</u>	<u>22.71</u>	<u>24.86</u>	<u>29.32</u>
Finished:				
For Transfer	6.0	6.0	6.0	6.0
Total Days Inventory	31.89	36.71	41.86	51.32
Mfg. Costs, $/60" yd.	0.47	0.49	0.52	0.56
Dyeing & Finishing				
Raw Material (incl. ship.)	4.0	6.0	9.0	12.0
Semi-Finished	6.5	6.5	6.5	6.5
Finished	<u>16.0</u>	<u>16.0</u>	<u>16.0</u>	<u>16.0</u>
Total Days Inventory	26.5	28.5	31.5	34.5
Mfg. Cost, $/60" yd.	0.19	0.20	0.22	0.25
Working Loss, etc. $/60" yd.	0.05	0.06	0.07	0.08
Finished Fabric				
Total Mfg. Cost, $/60" yd.	0.71	0.75	0.81	0.89
Total $ Inventory/60" yd.	0.13	0.14	0.16	0.19
Total Working Days Inv.	58.0	65.0	73.0	86.0
-Minus Fin. Goods	<u>16.0</u>	<u>16.0</u>	<u>16.0</u>	<u>16.0</u>
	42.0	49.0	57.0	70.0

Fabric Inventory and Cost Summary
Poplin
(Working Days & $)

	Diversity Level			
	1	2	3	4
Grey Fabric				
Raw Material				
Cotton	10.0	12.0	14.0	16.0
Polyester - Staple	6.0	8.0	10.0	12.0
65/35 Polyester/Cotton	7.4	9.4	11.4	13.4
Semi-Finished				
Yarn-Base	5.25	5.75	6.45	7.25
- Spinning: 18/1	2.08	2.08	3.52	3.55
26/1	3.84	3.88	2.13	3.55
Weave - Warp Base	5.55	6.90	8.50	10.60
- Weaving 5oz/sq yd	7.92	7.68	7.55	7.11
Fill	0.80	0.95	1.10	1.30
Cloth Room	1.15	1.25	1.40	1.60
Total @58% Warp	17.92	19.01	20.66	22.65
Finished:				
For Transfer	6.0	6.0	6.0	6.0
Total Days Inventory	31.32	34.41	38.06	42.05
Mfg. Cost $/60" yd.	1.02	1.08	1.18	1.35
Dyeing & Finishing				
Raw Material (incl. ship.)	4.0	6.0	9.0	12.0
Semi-Finished	7.5	7.5	7.5	7.5
Finished	16.0	16.0	16.0	16.0
Total Days Inventory	27.5	29.5	32.5	35.5
Mfg. Cost $/60" yd.	0.35	0.37	0.40	0.44
Working Loss etc. - $/60" yd	0.03	0.04	0.04	0.05
Finished Fabric				
Total Mfg. Cost $/60" yd.	1.40	1.49	1.62	1.84
Total $ Inventory/60" yd.	0.24	0.27	0.32	0.39
Total Working Days Inv.	59.0	64.0	71.0	78.0
-Minus Fin. Goods	16.0	16.0	16.0	16.0
	43.0	48.0	55.0	62.0

APPENDIX E1
Projected Sew & Finish Cost
Open Seam Casual Slack
USA Typical PBU

Diversity Level	Very Low	Low	Medium	High
SAH/Dozen	3.931	4.035	4.138	4.349
Std. $/Doz., $5.25 Base	20.64	21.18	21.72	22.83
Dir. Labor $/Std. $	0.10	0.15	0.20	0.35
Tot. Dir. Labor Cost	$22.70	$24.36	$26.07	$30.82
Ind. Labor $/DL $	0.144	0.144	0.144	0.144
Fr. Benefit $/DL $	0.284	0.284	0.284	0.284
Supp. & Util $/DL $	0.087	0.087	0.087	0.087
Tot. Var. Ovhd $/DL $	0.515	0.515	0.515	0.515
Var. Ovhd. Cost/Doz.	$11.69	$12.54	$13.43	$15.87
Mgmt. Supp. $/DL $	0.166	0.166	0.166	0.166
Misc. Ovhd. $/DL $	0.063	0.063	0.063	0.063
Insur. $/DL $	0.005	0.005	0.005	0.005
Depr. $/DL $	0.035	0.035	0.035	0.035
Local Tax $/DL $	0.004	0.004	0.004	0.004
Loss to Irregs. $/DL $	0.016	0.016	0.016	0.016
Other Ovhd. $/DL $	0.289	0.289	0.289	0.289
Other Ovhd. Cost/Doz.	$6.56	$7.04	$7.35	$8.91
Total Cost/Doz.	$40.95	$43.94	$47.03	$55.60
Total Cost/Unit	$3.41	$3.66	$3.92	$4.63
Mult: Total Cost/Std. $	1.98	2.07	2.16	2.44

APPENDIX E2
Projected Sew & Finish Cost
Open Seam Casual Slack
USA Best PBU

Diversity Level	Very Low	Low	Medium	High
SAH/Dozen	3.250	3.336	3.421	3.593
Std. $/Doz. $5.25 Base	17.06	17.51	17.96	18.86
Dir. Labor $/Std. $	0.100	0.150	0.200	0.350
Tot. Dir. Labor Cost	$18.77	$20.14	$21.55	$25.46
Ind. Labor $/DL $	0.150	0.150	0.150	0.150
Fr. Benefit $/DL $	0.285	0.285	0.285	0.285
Supp. & Util. $/DL $	0.091	0.091	0.091	0.091
Tot. Var. Ovhd. $/DL $	0.526	0.526	0.526	0.526
Var. Ovhd. Cost/Doz.	$9.87	$10.59	$11.34	$13.39
Mgmt. $ Supp $/DL $	0.172	0.172	0.172	0.172
Misc. Ovhd. $/DL $	0.066	0.066	0.066	0.066
Insur $/DL $	0.006	0.006	0.006	0.006
Depr. $/DL $	0.090	0.090	0.090	0.090
Local Tax $/DL $	0.010	0.010	0.010	0.010
Loss to Irregs. $/DL $	0.018	0.018	0.018	0.018
Other Ovhd. $/DL $	0.362	0.362	0.362	0.362
Other Ovhd. Cost/Doz.	$6.79	$7.29	$7.80	$9.22
Total Cost/Doz.	$35.44	$38.02	$40.70	$48.07
Total Cost/Unit	$2.95	$3.17	$3.39	$4.01
Mult.: Total Cost/Std. $	2.08	2.17	2.27	2.55

Projected Sew & Finish Cost
Open Seam Casual Slack
USA Best UPS

Diversity Level	Very Low	Low	Medium	High
SAH/Dozen	2.966	3.044	3.122	3.278
Std. $/Doz. $5.25 Base	15.57	15.98	16.39	17.21
Dir. Labor $/Std. $	0.100	0.150	0.200	0.350
Total Dir. Labor Cost	$17.13	$18.38	$19.67	$23.23
Ind. Labor $/DL $	0.150	0.150	0.150	0.150
Fr. Benefit $/DL $	0.285	0.285	0.285	0.285
Supp. & Util. $/DL $	0.091	0.091	0.091	0.091
Tot. Var. Ovhd. $/DL $	0.526	0.526	0.526	0.526
Var. Ovhd. Cost/Doz.	$9.01	$9.67	$10.34	$12.22
Mgmt. $ Supp. $/DL $	0.172	0.172	0.172	0.172
Misc. Ovhd. $/DL $	0.066	0.066	0.066	0.066
Insur. $/DL $	0.006	0.006	0.006	0.006
Depr. $/DL $	0.131	0.131	0.131	0.131
Local Tax $/DL $	0.010	0.010	0.010	0.010
Loss to Irregs. $/DL $	0.018	0.018	0.018	0.018
Other Ovhd. $/DL $	0.043	0.043	0.043	0.043
Other Ovhd. Cost/Doz.	$6.90	$7.41	$7.93	$9.36
Total Cost/Dozen	$33.04	$35.45	$37.94	$44.81
Total Cost/Unit	$2.75	$2.95	$3.16	$3.73
Mult: Total Cost/Std. $	2.12	2.22	2.31	2.60

APPENDIX E4
Projected Sew & Finish Cost
Ladies' Blouse
USA Typical PBU

Diversity Level	Very Low	Low	Medium	High
SAH/Dozen	3.096	3.178	3.259	3.585
Std. $/Doz. $5.25 Base	$16.25	$16.68	$17.11	$18.82
Dir. Labor $/Std. $	0.150	0.200	0.250	0.400
Total Dir. Labor Cost	$18.69	$20.02	$21.39	$26.35
Ind. Labor $/DL $	0.198	0.198	0.198	0.198
Fr. Benefit $.DL $	0.297	0.297	0.297	0.297
Supp. & Util. $/DL $	0.110	0.110	0.110	0.110
Tot. Var. Ovhd. $/DL $	0.605	0.605	0.605	0.605
Var. Ovhd. Cost/Dozen	$11.31	$12.11	$12.94	$15.94
Mgmt. $ Supp. $/DL $	0.160	0.160	0.160	0.160
Misc. Ovhd. $/DL $	0.070	0.070	0.070	0.070
Insur. $/DL $	0.004	0.004	0.004	0.004
Depr. $/DL $	0.019	0.019	0.019	0.019
Local Tax $/DL $	0.003	0.003	0.003	0.003
Loss to Irregs. $/DL $	0.014	0.014	0.014	0.014
Other Ovhd. $/DL $	0.270	0.270	0.270	0.270
Other Ovhd. Cost/Doz.	$5.05	$5.40	$5.77	$7.11
Total Cost/Dozen	$35.05	$37.53	$40.10	$49.40
Total Cost/Unit	$2.92	$3.13	$3.34	$4.12
Mult: Total Cost/Std. $	2.16	2.25	2.34	2.63

APPENDIX E5
Projected Sew & Finish Cost
Ladies' Blouse
USA Best PBU

Diversity Level	Very Low	Low	Medium	High
SAH/Dozen	2.370	2.4322	2.495	2.744
Std. $/Doz. $5.25 Base	12.44	12.77	13.10	14.41
Dir. Labor $/Std. $	0.150	0.200	0.250	0.400
Total Dir. Labor Cost	$14.31	$15.32	$16.37	$20.17
Ind. Labor $/DL $	0.201	0.201	0.201	0.201
Fr. Benefit $/DL $	0.298	0.298	0.298	0.298
Supp. & Util. $/DL $	0.127	0.127	0.127	0.127
Tot. Var. Ovhd. $/DL $	0.626	0.626	0.626	0.626
Var. Ovhd. Cost/Dozen	$8.96	$9.59	$10.25	$12.63
Mgmt. $ Supp. $/DL $	0.166	0.166	0.166	0.166
Misc. Ovhd. $/DL $	0.073	0.073	0.073	0.073
Insur. $/DL $	0.005	0.005	0.005	0.005
Depr. $/DL $	0.068	0.068	0.068	0.068
Local Tax $/DL $	0.008	0.008	0.008	0.008
Loss to Irregs. $/DL $	0.016	0.016	0.016	0.016
Other Ovhd. $/DL $	0.336	0.336	0.336	0.336
Other Ovhd. Cost/Dozen	$4.81	$5.15	$5.50	$6.78
Total Cost/Dozen	$28.07	$30.06	$32.16	$39.57
Total Cost/Unit	$2.34	$2.51	$2.68	$3.30
Mult: Total Cost/Std. $	2.26	2.35	2.45	2.75

Projected Sew & Finish Cost
Ladies' Blouse
USA Best UPS

Diversity Level	Very Low	Low	Medium	High
SAH/Dozen	2.261	2.320	2.380	2.618
Std. $/Doz. $5.25 Base	11.87	12.18	12.49	13.74
Dir. Labor $/Std. $	0.150	0.200	0.250	0.400
Total Dir. Labor Cost	$13.65	$14.62	$15.62	$19.24
Ind. Labor $/DL $	0.201	0.201	0.201	0.201
Fr. Benefit $/DL $	0.298	0.298	0.298	0.298
Supp. & Util. $/DL $	0.127	0.127	0.127	0.127
Tot. Var. Ovhd. $/DL $	0.626	0.626	0.626	0.626
Var. Ovhd. Cost/Doz.	$8.55	$9.15	$9.78	$12.05
Mgmt. $ Supp. $/DL $	0.166	0.166	0.166	0.166
Misc. Ovhd. $/DL $	0.073	0.073	0.073	0.073
Insur. $/DL $	0.006	0.006	0.006	0.006
Depr. $/DL $	0.088	0.088	0.088	0.088
Local Tax $/DL $	0.008	0.008	0.008	0.008
Loss to Irregs. $/DL $	0.016	0.016	0.016	0.016
Other Ovhd. $/DL $	0.357	0.357	0.357	0.357
Other Ovhd. Cost/Doz.	$4.87	$5.22	$5.58	$6.87
Total Cost/Dozen	$27.07	$28.99	$30.97	$38.16
Total Cost/Unit	$2.26	$2.42	$2.58	$3.18
Mult: Total Cost/Std. $	2.28	2.38	2.48	2.78

APPENDIX F1
Weighted Wholesale Cost
Men's Slack – Department Stores
UPS

Product Life:	50 Week			20 Week			10 Week		5 Wk
Resp. Time:	Pres.	6 Wk.	3 Wk.	Pres.	6 Wk.	3 Wk.	Pres.	3 Wk.	Pres.
Retail Distrib.	1.15	0.37	0.44	1.15	0.37	0.44	1.15	0.44	1.15
Freight Inv.	0.10	0.21	0.21	0.10	0.21	0.21	0.10	0.21	0.10
App. Sew/Fin	3.67	3.93	4.21	3.93	4.21	4.97	4.21	4.97	4.21
Apparel Cut	0.28	0.35	0.57	0.35	0.44	0.57	0.44	0.57	0.44
Trim $/Unit	0.87	0.87	0.89	0.87	0.89	0.92	0.89	0.92	0.89
Fabric $/Unit	2.19	2.25	2.45	2.35	2.41	2.69	2.37	2.69	2.57
Yards/Unit	1.25	1.26	1.29	1.26	1.27	1.29	1.27	1.29	1.27
Tex. Cost/Yard $									
Total	1.75	1.79	1.90	1.86	1.90	2.09	1.86	2.09	2.03
Finish	0.48	0.51	0.55	0.51	0.55	0.61	0.51	0.61	0.55
Greige	1.28	1.28	1.35	1.35	1.35	1.48	1.35	1.48	1.48
Initial Order	8.25	8.25	8.25	8.74	8.74	8.74	9.16	9.16	9.37
Reorder		7.98	8.78		8.54	9.81		9.81	
% Reorder		75	85		50	65		30	
Weighted Ave. Total Cost		8.05	8.70		8.64	9.44		9.36	
% of Present		98	105		99	108		102	

APPENDIX F2
Weighted Wholesale Costs
Ladies' Blouse – Department Stores
UPS

Product Life:	50 Week			20 Week			10 Week		5 Wk
Resp. Time:	Pres.	6 Wk.	3 Wk.	Pres.	6 Wk.	3 Wk.	Pres.	3 Wk.	Pres.
Retail Distrib.	0.78	0.26	0.25	0.78	0.26	0.25	0.78	0.25	0.78
Freight Inv.	0.08	0.18	0.18	0.08	0.18	0.18	0.08	0.18	0.08
App. Sew/Fin.	3.01	3.23	3.44	3.23	3.44	4.24	3.44	4.24	3.44
Apparel Cut	0.40	0.48	0.73	0.48	0.56	0.73	0.56	0.73	0.56
Trim $/Unit	0.35	0.35	0.36	0.35	0.36	0.37	0.36	0.37	0.36
Fabric $/Unit	1.22	1.26	1.38	1.30	1.36	1.50	1.28	1.50	1.41
Yards/Unit	1.375	1.382	1.416	1.382	1.396	1.416	1.369	1.416	1.396
Tex. Cost/Yd.									
Total	0.89	0.91	0.98	0.94	0.98	10.60	0.94	10.60	1.01
Finish	0.30	0.33	0.36	0.33	0.36	0.41	0.33	0.41	0.36
Greige	0.59	0.59	0.61	0.61	0.61	0.65	0.61	0.65	0.65
Initial Order	5.85	5.84	5.84	6.21	6.21	6.21	6.50	6.50	6.63
Reorder		5.75	6.34		6.16	7.27		7.27	
% Reorder		75	85		50	65		30	
Weighted Ave.									
Total Cost		5.78	6.27		6.19	6.90		6.73	
% of Present		99	107		100	111		104	

207

QR Economics – Model Data
Lead Times & Forecast Errors
Conditions: Traditional

	Product Life				
	5 Weeks	10 Weeks	20 Weeks	50+ Weeks	Weighted Total
Dept. & Speciality Stores					
% of Retail Sales	11	32	38	19	100
Initial Order					
Lead Time – Weeks	14	19	25	20	20.9
Commitment – Weeks	5	10	16	18	13.3
Total	19	29	41	38	34.2
Est. Forecast Error	45.0%	50.0%	60.0%	30.0%	49.5%
Reorder					
Lead Time	12	12	12	6	10.9
Reorderable Weeks	0	0	4	32	7.6
Est. Forecast Error	N/A	N/A	20	8	
% of Sales – Reorder	0	0	20	64	19.8
Combined Forecast Error	45.0%	50.0%	52.0%	16.0%	43.8%
Mass Merchants					
% of Retail Sales	3	20	52	25	100
Initial Order					
Lead Time – Weeks	14	19	20	20	19.6
Commitment – Weeks	5	10	16	18	15
Total	19	29	36	38	34.6
Est. Forecast Error	45.0%	50.0%	40.0%	25.0%	38.4%
Reorder					
Lead Time	12	12	12	6	10.5
Reorderable Weeks	0	0	4	32	10.1
Est. Forecast Error	N/A	N/A	13%	6%	
% of Sales – Reorder	0	0	20.0	64.0	26.4
Combined Forecast Error	45.0%	50.0%	35.0%	13.0%	32.8%

APPENDIX G2
QR Economics – Model Data
Markdowns
Conditions: Traditional

	Product Life				
	5 Weeks	10 Weeks	20 Weeks	50+ Weeks	Weighted Total
Dept. & Speciality Stores					
% of Retail Sales	11	32	38	19	100
Retail Markdowns					
% of Net Retail $	27.0	26.0	20.5	7.5	20.5
% of Retail Units	70	65	60	32	57.4
Forced M.D. – % Units	38	47	44	15	38.8
Forced M.D. – % Net $	16.6	20.2	15.6	2.9	14.8
Apparel Forced M.D.					
% of Net Retail $	5.8	5.4	4.1	2.6	4.4
Textile M.D.					
% of Net Retail $	0.9	0.7	0.6	0.4	0.6
Total Forced M.D.					
% of Net Retail $	23.3	26.3	20.3	5.9	19.8
Mass Merchants					
% of Retail Sales	3	20	52	25	100
Retail Markdowns					
% of Net Retail $	24.0	22.0	18.5	6.0	16.2
% of Retail Units	65	60	50	32	48
Forced M.D. – % Units	21	33	39	15	31.3
Forced M.D. – % of Net $	10.1	13.6	15.2	2.3	11.5
Apparel Forced M.D.					
% of Net Retail $	5.4	4.9	3.6	2.4	3.6
Textile M.D.					
% of Net Retail $	1.0	0.8	0.6	0.4	0.6
Total Forced M.D.					
% of Net Retail $	16.5	19.3	19.4	5.1	15.7

APPENDIX   G3
QR Economics – Model Data
Stock Outs
Conditions: Traditional

	Product Life				
	5 Weeks	10 Weeks	20 Weeks	50+ Weeks	Weighted Total
Dept. & Speciality Stores					
% Retail Sales	11	32	38	19	100
Sales Loss to Stock Outs as % of Net Retail					
Retail	16.6	20.2	15.6	2.9	14.8
Apparel	5.8	5.4	4.1	2.6	4.4
Textiles	0.9	0.7	0.6	0.4	0.6
Contribution Loss on 1/2 of Stock Outs as $ of Net Retail					
Retail	5.16	5.86	4.04	0.62	4.10
Apparel	0.59	0.49	0.34	0.19	0.39
Textiles	0.01	0.01	0.01	0.00	0.01
Total	5.76	6.36	4.39	0.81	4.50
Mass Merchants					
% Retail Sales	3	20	52	25	100
Sales Loss to Stock Outs as % of Net Retail					
Retail	10.0	13.6	15.2	2.3	11.5
Apparel	5.4	4.9	3.6	2.4	3.6
Textiles	1.0	0.8	0.6	0.4	0.6
Contribution Loss on 1/2 of Stock Outs as % of Net Retail					
Retail	2.88	3.56	3.60	0.43	2.78
Apparel	0.52	0.42	0.29	0.17	0.29
Textiles	0.01	0.01	0.01	0.01	0.01
Total	3.41	3.99	3.90	0.60	3.08

APPENDIX G4
QR Economics – Model Data
Inventory Weeks
Conditions: Traditional

| | Product Life | | | | |
	5 Weeks	10 Weeks	20 Weeks	50+ Weeks	Weighted Total
Dept. & Speciality Stores					
% of Retail Sales	11	32	38	19	100
Store Inventory	8.7	13.7	16.3	17.3	14.8
Retail D.C. Inventory	1.7	1.7	1.7	1.7	1.7
In-Transit to Retail	1.0	1.0	1.0	1.0	1.0
Apparel F.G. Inventory	9.5	11.6	13.0	13.7	12.3
Apparel W.I.P.	3.0	3.2	4.0	3.8	3.6
Apparel Fabric	4.0	5.0	6.0	10.0	6.2
Apparel Fabric In-Trans.	0.8	0.8	0.8	0.8	0.8
Textile Fabric Inventory	7.5	7.5	7.5	7.5	7.5
Textile W.I.P.	9.7	8.7	7.7	7.1	8.1
Textile Raw Materials	2.7	2.3	1.9	1.5	2.0
Fiber Finished Inventory	-	-	-	-	-
Total Inventory Weeks	55.3	62.2	66.6	62.1	64.1
Mass Merchants					
% of Retail Sales	3	20	52	25	100
Store Inventory	8.4	13.0	13.7	14.4	13.6
Retail D.C. Inventory	1.7	1.7	1.7	1.7	1.7
In-Transit to Retail	1.0	1.0	1.0	1.0	1.0
Apparel F.G. Inventory	9.5	11.6	13.0	13.7	12.8
Apparel W.I.P.	3.0	3.2	4.0	3.8	3.8
Apparel Fabric	4.0	5.0	6.0	10.0	6.7
Apparel Fabric In-Trans.	0.8	0.8	0.8	0.8	0.8
Textile Fabric Inventory	7.5	7.5	7.5	7.5	7.5
Textile W.I.P.	9.7	8.7	7.7	7.1	7.8
Textile Raw Materials	2.7	2.3	1.9	1.5	1.9
Fiber Finished Inventory	6.7	6.7	6.7	6.7	6.7
Total Inventory Units	55.0	61.5	64.0	68.2	64.3

APPENDIX G5
QR Economics – Model Data
Inventory Carrying Costs at 15%
Conditions: Traditional

| | Product Life | | | | |
	5 Weeks	10 Weeks	20 Weeks	50+ Weeks	W'ted Total
Dept. & Speciality Stores					
Carrying Costs as %					
of New Retail $					
Store	1.34	2.24	2.81	3.13	2.53
Retail D.C.	0.26	0.28	0.29	0.31	0.29
In-Transit to Retail	0.15	0.16	0.17	0.18	0.17
Apparel Finished Goods	1.10	1.43	1.65	1.79	1.55
Apparel W.I.P.	0.27	0.30	0.39	0.38	0.35
Apparel Fabric	0.25	0.33	0.41	0.71	0.42
Apparel Fabric In-Trans.	0.05	0.05	0.05	0.06	0.05
Textile Fabric	0.40	0.41	0.43	0.44	0.42
Textile W.I.P.	0.37	0.35	0.32	0.31	0.33
Textile Raw Materials	0.07	0.06	0.05	0.04	0.05
Fabric Finished Inventory	0.15	0.15	0.15	0.15	0.15
Total	4.41	5.76	6.72	7.50	6.31
Mass Merchants					
% of Retail Sales	3	20	52	25	100
Carrying Costs as %					
of Net Retail $					
Store	1.29	2.13	2.36	2.61	2.34
Retail D.C.	0.26	0.28	0.29	0.31	0.29
In-Transit to Retail	0.15	0.16	0.17	0.18	0.17
Apparel Finished Goods	1.10	1.43	1.65	1.79	1.62
Apparel W.I.P.	0.27	0.30	0.39	0.38	0.37
Apparel Fabric	0.25	0.33	0.41	0.71	0.46
Apparel Fabric In-Trans.	0.05	0.05	0.05	0.05	0.05
Textile Fabric	0.40	0.41	0.43	0.44	0.43
Textile W.I.P.	0.37	0.35	0.32	0.31	0.33
Textile Raw Materials	0.07	0.06	0.05	0.04	0.05
Fiber Finished Inventory	0.15	0.15	0.15	0.15	0.15
Total	4.36	5.65	6.27	6.98	6.26

QR Economics - Model Data
Lead Times & Forecast Errors
Conditions: 6-Week Response

			Product Life		
	5 Weeks	10 Weeks	20 Weeks	50+ Weeks	Weighted Total
Dept. & Speciality Stores					
% of Retail Sales	11	32	38	19	100
Initial Order					
Lead-Time Weeks	12	14	17	11	14.4
Commitment - Weeks	5	10	10	12	9.8
Total	17	24	27	23	24.2
Est. Forecast Error	31.0%	29.0%	33.0%	20.0%	29.0%
Reorder					
Lead Time	6	6	6	6	6
Reorderable Weeks	0	0	10	38	11
Est. Forecast Error	N/A	N/A	11%	5%	
% of Sales - Reorder	0	0	50	75	33.2
Combined Forecast Error	31.0%	29.0%	22.0%	9.0%	22.8%
Mass Merchants					
% of Retail Sales	3	20	52	25	100
Initial Order					
Lead Time - Weeks	12	14	11	11	11.6
Commitment - Weeks	5	10	10	12	10.4
Total	17	24	21	23	22
Est. Forecast Error	31.0%	29.0%	27.0%	15.0%	24.5%
Reorder					
Lead Time	6	6	6	6	6
Reorderable Weeks	0	0	10	38	6
Est. Forecast Error	N/A	N/A	9%	4%	
% of Sales - Reorder	0	0	50	75	44.7
Combined Forecast Error	31.0%	29.0%	18.0%	7.0%	17.8%

APPENDIX   G7
QR Economics – Model Data
Markdowns
Conditions: 6–Week Response

| | Product Life | | | | |
	5 Weeks	10 Weeks	20 Weeks	50+ Weeks	Weighted Total
Dept. & Speciality Stores					
% of Retail Sales	11	32	38	19	100
Retail Markdowns					
% of Net Retail $	20.6	16.0	10.7	6.0	12.6
% of Retail Units	58	45	35	25	38.8
Forced M.D. – % Units	26	27	19	8	20.2
Forced M.D. – % of Net $	10.8	10.7	6.2	1.5	7.3
Apparel Forced M.D.					
% of Net Retail $	3.2	2.5	1..4	0.9	1.9
Textile M.D.					
% of Net Retail $	0.6	0.4	0.2	0.2	0.3
Total Forced M.D.					
% of Net Retail $	14.6	13.6	7.8	2.6	9.5
Mass Merchants					
% of Retail Sales	3	20	52	25	100
Retail Markdowns					
% of Net Retail $	20.0	15.3	10.4	4.9	10.3
% of Retail Units	58	46	31	25	33.3
Forced M.D. – % Units	14	19	20	8	16.6
Forced M.D. – % Net $	6.5	7.4	7.3	1.2	5.8
Apparel Forced M.D.					
% of Net Retail $	3.6	2.7	1.7	1.3	1.9
Textile M.D.					
% of Net Retail $	0.6	0.4	0.3	0.2	0.3
Total Forced M.D.					
% of Net Retail $	10.7	10.5	9.3	2.7	8.0

QR Economics - Model Data
Stock Outs
Conditions: 6-Week Response

| | Product Life | | | | |
	5 Weeks	10 Weeks	20 Weeks	50+ Weeks	Weighted Total
Dept. & Speciality Stores					
% Retail Sales	11	32	38	19	100
Sales Loss to Stock Outs as % of Net Retail					
Retail	10.8	10.7	6.2	1.5	7.3
Apparel	3.2	2.5	1.4	0.9	1.9
Textiles	0.6	0.4	0.2	0.2	0.3
Contribution Loss of 1/2 of Stock Outs as % of Net Retail					
Retail	3.36	3.10	1.61	0.32	2.03
Apparel	0.33	0.23	0.12	0.07	0.17
Textile	0.01	0.00	0.00	0.00	0.00
Total	3.70	3.33	1.73	0.38	2.20
Mass Merchants					
% Retail Sales	3	20	52	25	100
Sales Loss to Stock Outs as % of Net Retail					
Retail	57.0	50.45	47.45	37.14	
Apparel	3.6	2.7	1.7	1.3	1.9
Textile	0.6	0.4	0.3	0.2	0.3
Contribution Loss on 1/2 of Stock Outs as % of Net Retail					
Retail	1.85	1.94	1.73	0.22	1.40
Apparel	0.34	0.23	0.14	0.09	0.15
Textile	0.01	0.00	0.00	0.00	0.00
Total	2.20	2.17	1.87	0.31	1.55

APPENDIX G9
QR Economics - Model Data
Inventory Weeks
Conditions: 6-Week Response

	Product Life				
	5 Weeks	10 Weeks	20 Weeks	50+ Weeks	Weighted Total
Dept. & Speciality Stores					
% of Retail Sales	11	32	38	19	100
Store Inventory	8.0	11.6	11.1	13.7	11.4
Retail D.C. Inventory	0.9	0.9	0.9	0.9	0.9
In-Transit to Retail	0.5	0.5	0.5	0.5	0.5
Apparel F.G. Inventory	8.7	10.4	11.6	12.4	11.0
Apparel W.I.P.	1.5	1.6	2.0	1.9	1.8
Apparel Fabric	3.0	3.0	3.0	6.0	3.6
Apparel Fabric In Trans.	0.4	0.4	0.4	0.4	0.4
Textile Fabric Inventory	7.0	6.0	5.0	2.0	5.0
Textile W.I.P.	8.1	7.1	5.9	5.0	6.4
Textile Raw Materials	2.1	1.8	1.5	1.1	1.6
Fiber Finished Inventory	3.8	3.8	3.8	3.8	3.8
Total Inventory Units	44.0	47.1	45.7	47.7	46.4
Mass Merchants					
% of Retail Sales	3	20	52	25	100
Store Inventory	7.6	10.8	10.2	11.3	10.5
Retail D.C. Inventory	0.9	0.9	0.9	0.9	0.9
In-Transit to Retail	0.5	0.5	0.5	0.5	0.5
Apparel F.G. Inventory	8.3	9.6	10.4	10.8	10.3
Apparel W.I.P.	1.5	1.6	2.0	1.9	1.9
Apparel Fabric	3.0	3.0	3.0	6.0	3.8
Apparel Fabric In Trans.	0.4	0.4	0.4	0.4	0.4
Textile Fabric Inventory	7.0	6.0	5.0	2.0	4.5
Textile W.I.P.	8.1	7.1	5.9	5.0	6.4
Textile Raw Materials	2.1	1.8	1.5	1.1	1.5
Fiber Finished Inventory	3.8	3.8	3.8	3.8	3.8
Total Inventory Weeks	43.2	45.5	43.6	43.7	44.1

QR Economics - Model Data
Inventory Carrying Costs at 15%
Conditions: 6-Week Response

	5 Weeks	10 Weeks	Product Life 20 Weeks	50+ Weeks	Weighted Total
Dept. & Speciality Stores					
% of Retail Sales	11	32	38	19	100
Carrying Costs as % of Net Retail $					
Store	1.23	1.89	1.91	2.48	1.94
Retail D.C.	0.14	0.15	0.15	0.16	0.15
In-Transit to Retail	0.08	0.08	0.08	0.09	0.08
Apparel Finished Goods	1.01	1.28	1.48	1.62	1.39
Apparel W.I.P.	0.13	0.15	0.20	0.19	0.17
Apparel Fabric	0.19	0.20	0.21	0.42	0.24
Apparel Fabric In Trans.	0.02	0.03	0.03	0.03	0.03
Textile Fabric	0.37	0.33	0.28	0.12	0.28
Textile W.I.P.	0.31	0.28	0.25	0.22	0.26
Textile Raw Materials	0.05	0.05	0.04	0.03	0.04
Fiber Finished Inventory	0.08	0.08	0.08	0.08	0.08
Total	3.61	4.52	4.71	5.44	4.66
Mass Merchants					
% of Retail Sales	3	20	52	25	100
Carrying Costs as % of Net Retail $					
Store	1.17	1.76	1.76	2.05	1.81
Retail D.C.	0.14	0.15	0.15	0.16	0.15
In-Transit to Retail	0.08	0.08	0.09	0.09	0.09
Apparel Finished Goods	0.96	1.19	1.32	1.41	1.31
Apparel W.I.P.	0.13	0.15	0.20	0.19	0.19
Apparel Fabric	0.19	0.20	0.21	0.42	0.26
Apparel Fabric In Trans.	0.02	0.03	0.03	0.03	0.03
Textile Fabric	0.37	0.33	0.28	0.12	0.25
Textile W.I.P.	0.31	0.28	0.25	0.22	0.25
Textile Raw Materials	0.05	0.05	0.04	0.03	0.04
Fiber Finished Inventory	0.08	0.08	0.08	0.08	0.08
Total	3.50	4.30	4.41	4.46	

APPENDIX G11
QR Economics – Model Data
Lead Times & Forecast Errors
Conditions: 3-Week Response

	5 Weeks	10 Weeks	20 Weeks	50+ Weeks	Weighted Total
			Product Life		
Dept. & Speciality Stores					
% of Retail Sales	11	32	38	19	100
Initial Order					
Lead Time – Weeks	12	14	17	11	14.4
Commitment – Weeks	5	7	7	9	7.2
Total	17	21	24	20	21.6
Est. Forecast Error	31.0%	29.0%	33.0%	20.0%	29.0%
Reorder					
Lead Time	3	3	3	3	3
Reorderable Weeks	0	0	13	41	13.7
Est. Forecast Error	N/A	15%	11%	5%	
% of Sales – Reorder	0	30	65	82	49.9
Combined Forecast Error	31.0%	25.0%	19.0%	80.0%	20.2%
Mass Merchants					
% of Retail Sales	3	20	52	25	100
Initial Order					
Lead Time – Weeks	12	14	11	11	11.6
Commitment – Weeks	5	7	7	9	7.4
Total	17	21	18	20	19
Est. Forecast Error	31.0%	29.0%	27.0%	15.0%	24.5%
Reorder					
Lead Time	3	3	3	3	3
Reorderable Weeks	0	3	13	41	17.6
Est. Forecast Error	N/A	10	9	4	
% of Sales – Reorder	0	30	65	82	60.3
Combined Forecast Error	31.0%	23.0%	15.0%	6.0%	14.8%

218

QR Economics – Model Data
Markdowns
Conditions: 3-Week Response

		Product Life			
	5 Weeks	10 Weeks	20 Weeks	50+ Weeks	Weighted Total
Dept. & Speciality Stores					
% of Retail Sales	11	32	38	19	100
Retail Markdowns					
% of Net Retail $	20.6	14.7	9.6	6.0	11.8
% of Retail Units	58	42	32	25	36.7
Forced M.D. – % Units	26	24	16	8	18.1
Forced M.D. – % Net $	10.8	9.4	5.2	1.5	6.5
Apparel Forced M.D.					
% of Net Retail $	3.2	2.2	1.3	0.99	1.8
Textile M.D.					
% of Net Retail $	0.6	0.3	0.2	0.2	0.3
Total Forced M.D.					
% of Net Retail $	14.6	11.9	6.7	2.6	8.5
Mass Merchants					
% of Retail Sales	3	20	52	25	100
Retail Markdowns					
% of Net Retail $	20.0	10.7	10.7	4.7	9.5
% of Retail Units	46	33	33	24	31
Forced M.D. – % Units	14	15	17	7	14
Forced M.D. – % of Net $	6.5	5.6	6.2	1.1	4.8
Apparel Forced M.D.					
% of Net Retail $	3.6	2	1.4	1.1	1.5
Textile M.D.					
% of Net Retail $	0.6	0.3	0.2	0.2	0.2
Total Forced M.D.					
% of Net Retail $	10.7	7.9	7.8	2.4	6.5

QR Economics – Model Data
Stock Outs
Conditions: 3-Week Response

	Product Life				
	5 Weeks	10 Weeks	20 Weeks	50+ Weeks	Weighted Total
Dept. & Speciality Stores					
% of Retail Sales	11	32	38	19	100
Sales Loss to Stock Outs as % of Net Retail					
Retail	10.8	9.4	5.2	1.5	6.5
Apparel	3.2	2.2	1.3	0.9	1.7
Textiles	0.6	0.3	0.2	0.2	0.3
Contribution Loss on 1/2 of Stock Outs as % of Net Retail					
Retail	3.36	2.73	1.35	0.32	1.82
Apparel	0.33	0.20	0.11	0.06	0.16
Textile	0.01	0.00	0.00	0.00	0.00
Total	3.70	2.93	1.46	0.38	1.97
Mass Merchants					
% of Retail Sales	3	20	52	25	100
Sales Loss to Stock Outs as % of Net Retail					
Retail	6.5	5.6	6.2	1.1	4.8
Apparel	3.6	2.0	1.4	1.1	1.5
Textiles	0.6	0.3	0.2	0.2	0.2
Contribution Loss on 1/2 of Stock Outs as % of Net Retail					
Retail	1.85	1.47	1.47	0.20	1.16
Apparel	0.34	0.17	0.11	0.08	0.12
Textiles	0.01	0.00	0.00	0.00	0.00
Total	2.20	1.64	1.58	0.28	1.28

QR Economics – Model Data
Inventory Weeks
Conditions: 3-Week Response

	Product Life				
	5 Weeks	10 Weeks	20 Weeks	50+ Weeks	Weighted Total
Dept. & Speciality Stores					
% of Retail Sales	11	32	38	19	100
Store Inventory	6.9	7.4	8.1	10.6	8.2
Retail D.C. Inventory	0.9	0.9	0.9	0.9	0.9
In-Transit to Retail	0.5	0.5	0.5	0.5	0.5
Apparel F.G. Inventory	7.4	8.7	9..5	10.4	9.2
Apparel W.I.P.	1.5	1.6	2.0	1.9	1.8
Apparel Fabric	3.0	3.0	3.0	6.0	3.6
Apparel Fabric In Trans.	0.4	0.4	0.4	0.4	0.4
Textile Fabric Inventory	7.0	6.0	5.0	2.0	5.0
Textile W.I.P.	8.1	7.1	5.9	5.0	6.4
Textile Raw Materials	2.1	1.8	1.5	1.1	1.6
Fiber Finished Inventory	3.8	3.8	3.8	3.8	3.8
Total Inventory Weeks	41.6	41.2	40.6	42.6	41.4
Mass Merchants					
% of Retail Sales	3	20	52	25	100
Store Inventory	6.8	7.3	7.6	8.8	7.8
Retail D.C. Inventory	0.9	0.9	0.9	0.9	0.9
In-Transit to Retail	0.5	0.5	0.5	0.5	0.5
Apparel F.G. Inventory	6.4	6.2	5.7	5.7	
Apparel W.I.P.	6.8	7.0	7.9	8.3	7.8
Apparel Fabric	3.0	3.0	3.0	6.0	3.8
Apparel Fabric In Trans.	0.4	0.4	0.4	0.4	0.4
Textile Fabric Inventory	7.0	6.0	5.0	2.0	4.5
Textile W.I.P.	8.1	7.1	5.9	5.0	6.0
Textile Raw Materials	2.1	1.8	1.5	1.1	1.5
Fiber Finished Inventory	3.8	3.8	3.8	3.8	3.8
Total Inventory Units	40.9	39.4	38.5	38.7	38.9

APPENDIX G15
QR Economics - Model Data
Inventory Carrying Costs at 15%
Conditions: 3-Week Response

	Product Life				
	5 Weeks	10 Weeks	20 Weeks	50+ Weeks	Weighted Total
Dept. & Speciality Stores					
% of Retail Sales	11	32	38	19	100
Carrying Costs as % of Net Retail $					
Store	1.06	1.21	1.39	1.92	1.40
Retail D.C.	0.14	0.15	0.15	0.16	0.15
In-Transit to Retail	0.08	0.08	0.08	0.09	0.08
Apparel Finished Goods	0.86	1.07	1.21	1.36	1.16
Apparel W.I.P.	0.13	0.15	0.20	0.19	0.17
Apparel Fabric	0.19	0.20	0.21	0.42	0.24
Apparel Fabric In Trans.	0.02	0.03	0.03	0.03	0.03
Textile Fabric	0.37	0.33	0.28	0.12	0.28
Textile W.I.P.	0.31	0.28	0.25	0.22	0.26
Textile Raw Materials	0.05	0.05	0.04	0.03	0.04
Fiber Finished Inventory	0.08	0.08	0.08	0.08	0.08
Total	3.29	3.63	3.92	4.62	3.89
Mass Merchants					
% of Retail Sales	3	20	52	25	100
Carrying Costs as % of Net Retail $					
Store	1.05	1.19	1.31	1.59	1.35
Retail D.C.	0.14	0.15	0.15	0.16	0.15
In-Transit to Retail	0.08	0.08	0.09	0.09	0.09
Apparel Finished Goods	0.79	0.86	0.84	1.08	0.90
Apparel W.I.P.	0.13	0.15	0.20	0.19	0.90
Apparel Fabric	0.19	0.20	0.21	0.42	0.26
Apparel Fabric I.T.	0.02	0.03	0.03	0.03	0.03
Textile Fabric	0.37	0.33	0.28	0.12	0.25
Textile W.I.P.	0.31	0.28	0.25	0.22	0.25
Textile Raw Materials	0.05	0.05	0.04	0.03	0.04
Fiber Finished Inventory	0.08	0.08	0.08	0.08	0.08
Total	3.21	3.40	3.48	4.01	3.59

APPENDICES H

Because of the amount of information contained in Appendices H, the following Tables are, for the most part, arranged in pairs. These are indicated by "a" and "b" and are to be found on facing pages.

The data cover two classes of garments distributed both by Department Stores and Chains. The economics are shown from both the manufacturer's and the retailer's points of view.

Manufacturers Cost Comparison – Imported Vs. Domestic
Men's Branded Slacks Sold By Department Stores

Domestic	Improved Low Div. PBU $/Unit	Med. Div. Typical PBU $/Unit	Medium Diversity QR $/Unit	Medium Diversity UPS $/Unit
Fabric	2.34	2.45	2.41	2.41
Trim	.65	.67	.67	.67
Cut	.26	.34	.33	.33
Ship to Sew	.02	.02	.04	.04
Sew and Finish	3.17	3.66	3.16	3.16
Pack and Ship	.07	.07	.05	.05
Contractor's G.P. and Quota	.00	.00	.00	.00
F.O.B.	.00	.00	.00	.00
Duty	.00	.00	.00	.00
Overseas Freight	.00	.00	.00	.00
Agent + L. of C.	.00	.00	.00	.00
Landed COGS	6.51	7.14	6.66	6.66
Gross Mark-Up		4.76	5.24	4.44
(%)		40.0%	44.0%	40.0%
Original Wholesale		11.90	11.90	11.10
Less Returns and Discounts		.60	.60	.56
Less Freight In		.04	.12	.12
Less Forced M.D.		.49	.17	.16
(%)		4.1%	1.4%	1.4%
Less Promo M.D.		.48	.48	.44
Subtotal		1.61	1.37	1.28
Average Wholesale $		10.29	10.53	9.82
Average Gross Margin		3.15	3.87	3.16
(%)		30.6%	36.8%	32.2%
Less Sales and Merchandising		1.03	1.05	.98
Less G & A		1.24	1.26	1.18
Less Distribution		.31	.14	.14
Operating Profit		.57	1.42	.86
(%)		5.5%	13.5%	8.8%
Total Assets		5.87	5.93	5.80
Cost of Inventory @ 15%		.39	.27	.27
Cost of Fixed Assets		.12	.25	.25
Cost Rec.., Cash & Misc.		.37	.37	.35
Sub Cost of Assets @ 15%		.88	.89	.87
Op. Prof. Less Cost of Assets		(.31)	.53	(.01)
Op. Prof. – % of Total Assets		9.7%	23.9%	14.8%

APPENDIX H1b
Manufacturers Cost Comparison – Imported Vs. Domestic
Men's Branded Slacks Sold by Department Stores

Imported	Typical Far East $/Unit	QR Far East $/Unit	807 $/Unit
Fabric	2.11	2.06	2.41
Trim	.47	.47	.67
Cut	.14	.12	.33
Ship to Sew	.00	.00	.00
Sew and Finish	1.43	1.04	1.04
Pack & Ship	.08	.08	.10
Contractor's G.P. and Quota	.32	.26	.10
F.O.B.	4.55	4.03	4.65
Duty	1.39	1.24	.36
Overseas Freight	.31	1.01	.30
Agent + L.C.	.25	.22	.04
Landed COGS	6.50	6.50	5.35
Gross Mark-Up	5.40	4.60	4.65
(%)	45.4%	41.4%	46.5%
Original Wholesale	11.90	11.10	10.00
Less Returns & Discounts	.60	.56	.50
Less Freight In	.06	.06	.12
Less Forced M.D.	.97	.39	.14
(%)	8.2%	3.5%	1.4%
Less Promo M.D.	.48	.44	.40
Subtotal	2.11	1.45	1.16
Average Wholesale $	9.79	9.65	8.84
Average Gross Margin	3.29	3.15	3.49
(%)	33.6%	32.6%	39.5%
Less Sales & Merchandising	.98	.96	.88
Less G & A	1.22	1.21	1.19
Less Distribution	.41	.41	.20
Operating Profit	.68	.57	1.22
(%)	6.9%	5.9%	13.8%
Total Assets	5.00	4.20	5.40
Cost of Inventory @ 15%	.38	.28	.30
Cost of Fixed Assets	.00	.00	.20
Cost Rec., Cash & Misc.	.37	.35	.31
Sub Cost of Assets @ 15%	.75	.63	.81
Op. Prof. Less Cost of Assets	(.07)	(.06)	.41
Op. Prof. – % of Total Assets	13.6%	13.6%	22.6%

225

Retailers Cost Comparison – Direct Import Vs. U.S. Manufacturers
Men's Branded Slacks Sold By Department Stores

	Domestic			Imported		
	Typical	QR		Typical F. East	QR F. East	807
	$/Unit	$/Unit	$/Unit	$/Unit	$/Unit	$/Unit
Cost (Org. Wholesale)	11.90	11.90	11.10	11.90	11.10	10.00
Mark On	11.66	11.66	10.25	11.66	10.25	11.35
(%)	49.5%	49.5%	48.0%	49.5%	48.0%	53.2%
Original Retail	23.56	23.56	21.35	23.56	21.35	21.35
Less Markdown – Forced	3.09	1.28	1.16	3.09	1.95	1.43
(%)	15.8%	6.0%	6.0	15.8%	10.5%	7.5%
Less Markdown – Promo.	.92	1.00	.91	.92	.87	.89
Average Retail Sale	19.55	21.28	19.28	19.55	18.53	19.03
(%)	20.5%	10.7%	10.7%	20.5%	15.2%	12.2%
Cum. Mark-On	9.67	10.53	9.25	9.67	8.90	10.12
(%)	49.5%	49.5%	48.0%	49.5%	48.0%	53.2%
Less Cost Value of M.D.	2.02	1.15	1.07	2.02	1.46	1.09
Less Stock Shortage	.18	.18	.17	.18	.17	.15
Less Freight In	.21	.20	.20	.21	.20	.20
Plus Discounts & Returns	(.60)	(.60)	(.56)	(.60)	(.56)	(.50)
Gross Margin	7.86	9.60	8.37	7.86	7.63	9.18
(%)	40.2%	45.1%	43.4%	40.2%	41.2%	48.2%
Less Warehousing	.50	.03	.03	.50	.03	.03
Less Local Transport						
Less Accounting & D.P.						
Less Adver. & Promotion						
Less Buying & Merchandising						
Less General Admin.						
Less Store, Field & Benefits						
Total Expense*	6.74	6.27	6.27	6.74	6.27	6.27
Operating Profit	1.12	3.33	2.10	1.12	1.36	2.91
(%)	5.7%	15.6%	10.9%	5.7%	7.3%	15.3%
Total Assets	9.67	8.20	8.00	9.67	8.33	7.80
Inv. Cost of Assets @ 15%	.65	.43	.40	.65	.45	.37
Other Assets @ 15%	.80	.80	.80	.80	.80	.80
Op. Prof. Less Cost of Assets	(.33)	2.10	.95	(.33)	.11	1.74
Op. Prof. – % Total Assets	11.6%	40.6%	26.3%	11.6%	16.3%	37.3%

* Detail not available

Manufacturers Cost Comparison - Imported & Domestic
Ladies' Branded Blouses Sold by Department Stores

Domestic	Improved Low Div. PBU $/Unit	Med. Div. Typical PBU $/Unit	Medium Diversity QR $/Unit	UPS $/Unit
Fabric	1.42	1.50	1.46	1.46
Trim	.26	.26	.26	.26
Cut	.28	.37	.36	.36
Ship to Sew	.04	.02	.04	.04
Sew and Finish	2.51	3.34	2.58	2.58
Pack and Ship	.05	.07	.05	.05
Contr. G.P. & Quota	.00	.00	.00	.00
F.O.B.	.00	.00	.00	.00
Duty	.00	.00	.00	.00
Overseas Freight	.00	.00	.00	.00
Agent + L.C.	.00	.00	.00	.00
Landed COGS	4.56	5.56	4.75	4.75
Gross Mark-up		4.74	5.55	4.05
(%)		46.0%	53.9%	46.0%
Original Wholesale		10.30	10.30	8.80
Less Returns & Discounts		.82	.82	.70
Less Freight In		.03	.09	.09
Less Forced M.D.		.56	.26	.22
(%)		5.4%	2.5%	2.5%
Less Promo M.D.		.51	.52	.44
Subtotal		1.92	1.69	1.45
Average Wholesale $		8.38	8.61	7.35
Average Gross Margin		2.82	3.86	2.60
(%)		33.7%	44.8%	35.4%
Less Sales & Merchandising		.88	.90	.77
Less G & A		1.05	1.08	.92
Less Distribution		.35	.16	.16
Operating Profit		.54	1.72	.75
(%)		6.4%	20.0%	10.2%
Total Assets		4.47	4.73	4.40
Cost of Inventory @ 15%		.25	.16	.16
Cost of Fixed Assets		.08	.21	.21
Cost Rec., Cash & Misc.		.34	.34	.29
Sub Cost of Assets @ 15%		.67	.71	.66
Op. Prof. Less Cost of Assets		(1.13)	1.01	.09
Op. Prof. - % of Total Assets		12.1%	36.3%	17.0%

Manufacturers Cost Comparison - Imported & Domestic
Ladies' Branded Blouses Sold by Department Stores

Imported	Typical Far East $/Unit	QR Far East $/Unit	807 $/Unit
Fabric	1.03	1.00	1.46
Trim	.18	.18	.26
Cut	.15	.13	.36
Ship to Sew	.00	.00	.00
Sew and Finish	1.45	1.10	1.00
Pack and Ship	.08	.08	.10
Contr. G.P. & Quota	.28	.22	.10
F.O.B.	3.17	2.71	3.28
Duty	.94	.82	.33
Overseas Freight	.35	1.14	.34
Agent + L.C.	.17	.15	.04
Landed COGS	4.63	4.82	3.99
Gross Mark-up	5.67	3.98	4.01
(%)	55.0%	45.2%	50.1%
Original Wholesale	10.30	8.80	8.00
Less Returns & Discounts	.82	.70	.64
Less Freight In	.07	.007	.09
Less Forced M.D.	1.11	.42	.21
(%)	10.8%	4.8%	2..6%
Less Promo M.D.	.51	.44	.40
Subtotal	2.51	1.63	1.34
Average Wholesale $	7.79	7.17	6.66
Average Gross Margin	3.16	2.35	2.67
(%)	40.6%	32..8%	40.1%
Less Sales & Merchandising	.82	.75	.70
Less G & A	1.05	1.00	.93
Less Distribution	.45	.45	.23
Operating Profit	.84	.15	.81
(%)	10.8%	2.1%	12.2%
Total Assets	4.00	3.33	4.07
Cost of Inventory @ 15%	.27	.21	.18
Cost of Fixed Assets	.00	.00	.17
Cost Rec., Cash & Misc.	.33	.29	.26
Sub Cost of Assets @ 15%	.60	.50	.61
Op. Prof. Less Cost of Assets	.24	(.35)	.20
Op. Prof. - % of Total Assets	21.0%	4.5%	19.9%

Retailers Cost Comparison – Direct Import Vs. U.S. Manufacturers
Ladies' Branded Blouses Sold By Department Stores

	Domestic			Imported		
	Typical	QR		Typical F. East	QR F. East	807
	$/Unit	$/Unit	$/Unit	$/Unit	$/Unit	$/Unit
Cost (Org. Wholesale)	10.30	10.30	8.80	10.30	8.80	8.00
Mark-On	11.20	11.20	10.20	11.20	10.20	11.00
(%)	52.1%	52.1%	53.7%	52.1%	53.7%	57.9%
Original Retail	21.50	21.50	19.00	21.50	19.00	19.00
Less Markdown - Forced	3.48	1.93	1.70	3.48	2.28	1.85
(%)	20.4%	10.4%	10.4%	20.4%	14.4%	11.4%
Less Markdown - Promo.	.96	1.04	.92	.96	.89	.91
Average Retail Sales	17.6	18.53	16.38	17.06	15.83	16.24
(%)	26.0%	16.0%	16.0%	26.0%	20.0%	17.0%
Cum. Mark-On	8.89	9.65	8.79	8.89	8.50	9.40
(%)	52.1%	52.1%	53.7%	52.1%	53.7%	57.9%
Less Cost Value of M.D.	2.12	1.42	1.21	2.12	1.47	1.16
Less Stock Shortage	.23	.23	.19	.23	.19	.18
Less Freight In	.14	.13	.13	.14	.13	.13
Plus Discounts & Returns	(.82)	(.82)	(.70)	(.82)	(.70)	(.64)
Gross Margin	7.22	8.69	7.96	7.22	7.41	8.57
(%)	42.3%	47.0%	48.6%	42.3%	46.8%	52.8%
Less Warehousing	.34	.03	.03	.34	.03	.03
Less Local Transport						
Less Accounting & D.P.						
Less Adver. & Promotion						
Less Buying & Mdsg.						
Less General Admin.						
Less Store, Field & Benefits						
Total Expense*	5.88	5.57	5.57	5.88	5.57	5.57
Operating Profit	1.34	3.12	2.39	1.34	1.84	3.00
(%)	7.9%	16.8%	14.6%	7.9%	11..6%	18.5%
Total Assets	7.93	7.27	6.87	7.93	7.13	6.73
Inv. Cost of Assets @ 15%	.49	.39	.33	.49	.37	.31
Other Assets @ 15%	.70	.70	.70	.70	.70	.70
Op. Prof. Less Cost of Assets	.15	2.03	1.36	.15	.77	1.99
Op. Prof. - % Total Assets	16.9%	42.9%	34.8%	16.9%	25.8%	44.6%

* Detail not available.

Manufacturers Cost Comparison – Imported Vs. Domestic
Men's Private Label Slacks Sold By Mass Merchants

Domestic	Improved Low Div. PBU $/Unit	Low Div. Typical PBU $/Unit	Medium Diversity QR $/Unit	UPS $/Unit
Fabric	2.34	2.45	2.41	2.41
Trim	.65	.67	.67	.67
Cut	.26	.34	.33	.33
Ship to Sew	.02	.02	.04	.04
Sew and Finish	3.17	3.66	3.16	3.16
Pack and Ship	.07	.07	.05	.05
Contr. G.P. & Quota	.00	.00	.00	.00
F.O.B.	.00	.00	.00	.00
Duty	.00	.00	.00	.00
Overseas Freight	.00	.00	.00	.00
Agent + L.C.	.00	.00	.00	.00
Landed COGS	6.51	7.14	6.66	6.66
Gross Mark-up		2.38	2.86	2.22
(%)		25.0%	30.0%	25.0%
Original Wholesale		9.52	9.52	8.88
Less Returns & Discounts		.19	.19	.18
Less Freight In		.04	.12	.12
Less Forced M.D.		.34	.16	.15
(%)		3.6%	1.7%	1.7%
Less Promo M.D.		.29	.29	.27
Subtotal		.86	.76	.72
Average Wholesale $		8.66	8.76	8.16
Average Gross Margin		1.52	2.10	1.50
(%)		17.5%	24.0%	18.4%
Less Sales & Merchandising		.26	.26	.24
Less G & A		.69	.70	.65
Less Distribution		.18	.08	.08
Operating Profit		.39	1.06	.53
(%)		45.%	12.1%	6.5%
Total Assets		4.73	4.80	4.73
Cost of Inv. @ 15%		.39	.27	.27
Cost of Fixed Assets		.12	.25	.25
Cost Rec., Cash & Misc.		.20	.20	.19
Sub Cost of Assets @ 15%		.71	.72	.71
Op. Profits Less Cost of Assets		(.32)	.34	(.18)
Op. Profits – % of Total Assets		8.2%	22..1%	11.2%

Manufacturers Cost Comparison – Imported Vs. Domestic
Men's Private Label Slacks Sold By Mass Merchants

Imported	Typical Far East	QR Far East	807	Far East Direct Import Typical	QR
	$/Unit	$/Unit	$/Unit	$/Unit	$/Unit
Fabric	2.11	2.06	2.41	2.11	2.06
Trim	.47	.47	.67	.47	.47
Cut	.14	.12	.33	.14	.12
Ship to Sew	.00	.00	.00	.00	.00
Sew and Finish	1.43	1.04	1.04	1.43	1.04
Pack and Ship	.08	.08	.10	.08	.08
Contr. G.P. & Quota	.32	.26	.10	.32	.26
F.O.B.	4.55	4.03	4.65	4.55	4.03
Duty	1.39	1.24	.36	1.39	1.24
Overseas Freight	.31	1.01	.30	.31	1.01
Agent + L.C.	.25	.22	.04	.25	.22
Landed COGS	6.50	6.50	5.35	6.50	6.50
Gross Margin	3.02	2.38	2.65		
(%)	31.7%	26.8%	33.1%		
Original Wholesale	9.52	8.88	8.00		
Less Returns & Discounts	.19	.18	.16		
Less Freight In	.06	.06	.12		
Less Forced M.D.	.68	.28	.14		
(%)	7.2%	3.2%	1.8%		
Less Promo M.D.	.29	.27	.24		
Subtotal	1.22	.79	.66		
Average Wholesale $	8.30	8.09	7.34		
Average Gross Margin	1.80	1.59	1.99		
(%)	21.7%	19.7%	27.1%		
Less Sales & Merchandising	.25	.24	.22		
Less G & A	.70	.69	.70		
Less Distribution	.24	.24	.12		
Operating Profit	.61	.42	.95		
(%)	7.3%	5.2%	12.9%		
Total Assets	3.87	3.20	4.40		
Cost of Inv. @ 15%	.38	.29	.30		
Cost of Fixed Assets	.00	.00	.20		
Cost Rec., Cash & Misc.	.20	.19	.16		
Sub Cost of Assets @ 15%	.58	.48	.66		
Op. Prof. Less Cost of Assets	.03	(.06)	.29		
Op. Prof.-% of Total Assets	15.8%	13.1%	21.6%		

APPENDIX H6a

Retailers Cost Comparison – Direct Import Vs. U.S. Manufacturers
Men's Private Label Slacks Sold By Mass Merchants

Domestic	Typical $/Unit	Q R $/Unit	$/Unit
Cost (Original Wholesale)	9.52	9.52	8.88
Mark-On	6.46	6.46	5.61
(%)	40.4%	40.4%	38.7%
Original Retail	15.98	15.98	14.49
Less Markdown - Forced	2.05	1.05	.96
(%)	15.2%	7.3%	7.3%
Less Markdown - Promotion	.45	.48	.43
Average Retail Sales	13.48	14.45	13.10
Cum. Mark-On	5.45	5.84	5.07
(%)	40.4%	40.4%	38.7%
Less Cost Value of M.D.	1.49	.91	.85
Less Stock Shortage	.10	.10	.09
Less Freight In	.21	.20	.20
Plus Discounts & Returns	(.19)	(.19)	(.18)
Gross Margin	3.84	4.82	4.11
(%)	28.5%	33.4%	31.4%
Less Warehousing	.40	.02	.02
Less Local Transport	.10	.10	.10
Less Accounting & D.P.	.09	.09	.09
Less Adver. & Promotion	.30	.30	.30
Less Buying & Merchandising	.07	.07	.07
Less General Administration	.13	.13	.13
Less Store, Field & Benefits	2.21	2.21	2.21
Total Expense	3.30	2.92	2.92
(%)	24.5%	20.2%	22.3%
Operating Profit	.54	1.90	1.19
(%)	4.0%	13.1%	9.1%
Total Assets	5.60	4.73	4.60
Inv. Cost of Assets @ 15%	.45	.32	.30
Other Assets @ 15%	.39	.39	.39
Op. Profits Less Cost of Assets	(.30)	1.19	.50
Op. Profits - % of Total Assets	9.6%	40.1%	25.9%

APPENDIX H6b
Retailers Cost Comparison – Direct Import Vs. U.S. Manufacturers
Men's Private Label Sold By Mass Merchants

Imported	Typical Far East $/Unit	QR F. East $/Unit	807 $/Unit	Direct Import Far East Typical $/Unit	Direct Import Far East QR $/Unit
Cost (Original Wholesale)	9.52	8.88	8.00	6.50	6.50
Mark-On	6.46	5.61	6.49	7.99	7.99
(%)	40.4%	38.7%	44.8%	55.1%	55.1%
Original Retail	15.58	14.49	14.49	14.49	14.49
Less Markdown – Forced	2.05	1.51	1.10	2.30	1.78
(%)	15.2%	12.05	8.5%	19.5%	14.5%
Less Markdown – Promotion	.45	.41	.43	.39	.41
Average Retail Sales	13.48	12.57	12.96	11.80	12.30
Cum. Mark-On	5.45	4.87	5.80	6.51	6.78
(%)	40.4%	38.7%	44.8%	55.1%	55.1%
Less Cost Value of M.D.	1.49	1.18	.84	1.21	.98
Less Stock Shortage	.10	.09	.08	.08	.08
Less Freight In	.21	.20	.20	.21	.20
Plus Discounts & Returns	(.19)	(.18)	(.16)	.00	.00
Gross Margin	3.84	3.58	4.84	5.01	5.52
Less Warehousing	.40	.02	.02	.60	.60
Less Local Transport	.10	.10	.10	.10	.10
Less Accounting & D.P.	.09	.09	.09	.12	.11
Less Adver. & Promotion	.30	.30	.30	.30	.30
Less Buying & Merchandising	.07	.07	.07	.18	.16
Less General Administration	.13	.13	.13	.16	.15
Less Store, Field & Benefits	2.21	2.21	2.21	2.21	2.21
Total Expense	3.30	2.92	2.92	3.67	3.63
Operating Profit	.54	.66	1.92	1.34	1.89
(%)	4.0%	5.3%	14.8%	11.4%	15.4%
Total Assets	5.60	5.07	4.47	5.40	4.87
Inv. Cost of Assets @ 15%	.45	.37	.28	.42	.34
Other Assets @ 15%	.39	.39	.39	.39	.39
Op. Profits Less Cost of Ass.	(.30)	(.10)	1.25	.53	1.16
Op. Profits – % of Total Ass.	9.6%	13.0%	43.0%	24.8%	38.8%

233

APPENDIX H7a
Manufacturers Cost Comparison - Imported Vs. Domestic
Ladies' Private Label Blouses Sold By Mass Merchants

Domestic	Improved Low Div. PBU $/Unit	Med. Div. Typical PBU $/Unit	Medium Diversity QR $/Unit	Medium Diversity UPS $/Unit
Fabric	1.42	1.50	1.46	1.46
Trim	.26	.26	.26	.26
Cut	.28	.37	.36	.36
Ship to Sew	.04	.02	.04	.04
Sew and Finish	2.51	3.34	2.58	2.58
Pack and Ship	.05	.07	.05	.05
Contr. G.P. & Quota	.00	.00	.00	.00
F.O.B.	.00	.00	.00	.00
Duty	.00	.00	.00	.00
Overseas Freight	.00	.00	.00	.00
Agent + L.C.	.00	.00	.00	.00
Landed COGS	4.56	5.56	4.75	4.75
Gross Mark-up		2.38	3.19	2.04
(%)		30.0%	40.2%	30.0%
Original Wholesale		7.94	7.94	6.79
Less Returns & Discounts		.24	.24	.20
Less Freight In		.03	.009	.09
Less Forced M.D.		.39	.21	.18
(%)		4.9%	2.7%	2.7%
Less Promo M.D.		.32	.32	.27
Subtotal		.98	.86	.74
Average Wholesale $		6.96	7.08	6.05
Average Gross Margin		1.40	2.33	1.30
(%)		20.1%	32.9%	21.5%
Less Sales & Merchandising		.24	.25	.21
Less G & A		.59	.60	.51
Less Distribution		.22	.10	.10
Operating Profit		.35	1.38	.48
(%)		5.0%	19.5%	7.9%
Total Assets		3.33	3.53	3.40
Cost of Inv. @ 15%		.25	.16	.16
Cost of Fixed Assets		.08	.21	.21
Cost Rec., Cash & Misc.		.17	.16	.14
Sub Cost of Assets @ 15%		.50	.53	.51
Op. Profits Less Cost of Assets		(.15)	.85	(.03)
Op. Profits - % of Total Assets		10.5%	39.1%	14.1%

Manufacturers Cost Comparison – Imported Vs. Domestic
Ladies' Private Label Blouses Sold By Mass Merchants

Imported	Typical Far East $/Unit	QR F. East $/Unit	QR 807 $/Unit	Far East Direct Import Typical $/Unit	Far East Direct Import QR $/Unit
Fabric	1.03	1.00	1.46	1.03	1.00
Trim	.18	.18	.26	.18	.18
Cut	.15	.13	.36	.15	.13
Ship to Sew	.00	.00	.00	.00	.00
Sew and Finish	1.45	1.10	1.00	1.45	1.10
Pack and Ship	.08	.08	.10	.08	.08
Contr. G.P. & Quota	.28	.22	.10	.28	.22
F.O.B.	3.17	2.71	3.28	3.17	2.71
Duty	.94	.82	.33	.94	.82
Overseas Freight	.35	1.14	.34	.35	1.14
Agent + L.C.	.17	.15	.04	.17	.15
Landed COGS	4.63	4.82	3.99	4.63	4.82
Gross Mark-up	3.31	1.97	2.16		
(%)	41.7%	29.0%	35.1%		
Original Wholesale	7.94	6.79	6.15		
Less Returns & Discounts	.24	.20	.18		
Less Freight In	.07	.07	.09		
Less Forced M.D.	.78	.30	.18		
(%)	9.8%	4.4%	2.9%		
Less Promo M.D.	.32	.27	.25		
Subtotal	1.41	.84	.70		
Average Wholesale $	6.53	5.95	5.45		
Average Gross Margin	1.90	1.13	1.46		
(%)	29.1%	19.0%	26.8%		
Less Sales & Merchandising	.23	.21	.19		
Less G & A	.59	.53	.55		
Less Distribution	.29	.29	.15		
Operating Profit	.79	.10	.57		
(%)	12.1%	1.7%	10.5%		
Total Assets	2.87	2.33	3.13		
Cost of Inv. @ 15%	.27	.21	.18		
Cost of Fixeds Assets	.00	.00	.00		
Cost Rec., Cash & Misc.	.16	.14	.12		
Sub Cost of Assets @ 15%	.43	.35	.47		
Op. Profits Less Cost of Assets	.36	(.25)	.10		
Op. Profits – % of Total Assets	27.6%	4.3%	18.2%		

Retailers Cost Comparison – Direct Import Vs. U.S. Manufacturers
Ladies' Private Label Blouses Sold By Mass Merchants

Domestic	Typical $/Unit	$/Unit	QR $/Unit
Cost (Original Wholesale)	7.94	7.94	6.79
Mark-On	6.06	6.06	5.21
(%)	43.3%	43.3%	43.4%
Original Retail	14.00	14.00	12.00
Less Markdown – Forced	2.12	1.43	1.23
(%)	18.5%	11.8%	11.8%
Less Markdown – Promotion	.40	.43	.36
Average Retail Sales	11.48	12.14	10.41
Cum. Mark-On	4.97	5.25	4.52
(%)	43.3%	43.3%	43.4%
Less Cost Value of M.D.	1.43	1.05	.90
Less Stock Shortage	.12	.12	.12
Less Freight In	.14	.13	.13
Plus Discounts & Returns	(.24)	(.24)	(.20)
Gross Margin	3.52	4.19	3.57
(%)	30.6%	34.5%	34.3%
Less Warehousing	.27	.02	.02
Less Local Transport	.06	.06	.06
Less Accounting & D.P.	.08	.08	.08
Less Adver. & Promotion	.25	.25	.25
Less Buying & Merchandising	.06	.06	.06
Less General Administration	.11	.11	.11
Less Store, Field & Benefits	1.95	1.95	1.95
Total Expense	2.78	2.53	2.53
(%)	24.2%	20.8%	24.3%
Operating Profit	.74	1.66	1.04
(%)	6.4%	13.7%	10.0%
Total Assets	4.67	4.13	3.87
Inv. Cost of Assets @ 15%	.36	.28	.24
Other Assets @ 15%	.34	.34	.34
Op. Profits Less Cost of Assets	.04	1.04	.46
Op. Profits – % of Total Assets	15.9%	40.2%	26.9%

Retailers Cost Comparison – Direct Import Vs. U.S. Manufacturers
Ladies' Private Label Blouses Sold By Mass Merchants

Imported	Imported			Direct Import	
	Typical	QR		Far East	
	Far East	F. East	807	Typical	QR
	$/Unit	$/Unit	$/Unit	$/Unit	$/Unit
Cost (Original Wholesale)	7.94	6.79	6.15	4.63	4.82
Mark-On	6.06	5.21	5.85	7.37	7.18
(%)	43.3%	43.4%	48.8%	61.4%	59.8%
Original Retail	14.00	12.00	12.00	12.00	12.00
Less Markdown – Forced	2.12	1.52	1.38	2.22	1.74
(%)	18.5%	15.0%	13.5%	23.5%	17.5%
Less Markdown – Promotion	.40	.35	.36	.33	.35
Average Retail Sales	11.48	10.13	10.26	9.45	9.91
Cum. Mark-On	4.97	4.40	5.00	5.80	5.93
(%)	43.5%	43.4%	48.8%	61.4%	59.8%
Less Cost Value of M.D.	1.43	1.06	.89	.98	.84
Less Stock Shortage	.12	.10	.09	.08	.09
Less Freight In	.14	.13	.13	.14	.13
Plus Discounts & Returns	(.24)	(.20)	(.18)	.00	.00
Gross Margin	3.52	3.31	4.07	4.60	4.87
(%)	30.7%	32.1%	39.7%	48.8%	49.3%
Less Warehousing	.27	.02	.02	.41	.41
Less Local Transport	.06	.06	.06	.06	.06
Less Accounting & D.P.	.08	.08	.08	.11	.10
Less Adver. & Promotion	.25	.25	.25	.25	.25
Less Buying & Merchandising	.06	.06	.06	.15	.14
Less General Administration	.11	.11	.11	.14	.13
Less Store, Field & Benefits	1.95	1.95	1.95	1.95	1.95
Total Expense	2.78	2.53	2.53	3.07	3.04
Operating Profit	.74	.78	1.54	1.53	1.83
(%)	6.4%	7.7%	15.0%	16.2%	18.5%
Total Assets	4.67	4.20	3.80	4.20	3.93
Inv. Cost of Assets @ 15%	.36	.29	.23	.29	.25
Other Assets @ 15%	.34	.34	.34	.34	.34
Op. Profits Less Cost of Ass.	.04	.15	.97	.90	1.24
Op. Profits – % of Total Ass.	15.9%	18.6%	40.5%	36.4%	46.5%

Economic Summary of Quick Response
Apparel Ventures for Women's Slacks

	Bundle	Seasonal UPS	Modular
Annual Dozens Produced (M)	83.76	89.89	89.12
SAH	4.40	4.10	4.00
Cost ($/Dozen)			
Labor	38.37	35.90	34.25
Material	78.18	78.18	78.18
Overhead Salary	10.68	10.30	8.48
Other Overhead	5.76	5.36	4.43
Depreciation	2.31	2.81	2.08
Total Manufacturing Costs	135.32	132.55	127.41
S.G. & A.	41.34	41.34	41.98
Cost of Sales	176.66	173.89	169.39
Pre-tax Profit	30.04	32.81	40.49
Net Selling Price	206.70	206.70	209.88*
Manufacturing Cost Multiplier	2.52	2.57	2.39
Plant Summary ($M)			
Total Net Sales	17,314	18,581	18,705
Pre-tax Profit	2,516	2,950	3,608
After-tax Profit	1,258	1,475	1,804
Investment ($M)			
Permanent	1,721	2,248	1,649
Working Capital	2,716	2,586	2,520
Total	4,437	4,834	4,169
After-tax ROI	28.4%	30.5%	43.3%
Fifth Year Summary			
Net Cash Flow – Year 1	(5747)	(5976)	(5120)
($M) – Year 2	(3396)	(3420)	(2433)
– Year 3	(1977)	(1735)	(474)
– Year 4	(573)	(70)	1470
– Year 5	818	1579	3402
Net Return on Equity	34.4%	38.6%	52.9%
Internal Rate of Return	23.4%	26.9%	38.8%

* 98% 1st. quality vs. 95% for Bundle and UPS

APPENDIX 12
Economic Summary of Quick Response
Apparel Ventures for Women's Slacks

	Fashion		
	Bundle	UPS	Modular
Annual Dozens Produced (M)	72.27	77.08	74.79
SAH	4.80	4.50	4.40
Cost ($/Dozen)			
Labor	44.42	41.81	39.42
Material	78.62	78.62	78.62
Overhead Salary	13.28	12.85	10.75
Other Overhead	7.58	7.07	5.89
Depreciation	2.83	3.48	2.57
Total Manufacturing Costs	146.74	143.83	137.25
S.G. & A.	45.63	45.63	46.33
Cost of Sales	192.37	189.46	183.58
Pre-tax Profit	35.78	38.69	48.08
Net Selling Price	228.15	228.15	231.66*
Manufacturing Cost Multiplier	2.76	2.81	2.59
Plant Summary ($M)			
Total Net Sales	16,487	17,587	17,325
Pre-tax Profit	2,586	2,982	3,596
After-tax Profit	1,293	1,491	1,798
Investment ($M)			
Permanent	1,825	2,389	1,710
Working Capital	2,615	2,488	2,382
Total	4,440	4,877	4,092
After-tax ROI	29.1%	30.6%	43.9%
Fifth Year Summary			
Net Cash Flow – Year 1	(5573)	(5782)	(4825)
($M) – Year 2	(3242)	(3289)	(2229)
– Year 3	(1778)	(1575)	(272)
– Year 4	(331)	119	1672
– Year 5	1103	1794	3601
Net Return on Equity	35.8%	39.3%	54.4%
Internal Rate of Return	25.2%	28.4%	41.2%

* 98% 1st. quality vs. 95% for Bundle and UPS

APPENDIX 13
Economic Summary of Quick Response
Apparel Ventures for Women's Blouses

	Bundle	Seasonal UPS	Modular
Annual Dozens Produced (M)	73.71	77.43	76.66
SAH	5.00	4.76	4.65
Cost ($/Dozen)			
Labor	43.97	42.00	40.13
Material	34.97	34.97	34.97
Overhead Salary	12.14	11.95	9.85
Other Overhead	6.60	6.25	5.16
Depreciation	2.68	3.37	2.48
Total Manufacturing Costs	100.35	98.54	92.59
S.G. & A.	29.64	29.64	30.10
Cost of Sales	129.99	128.18	122.69
Pre-tax Profit	18.21	20.02	27.79
Net Selling Price	148.20	148.20	150.48*
Manufacturing Cost Multiplier	2.54	2.59	2.41
Plant Summary ($M)			
Total Net Sales	10,924	11,475	11,563
Pre-tax Profit	1,342	1,550	2,130
After-tax Profit	671	775	1,065
Investment ($M)			
Permanent	1,763	2,326	1,694
Working Capital	1,660	1,558	1,515
Total	3,423	3,884	3,209
After-tax ROI	19.6%	20.0%	33.2%
Fifth Year Summary			
Net Cash Flow – Year 1	(4829)	(5163)	(4323)
($M) – Year 2	(3306)	(3375)	(2287)
– Year 3	(2175)	(2234)	(1064)
– Year 4	(1354)	(1262)	146
– Year 5	(547)	(307)	1342
Net Return on Equity	25.5%	27.2%	43.7%
Internal Rate of Return	13.5%	15.4%	27.2%

* 98% 1st. quality vs. 95% for Bundle and UPS

240

APPENDIX 14
Economic Summary of Quick Response
Apparel Ventures for Women's Blouses

	Bundle	Fashion UPS	Modular
Annual Dozens Produced (M)	63.07	66.45	64.40
SAH	5.50	5.22	5.11
Cost ($/Dozen)			
Labor	51.24	48.80	46.07
Material	35.21	35.21	35.21
Overhead Salary	15.22	14.91	12.49
Other Overhead	8.71	8.23	6.88
Depreciation	3.33	4.19	3.18
Total Manufacturing Costs	113.70	111.34	103.83
S.G. & A.	34.13	34.13	34.65
Cost of Sales	147.83	145.47	138.48
Pre-tax Profit	22.80	25.16	34.77
Net Selling Price	170.63	170.63	173.25*
Manufacturing Cost Multiplier	2.77	2.83	2.61
Plant Summary ($M)			
Total Net Sales	10,761	11,338	11,157
Pre-tax Profit	1,438	1,672	2,238
After-tax Profit	719	836	1,119
Investment ($M)			
Permanent	1,873	2,480	1,824
Working Capital	1,632	1,550	1,473
Total	3,505	4,030	3,297
After-tax ROI	20.5%	20.7%	30.3%
Fifth Year Summary			
Net Cash Flow – Year 1	(4782)	(5112)	(4233)
($M) – Year 2	(3153)	(3186)	(2197)
– Year 3	(2052)	(2105)	(907)
– Year 4	(1174)	(1058)	367
– Year 5	(311)	(31)	1627
Net Return on Equity	27.0%	28.6%	45.4%
Internal Rate of Return	15.4%	17.4%	29.7%

* 98% 1st. quality vs. 95% for Bundle and UPS

APPENDIX 15
Fixed Assumptions
Quick Response Apparel Ventures
Women's Slacks and Blouses

Total Work Hours/Year	1875
Assembly Base Rate/Hour	$5.15
Cutting Base Rate/Hour	$7.00
Management % Fringe Benefits	25%
Labor % Fringe Benefits	35%
Additional UPS Cost/Workplace	$3,500
Annual Rent/Sq. Ft.	$5.00
Receivable Cal. Day	35
Cash Cal. Days	7
Years Depreciation	9.0
Start-up Expense	$400M
$/KWH	$.065
Taxes & Insurance - % Perm. Invest.	2.0%
Insurance - % D.L. Cost Incl. E.B.	0.75%

APPENDIX 16
Variable Product, Season, & System Assumptions
Quick Response Apparel Ventures

	Seasonal		
	Bundle	UPS	Modular
Women's Slacks			
Piecegoods Cost/Yard $	1.85	1.85	1.85
Trim Cost Per Dozen $	36.00	36.00	36.00
Cutting Operators	12	13	13
Selling Price/Dozen $	212.00	212.00	212.00
Yards/Dozen	22.80	22.80	22.80
Cutting SAH	0.20	0.20	0.20
Assembly SAH	4.40	4.10	4.00
Workplace Utilization	80%	80%	72%
Storage & Office Equipment $	122.0M	112.0M	115.0M
Women's Blouses			
Piecegoods Cost/Yard $	1.20	1.20	1.20
Trim Cost Per Dozen	5.45	5.45	5.45
Cutting Operators	14	14	14
Selling Price/Dozen $	152.00	152.00	152.00
Yards/Dozen	24.6	24.6	24.6
Cutting SAH	0.26	0.26	0.26
Assembly SAH	5.00	4.76	4.65
Workplace Utilization	75%	75%	67%
Storage & Office Equipment $	116.0M	106.0M	108.0M

APPENDIX I7
Variable Product, Season, & System Assumptions
Quick Response Apparel Ventures

		Fashion	
	Bundle	UPS	Modular

Women's Slacks

	Bundle	UPS	Modular
Piecegoods Cost/Yard $	1.85	1.85	1.85
Trim Cost Per Dozen $	36.00	36.00	36.00
Cutting Operators	12	13	13
Selling Price/Dozen $	234.00	234.00	234.00
Yards/Dozen	23.04	23.04	23.04
Cutting SAH	0.22	0.22	0.22
Assembly SAH	4.80	4.50	4.40
Workplace Utilization	75%	75%	70%
Storage & Office Equipment $	123.0M	114.0M	106.0M

Women's Blouses

	Bundle	UPS	Modular
Piecegoods Cost/Yard $	1.20	1.20	1.20
Trim Cost Per Dozen $	5.45	5.45	5.45
Cutting Operators	14	14	14
Selling Price/Dozen $	175.00	175.00	175.00
Yards/Dozen	24.8	24.8	24.8
Cutting SAH	0.28	0.28	0.28
Assembly SAH	5.50	5.22	5.11
Workplace Utilization	70%	70%	60%
Storage & Office Equipment $	116.0M	109.0M	101.0M

APPENDIX 18
Variable Season & System Assumptions
Quick Response Apparel Ventures
Women's Slacks & Blouses

	Seasonal		
	Bundle	UPS	Modular
% Absentee	7.5%	7.5%	2.5%
% 1st. Quality	95%	95%	98%
ASSY Prod. Factor (%)	-	-	-
1st. Quarter	20%	20%	20%
2nd. Quarter	39%	47%	39%
3rd. Quarter	55%	57%	55%
4th. Quarter	68%	67%	68%
ASSY Operators	-	-	-
1st. Quarter	100	100	100
2nd. Quarter	200	200	200
After 3rd. Quarter	250	250	250
Cutting Excesses	20%	20%	20%
Assembly Excesses	18%	18%	15%
% Workplace w/UPS	0%	50%	0%
Ave. Cost/Standard Workplace	$2,300	$2,300	$2,000
Cutting Investment	$530M	$530M	$530M
Utility & Bldg. Improv. Investment	$350M	$340M	$310M
Total Square Feet	45M	40M	32M
Mixed Management Staffing	8	8	8
Sewing Supervisor	7	8	5
Fixed Indirect Staffing	18	18	18
Mechanic Staffing	2	3	2
Service Person Staffing	5	4	1
Q.C. Samples Staffing	4	3	1
Maintenance Staffing	1	2	1
Raw Material Work Days	6	6	6
W.I.P. Work Days	15	7	5
Acct. Payable % of Raw Mat. Invest.	120%	80%	70%
Power - KW/Assy. SAH	3.8	3.8	3.1
Spare Parts -$/Assy. SAH	$0.30	$0.33	\$0.30

APPENDIX 19
Variable Season & System Assumptions
Quick Response Apparel Ventures
Women's Slacks & Blouses

		Fashion	
	Bundle	UPS	Modular
% Absentee	7.5%	7.5%	2.5%
% 1st. Quality	95%	95%	98%
ASSY Prod. Factor (%)	–	–	–
1st. Quarter	15%	15%	15%
2nd. Quarter	38%	47%	38%
3rd. Quarter	54%	57%	54%
4th. Quarter	67%	67%	67%
After 4th. Quarter	80%	80%	72%
ASSY Operators	–	–	–
1st. Quarter	100	100	100
2nd. Quarter	200	200	200
After 3rd. Quarter	250	250	250
Cutting Excesses	30%	30%	30%
Assembly Excesses	25%	25%	20%
% Workplace w/UPS	0%	50%	0%
Ave. Cost/Std. Workplace	$2,300	$2,300	$2,000
Cutting Investment	$550M	$550M	$550M
Utility & Bldg. Improv. Invest.	$385M	$375M	$340M
Total Square Feet	55M	50M	40M
Mixed Management Staffing	8	8	8
Sewing Supervisor	11	12	8
Fixed Indirect Staffing	18	18	18
Mechanic Staffing	2	3	2
Service Person Staffing	5	4	1
Q.C. Samples Staffing	4	3	1
Maintenance Staffing	1	2	1
Raw Material Work Days	10	10	10
W.I.P. Work Days	15	7	5
Finished Good Work Days	7	5	5
Acct. Payable % of Raw Matl. Invest.	85%	60%	50%
Power –KW/Assy. SAH	4.5	4.5	3.7
Spare Parts –$/Assy. SAH	$0.32	$0.35	$0.32

APPENDIX J
Apparel Cost Model Assumptions

General

- Medium size plant with 255 assembly operators.
- Labor pay rates (1988)
    Assembly - $5.00/hr.
    Cutting   - $6.50/hr.
- Fringe benefits
    Operators - 26%
    Management/Indirect - 22%
- Annual turnover = 35%
- Scheduled work week = 47.2 (1,888) hours
- Investment
    Cutting - $30.0M (1979)
             - $70.8M (1980)
    Marking - $100.0M (1984)
    Office equipment, etc. - $58.0M (1979)
    Building/utility improvements - $314.0M (1979)
- Working capital:
    Cash - 21 days
    Accounts Rec. - 45 days
    Accounts Pay - 0 days
- Power cost = $0.65/kwh
- Oil = $.60/gallon
- Other maintenance cost = $.34/sq. ft.
- Office supplies = $125/SAH + .2975 dozen
- Equipment power consumption = 0.5 kw/SAH
- Oil consumption = 0.05 gallons/SAH
- Location = middle America
- Taxes/Insurance = 2% of investment
- Building investment = $21/sq. ft. (1979)

Quick Response - I

As above, plus:
- Increase assembly SAH by 0.02 for TALC labeling.
- Lot up/inspection occurs at textile mill. Piece goods inventory reduced 50% (40 to 15 days for fashion)
- Workplaces added for increased production (rent additional space at $3.50/sq. ft.).

Quick Response - II

Same as QR I, plus:
- Attendance from 93 to 97%.
- Mill size adjusted by utilization (excess space leased out at $4.00/sq. ft.).
- Added QC manager for TQC implementation.
- Consulting charge of $150K for 1986 and 1987.
- Additional $20,000 cutting investment in 1986.
- Work places added for increased production.

Product Group

	Basic	Seasonal	Fashion
• Markdowns reduced by 50%			
• Inventory levels			
Raw Material	10	10	15
WIP	5	5	5/8
FG's	12	20	20/25
• Piece good			
Shipments received weekly, by cut lot			
Contract size (dozen)	30,000	12,000	6,000
% excess lost	8.5	12.5	16.0/18.0
% efficiency	88	86	80/84
1st. quality	99	98.5	97.5/98.5

- Excess and efficiency adjusted

APPENDIX K1a
Apparel Manufacturing Economics
Basic – Long Sleeve Shirt

	Typical	QR I	QR II
Labor			
– Operators	255	308	301
– Indirect	39	43	27
Management	15	17	14
Total	309	368	342
SAH/doz.	2.60	2.62	2.76
Ann. dozen, M	146	175	176
Workplace Utilization, %	0.85	0.95	0.75
S&F Invest., $M	1,350	1,683	2,180
Gen. Invest. & Fees, $M	372	602	822
Cutting Invest., $M	201	201	221
Total Invest., $M 1988	1,923	2,486	3,223
Mill, M Sq. Ft.	72.3	78.2	54.8
– Sew/Finish	33.0	35.6	30.1
– Cutting	10.5	11.3	11.3
– Storage	28.8	31.3	13.4
Fabric – $/yd.	1.54	1.56	1.56
– Yds./doz.	18.75	18.75	18.75
Trim, $/doz.	4.10	4.10	4.10
Lining, $/doz.	4.31	4.31	4.31
Inventory (days)			
– Raw Material	20	10	10
– WIP	20	20	5
– Fin. goods	35	35	12
1st. Qual. Prod., %	0.99	0.99	0.99
Markdowns, %	0.02	0.01	0.01
Selling Price, $/doz.	95.40	95.40	95.40

APPENDIX K1b
Apparel Manufacturing Economics
Basic – Long Sleeve Shirt

	Typical	QR I	QR II
Revenue – $/doz.			
Gross Sales	95.40	95.40	95.40
– seconds	-0.72	-0.71	-0.48
– markdowns	-1.42	-0.95	-0.48
Net Sales	93.26	93.74	94.44
Costs – $/doz.			
Fabric	28.89	29.16	29.16
Other Material	8.41	8.41	8.41
Labor			
– Standard	13.68	13.81	14.91
– Excess	2.02	2.04	1.36
– Indirect	3.49	3.22	2.13
– Management	2.06	1.86	1.72
– Fringe benefits	5.30	5.24	5.08
Utilities	0.78	0.69	0.67
Depreciation	1.46	1.37	1.66
All Other	2.08	2.06	1.66
Mfg. Costs	68.17	67.86	66.76
S,G, &A	17.38	17.38	17.42
Total Cost/doz $.	85.55	85.24	84.18
Pre-Tax Earnings, $M	7,735	8,502	10,280
Investment, $M			
Fixed	1,649	1,927	2,423
Building	1,446	1,446	1,446
Inventory	2,340	2,549	965
Work Cap., other	2,440	2,923	2,915
Total	7,875	8,845	7,749
Equity, $M	6,119	7,005	5,761
Net ROS	5.2%	5.7%	6.9%
Net ROE	11.7%	13.4%	19.7%
Net ROI	9.1%	10.6%	14.7%

APPENDIX K2a
Apparel Manufacturing Economics
Basic - Long Sleeve Oxford Shirt

	Typical	QR I	QR II
Labor			
– Operators	255	310	301
– Indirect	37	43	28
Management	15	16	14
Total	307	369	343
SAH/doz.	2.20	2.22	2.33
Ann. dozen, M	173	208	208
Workplace Utilization, %	0.85	0.95	0.75
S&F Invest., $M	1,350	1,692	2,180
Gen. Invest. & Fees, $M	372	602	822
Cutting Invest., $M	201	201	221
Total Invest., $M 1988	1,923	2,495	3,223
Mill, M Sq. Ft.	76.4	83.5	56.5
– Sew/Finish	33.0	35.9	30.1
– Cutting	10.5	11.3	11.3
– Storage	32.9	36.3	15.1
Fabric – $/yd.	1.40	1.41	1.41
– Yds./doz.	14.40	14.40	14.40
Trim, $/doz.	3.50	3.50	3.50
Lining, $/doz.	2.50	2.50	2.50
Inventory (days)			
– Raw Material	20	10	10
– WIP	20	20	5
– Fin. goods	35	35	12
1st. Qual. Prod., %	0.99	0.99	0.99
Markdowns, %	0.02	0.01	0.01
Selling Price, $/doz.	66.60	66.60	66.60

Apparel Manufacturing Economics
Basic - Long Sleeve Oxford Shirt

	Typical	QR I	QR II
Revenue - $/doz.			
Gross Sales	66.60	66.60	66.60
- seconds	-0.50	-0.50	-0.33
- markdowns	-0.92	-0.66	-0.33
Net Sales	65.18	65.44	65.94
Costs - $/doz.			
Fabric	20.16	20.23	20.23
Other Material	6.00	6.00	6.00
Labor			
- Standard	11.65	11.78	12.68
- Excess	1.73	1.75	1.17
- Indirect	2.77	2.66	1.82
- Management	1.74	1.51	1.45
- Fringe Benefits	4.47	4.44	4.32
Utilities	0.68	0.60	0.57
Depreciation	1.25	1.17	1.41
All Other	1.74	1.75	1.42
Mfg. Costs	52.19	51.89	51.07
S,G, &A	12.13	12.13	12.16
Total Cost/doz. $	64.32	64.02	63.23
Pre-Tax Earnings, $M	806	1,422	2,690
Investment, $M			
Fixed	1,649	1,936	2,423
Building	1,528	1,528	1,528
Inventory	2,068	2,273	849
Work Cap., other	2,057	2,475	2,461
Total	7,302	8,212	7,261
Equity, $M	5,519	6,343	5,246
Net ROS	0.8%	1.4%	2.6%
Net ROE	1.6%	2.9%	6.7%
Net ROI	1.2%	2.3%	4.9%

	Typical	QR I	QR II
Labor			
– Operators	255	334	270
– Indirect	33	40	26
Management	14	16	14
Total	302	390	310
SAH/doz.	3.12	3.14	2.80
Adj. Ann. SAH	365	475	474
Ann. dozen, M	117	152	152
Workplace Utilization, %	0.75	0.90	0.73
S&F Invest., $M	833	1,018	1,438
Gen. Invest. & Fees, $M	372	602	822
Cutting Invest., $M	201	201	221
Total Invest., $M 1988	1,406	1,821	2,481
Mill, M Sq. Ft.	91.7	101.3	65.0
– Sew/Finish	34.0	37.1	24.2
– Cutting	12.0	13.9	13.9
– Storage	45.7	50.3	26.9
Fabric – $/yd.	2.50	2.57	2.65
– Yds./doz.	16.10	16.10	16.10
Trim, $/doz.	4.63	4.63	4.63
Lining, $/doz.	1.50	1.50	1.50
Inventory (days)			
– Raw Material	30	15	10
– WIP	25	25	5
– Fin. goods	40	40	20
1st. Qual. Prod., %	0.98	0.98	0.99
Markdowns, %	0.03	0.02	0.01
Selling Price, $/doz.	133.20	133.20	133.20

	Typical	QR I	QR II
Revenue – $/doz			
Gross Sales	133.20	133.20	133.20
- seconds	-1.67	-1.67	-1.00
- markdowns	-3.95	-2.63	-1.32
Net Sales	127.58	128.90	130.88
Costs –$/doz.			
Fabric	40.25	41.38	42.67
Other Material	6.13	6.13	6.13
Labor			
- Standard	16.51	16.66	15.08
- Excess	3.22	3.25	1.97
- Indirect	3.66	3.45	2.28
- Management	2.46	2.06	1.99
- Fringe Benefits	6.48	6.39	5.37
Utilities	1.15	0.96	0.85
Depreciation	1.46	1.29	1.58
All Other	2.37	2.33	1.40
Mfg. Costs	83.69	83.90	79.32
S,G, &A	26.31	26.31	26.44
Total Cost/doz.	110.00	110.21	105.76
Pre-Tax Earnings, $M	17,596	18,697	25,128
Investment, $M			
Fixed	1,096	1,354	1,793
Building	1,834	1,834	1,834
Inventory	2,844	3,320	1,395
Work Cap., other	2,653	3,456	3,423
Total	8,427	9,964	8,445
Equity, $M	6,884	8,343	6,701
Net ROS	8.7%	9.1%	12.1%
Net ROE	18.8%	21.5%	35.9%
Net ROI	15.4%	18.0%	28.5%

Apparel Manufacturing Economics
Seasonal – Women's Slacks

	Typical	QR I	QR II
Labor			
– Operators	255	334	280
– Indirect	34	40	27
Management	14	16	14
Total	303	390	321
SAH/doz.	2.80	2.82	2.60
Ann. dozen, M	130	170	170
Workplace Utilization, %	0.77	0.92	0.70
S&F Invest., $M	960	1,189	1,546
Gen. Invest. & Fees, $M	372	602	822
Cutting Invest., $M	201	201	221
Total Invest., $M 1988	1,533	1,992	2,589
Mill, M Sq. Ft.	94.6	105.5	69.3
– Sew/Finish	33.1	36.3	26.0
– Cutting	8.9	13.9	13.9
– Storage	52.6	55.3	29.4
Fabric – $/yd.	2.00	2.04	2.10
– Yds./doz.	15.00	15.00	15.00
Trim, $/doz.	3.85	3.85	3.85
Lining, $/doz.	0.80	0.80	0.80
Inventory (days)			
– Raw Material	30	15	10
– WIP	25	25	5
– Fin. goods	40	40	20
1st. Qual. Prod., %	0.98	0.98	0.99
Markdowns, %	0.03	0.02	0.01
Selling Price, $/doz.	102.00	102.00	102.00

APPENDIX K4b
Apparel Manufacturing Economics
Seasonal – Women's Slacks

	Typical	QR I	QR II
Revenue- $/doz.			
Gross Sales	102.00	102.00	102.00
- seconds	-1.28	-1.28	-0.77
- markdowns	-3.02	-2.01	-1.01
Net Sales	97.70	98.71	100.22
Costs – $/doz.			
Fabric	30.00	30.60	31.50
Other Material	4.65	4.65	4.65
Labor			
- Standard	14.53	14.65	13.64
- Excess	2.84	2.86	1.75
- Indirect	3.43	3.10	2.16
- Management	2.21	1.85	1.78
- Fringe Benefits	5.75	5.64	4.87
Utilities	1.07	0.90	0.82
Depreciation	1.47	1.28	1.49
All Other	2.18	2.17	1.40
Mfg. Costs	68.13	67.70	64.06
S,G, &A	20.15	20.15	20.25
Total Cost/doz.	88.28	87.85	84.31
Pre-Tax Earnings, $M	9,443	10,865	15,917
Investment, $M			
Fixed	1,280	1,530	1,888
Building	1,892	1,892	1,892
Inventory	2,512	2,925	1,229
Work Cap., other	2,291	2,978	2,952
Total	7,975	9,325	7,961
Equity, $M	6,331	7,606	6,135
Net ROS	6.1%	6.9%	10.0%
Net ROE	12.2%	15.3%	27.7%
Net ROI	9.7%	12.4%	21.4%

Apparel Manufacturing Economics
Fashion – Men's Knit Shirt

	QR I	QR II
Labor		
– Operators	255	268
– Indirect	34	26
Management	14	13
Total	303	307
SAH/dozen	2.14	1.92
Ann. dozen, M	157	212
Workplace Utilization, %	0.79	0.70
S & F Investment, $M	864	1,345
Gen. Investment & Fees, $M	372	822
Cutting Investment, $M	201	221
Total Investment, $M 1988	1,437	2,388
Mill, M Sq. Ft.	79.4	63.0
– Sew/Finish	27.5	24.9
– Cutting	10.5	12.3
– Storage	41.4	25.8
Fabric – $/yd.	2.75	3.01
– Yds./dozen	13.82	13.82
Trim, $/dozen	2.90	2.90
Lining, $/dozen	2.12	2.12
Inventory (days)		
– Raw Material	40	15
– WIP	20	5
– Finished goods	45	25
1st. Quality Prod., %	0.96	0.98
Markdowns, %	0.05	0.02
Selling Price, $/dozen	120.00	120.00

Apparel Manufacturing Economics
Fashion – Men's Knit Shirt

	QR I	QR II
Revenue – $/dozen		
Gross Sales	120.00	120.00
– seconds	–2.70	–1.50
– markdowns	–5.87	–2.01
Net Sales	111.43	116.49
Costs – $/dozen		
Fabric	38.01	41.60
Other Material	5.02	5.02
Labor		
– Standard	11.41	10.47
– Excess	2.82	1.71
– Indirect	2.84	1.68
– Management	1.83	1.36
– Fringe Benefits	4.73	3.84
Utilities	0.68	0.51
Depreciation	1.01	1.06
All Other	1.52	1.14
Manufacturing Costs	69.87	68.39
S, G, & A	29.33	29.63
Total Cost/dozen	99.20	98.02
Pre-Tax Earnings, $M	12,248	18,468
Investment, $M		
Fixed	1,062	1,712
Building	1,588	1,588
Inventory	3,603	2,189
Work Cap., other	3,190	4,319
Total	9.443	9.808
Equity, $M	8,009	8,188
Net ROS	6.9%	10.0%
Net ROE	15.1%	30.1%
Net ROI	12.8%	25.1%

APPENDIX K6a
Apparel Manufacturing Economics
Fashion- Women's Blouse

	QR I	QR II
Labor		
– Operators	255	269
– Indirect	40	27
Management	17	15
Total	312	311
SAH/dozen	2.13	1.94
Ann. dozen, M	158	213
Workplace Utilization, %	0.74	0.70
S & F Investment, $M	776	1,342
Gen. Investment & Fees, $M	372	822
Cutting Investment, $M	201	221
Total Investment, $M 1988	1,349	2,385
Mill, M Sq. Ft.	83.5	61.1
– Sew/Finish	34.5	26.9
– Cutting	10.5	12.3
– Storage	38.5	21.9
Fabric – $/yd.	1.45	1.57
– Yds./dozen	12.38	12.38
Trim, $/dozen	2.90	2.90
Lining, $/dozen	0.50	0.50
Inventory (days)		
– Raw Material	40	15
– WIP	30	7
– Finished goods	45	20
1st. Quality Prod., %	0.97	0.98
Markdowns, %	0.05	0.02
Selling Price, $/dozen	84.60	84.60

Apparel Manufacturing Economics
Fashion- Women's Blouse

	QR I	QR II
Revenue - $/dozen		
Gross Sales	84.60	84.60
- seconds	-1.27	-0.85
- markdowns	-4.17	-1.42
Net Sales	79.16	82.33
Costs - $/dozen		
Fabric	17.95	19.44
Other Material	3.40	3.40
Labor		
- Standard	11.18	10.39
- Excess	2.77	1.69
- Indirect	3.23	1.75
- Management	2.07	1.48
- Fringe Benefits	4.79	3.85
Utilities	0.75	0.54
Depreciation	0.98	1.15
All Other	1.65	1.15
Manufacturing Costs	48.77	44.84
S, G, & A	20.83	20.94
Total Cost/dozen	69.60	65.78
Pre-Tax Earnings, $M	9,575	16,556
Investment, $M		
Fixed	988	1,901
Building	1,670	1,670
Inventory	2,475	1,204
Work Cap., other	2,272	3,024
Total	7,405	7,799
Equity, $M	5,989	6,120
Net ROS	7.6%	12.7%
Net ROE	15.9%	36.3%
Net ROI	12.9%	28.5%

Apparel Manufacturing Economics
Fashion – Women's Skirt

	QR I	QR II
Labor		
– Operators	255	285
– Indirect	40	27
Management	17	15
Total	312	327
SAH/dozen	2.48	2.29
Ann. dozen, M	135	183
Workplace Utilization, %	0.69%	0.65%
S & F Investment, $M	833	1,283
Gen. Investment & Fees, $M	372	822
Cutting Investment, $M	201	221
Total Investment, $M 1988	1,406	2,326
Mill, M Sq. Ft.	79.5	58.6
– Sew/Finish	33.3	28.5
– Cutting	8.5	10.0
– Storage	37.7	20.1
Fabric – $/yd.	1.53	1.98
– yds./dozen	18.61	18.61
Trim, $/dozen	3.65	3.65
Lining, $/dozen	0.00	0.00
Inventory (days)		
– Raw Material	40	15
– WIP	30	8
– Finished goods	45	20
1st. Quality Prod., %	0.98	0.99
Markdowns, %	0.05	0.02
Selling Price, $/dozen	110.40	110.40

APPENDIX K7b
Apparel Manufacturing Economics
Fashion – Women's Skirt

	QR I	QR II
Revenue – $/dozen		
Gross Sales	110.40	110.40
– seconds	-1.38	-0.83
– markdowns	-5.45	-1.86
Net Sales	103.57	107.71
Costs – $/dozen		
Fabric	28.47	35.73
Other Material	3.65	3.65
Labor		
– Standard	12.86	11.97
– Excess	3.19	2.17
– Indirect	3.78	2.05
– Management	2.42	1.79
– Fringe Benefits	5.54	4.50
Utilities	0.85	0.63
Depreciation	1.15	1.19
All Other	1.89	1.36
Manufacturing Costs	63.80	65.04
S, G, & A	27.26	27.39
Total Cost/dozen	91.06	92.43
Pre-Tax Earnings, $M	12,512	15,338
Investment, $M		
Fixed	1,029	1,648
Building	1,590	1,590
Inventory	2,889	1,613
Work Cap., other	2,541	3,456
Total	8,049	8,307
Equity, $M	6,624	6,703
Net ROS	7.6%	9.0%
Net ROE	16.1%	26.3%
Net ROI	13.2%	21.2%

APPENDIX L1
Textile Economics – Poplin In Basic & Fashion Products.

	Typical	Basic QR II	Fash. QR II
Greige Mfg. Cost ($/yd.)			
Fiber	0.41	0.41	0.41
Other	0.04	0.04	0.04
Total	0.45	0.45	0.45
Direct Cost			
Operating Labor	0.26	0.28	0.34
Direct Supervision	0.03	0.03	0.03
Power & Supplies	0.13	0.12	0.13
Plant Burden	0.08	0.07	0.07
Depreciation	0.09	0.08	0.07
Total Mfg. Cost	1.04	1.02	1.09
Freight	0.01	0.01	0.01
Shrinkage & Waste	0.06	0.06	0.08
Total Adj. Cost	1.11	1.09	1.18
D & F Cost			
Dyes & Chemicals	0.07	0.07	0.07
Other	0.02	0.02	0.02
Total	0.09	0.09	0.09
Direct Cost			
Labor	0.08	0.09	0.12
Direct Supervision	0.01	0.01	0.02
Power & Supplies	0.08	0.08	0.09
Plant Burden	0.03	0.03	0.05
Depreciation	0.02	0.01	0.02
Total D&F Cost	0.31	0.31	0.39
S, G, &A	0.16	0.14	0.16
Gross Selling Price	1.74	1.74	1.93
Markdowns, etc.	0.04	0.03	0.02
Net Selling Price	1.70	1.71	1.91
Pre-Tax Profits	0.14	0.16	0.19
Investments ($/Ann. Yd.)			
Fixed	0.53	0.45	0.50
Inventory	0.22	0.20	0.18
Other WC	0.19	0.19	0.21
Total Investment	0.94	0.84	0.89
ROS	5.0%	6.0%	6.2%
ROA	9.0%	12.2%	13.4%

APPENDIX L2
Textile Economics – Poplin In Seasonal Products.

	Typical	Seas. QRI	Seas. QR II
Greige Mfg. Cost ($/Yd.)			
Fiber	0.41	0.41	0.41
Other	0.04	0.04	0.04
Total	0.45	0.45	0.45
Direct Cost			
Operating Labor	0.26	0.30	0.33
Direct Supervision	0.03	0.03	0.03
Power & Supplies	0.13	0.12	0.12
Plant Burden	0.08	0.07	0.07
Depreciation	0.09	0.07	0.07
Total Mfg. Cost	1.04	1.04	1.07
Freight	0.01	0.01	0.01
Shrinkage & Waste	0.06	0.07	0.07
Total Adj. Cost	1.11	1.12	1.15
D & F Cost			
Dyes & Chemicals	0.07	0.07	0.07
Other	0.02	0.02	0.02
Total	0.09	0.09	0.09
Direct Cost			
Labor	0.08	0.10	0.10
Direct Supervision	0.01	0.01	0.01
Power & Supplies	0.08	0.08	0.08
Plant Burden	0.03	0.04	0.04
Depreciation	0.02	0.02	0.02
Total D&F Cost	0.31	0.34	0.34
S, G, &A	0.16	0.15	0.15
Gross Selling Price	1.74	1.78	1.84
Markdowns, etc.	0.04	0.02	0.02
Net Selling Price	1.70	1.76	1.82
Pre-Tax Profits	0.14	0.16	0.17
Investments ($/Ann. Yd.)			
Fixed	0.53	0.43	0.45
Inventory	0.22	0.18	0.17
Other WC	0.19	0.20	0.20
Total Investment	0.94	0.81	0.82
ROS	5.0%	5.8%	5.8%
ROA	9.0%	12.7%	12.8%

Textile Economics – Basic Goods

	Broadcloth		Yarn-Dyed Oxford	
	Typical	QR II	Typical	QR II
Greige Mfg. Cost ($/Yd.)				
Fiber	0.27	0.27	0.30	0.30
Other	0.02	0.02	0.05	0.05
Total	0.29	0.29	0.35	0.35
Direct Cost				
Operating Labor	0.29	0.31	0.29	0.31
Direct Supervision	0.03	0.03	0.03	0.03
Power & Supplies	0.15	0.15	0.13	0.12
Plant Burden	0.09	0.09	0.09	0.08
Depreciation	0.11	0.09	0.06	0.05
Total Mfg. Cost	0.96	0.96	0.95	0.94
Freight	0.01	0.01	0.01	0.01
Shrinkage & Waste	0.04	0.04	0.01	0.01
Total Adj. Cost	1.01	1.01	0.97	0.96
D & F Cost				
Dyes & Chemicals	0.04	0.04	0.03	0.03
Other	0.01	0.01	0.01	0.01
Total	0.05	0.05	0.04	0.04
Direct Cost				
Labor	0.04	0.05	0.04	0.05
Direct Supervision	0.01	0.01	0.01	0.01
Power & Supplies	0.04	0.04	0.04	0.04
Plant Burden	0.02	0.02	0.02	0.02
Depreciation	0.01	0.01	0.01	0.01
Total D&F Cost	0.17	0.18	0.16	0.17
S, G, & A	0.15	0.13	0.14	0.12
Gross Selling Price	1.45	1.46	1.41	1.40
Markdowns, etc.	0.03	0.02	0.03	0.02
Net Selling Price	1.42	1.44	1.38	1.38
Pre-Tax Profits	0.11	0.15	0.11	0.13
Investments ($/Ann. Yd.)				
Fixed	0.51	0.43	0.43	0.36
Inventory	0.19	0.17	0.20	0.18
Other WC	0.17	0.16	0.15	0.15
Total Investment	0.87	0.76	0.78	0.69
ROS	5.0%	6.5%	5.0%	6.1%
ROA	8.3%	12.1%	8.8%	12.1%

APPENDIX L4
Textile Economics – Seasonal Goods

	65/35 P/C Twill		
	Typical	QR I	QR II
Greige Mfg. Cost ($/Yd.)			
Fiber	0.74	0.74	0.74
Other	0.05	0.05	0.05
Total	0.79	0.79	0.79
Direct Cost			
Operating Labor	0.26	0.31	0.34
Direct Supervision	0.03	0.03	0.03
Power & Supplies	0.12	0.11	0.12
Plant Burden	0.08	0.06	0.07
Depreciation	0.05	0.03	0.04
Total Mfg. Cost	1.33	1.33	1.39
Freight	0.02	0.02	0.02
Shrinkage & Waste	0.08	0.08	0.08
Total Adj. Cost	1.43	1.43	1.49
D & F Cost			
Dyes & Chemicals	0.14	0.14	0.14
Other	0.02	0.02	0.02
Total	0.16	0.16	0.16
Direct Cost			
Labor	0.08	0.11	0.11
Direct Supervision	0.01	0.01	0.01
Power & Supplies	0.09	0.09	0.09
Plant Burden	0.03	0.04	0.04
Depreciation	0.01	0.01	0.01
Total D&F Cost	0.38	0.42	0.42
S, G, & A	0.15	0.14	0.15
Gross Selling Price	2.13	2.18	2.23
Markdowns, etc.	0.03	0.03	0.03
Net Selling Price	2.10	2.15	2.20
Pre-Tax Profits	0.17	0.16	0.17
Investments ($/Ann. Yd.)			
Fixed	0.38	0.32	0.34
Inventory	0.29	0.23	0.22
Other WC	0.22	0.24	0.24
Total Investment	0.89	0.79	0.80
ROS	5.0%	4.8%	4.7%
ROA	11.7%	13.0%	13.0%

Textile Economics – Seasonal Goods

	100% Cotton Twill		
	Typical	QR I	QR II
Greige Mfg. Cost ($/Yd.)			
Fiber	0.61	0.61	
Other	0.02	0.02	
Total	0.63	0.63	
Direct Cost			
Operating Labor	0.35	0.42	
Direct Supervision	0.03	0.03	
Power & Supplies	0.14	0.14	
Plant Burden	0.09	0.08	
Depreciation	0.06	0.04	
Total Mfg. Cost	1.30	1.34	
Freight	0.02	0.02	
Shrinkage & Waste	0.08	0.08	
Total Adj. Cost	1.40	1.44	
D & F Cost			
Dyes & Chemicals	0.21	0.21	
Other	0.03	0.03	
Total	0.24	0.24	
Direct Cost			
Labor	0.10	0.13	
Direct Supervision	0.01	0.02	
Power & Supplies	0.11	0.12	
Plant Burden	0.03	0.04	
Depreciation	0.02	0.02	
Total D&F Cost	0.51	0.57	
S, G, & A	0.18	0.17	0.17
Gross Selling Price	2.30	2.37	2.44
Markdowns, etc.	0.04	0.03	0.03
Net Selling Price	2.26	2.34	2.41
Pre-Tax Profits	0.18	0.18	0.19
Investments ($/Ann. Yd.)			
Fixed	0.46	0.38	0.41
Inventory	0.31	0.25	0.24
Other WC	0.26	0.25	0.26
Total Investment	1.03	0.88	0.91
ROS	5.0%	4.9%	4.9%
ROA	11.3%	13.0%	12.9%

267

Textile Economics – Fashion Goods

	Polyester Pongee		Yarn-Dyed Madras	
	Typical	QR II	Typical	QR II
Greige Mfg. Cost				
Fiber	0.39	0.39	0.16	0.16
Other	0.01	0.01	0.03	0.03
Total	0.40	0.40	0.19	0.19
Direct Cost				
Operating Labor	0.09	0.13	0.46	0.66
Direct Supervision	0.01	0.01	0.05	0.06
Power & Supplies	0.06	0.06	0.19	0.23
Plant Burden	0.05	0.05	0.10	0.10
Depreciation	0.06	0.05	0.06	0.05
Total Mfg. Cost	0.67	0.70	1.05	1.29
Freight	0.00	0.00	0.01	0.01
Shrinkage	0.05	0.05	0.01	0.01
Total Adj. Cost	0.72	0.75	1.07	1.31
D & F Cost				
Dyes & Chemicals	0.01	0.01	0.02	0.02
Other	0.01	0.01	0.01	0.01
Total	0.02	0.02	0.03	0.03
Direct Cost				
Labor	0.07	0.10	0.04	0.05
Direct Supervision	0.01	0.01	0.01	0.01
Power & Supplies	0.04	0.04	0.03	0.03
Plant Burden	0.03	0.04	0.02	0.03
Depreciation	0.01	0.01	0.01	0.01
Total D&F Cost	0.18	0.22	0.14	0.16
S, G, & A	0.09	0.09	0.16	0.18
Gross Selling Price	1.11	1.20	1.48	1.86
Markdowns, etc.	0.03	0.03	0.03	0.04
Net Selling Price	1.08	1.17	1.45	1.82
Pre-Tax Profits	0.09	0.11	0.12	0.18
Investments ($/Ann. Yd.)				
Fixed	0.27	0.25	0.42	0.44
Inventory	0.11	0.10	0.24	0.22
Other WC	0.15	0.14	0.16	0.16
Total Investment	0.53	0.49	0.82	0.82
ROS	5.0%	5.7%	5.0%	6.4%
ROA	10.4%	13.5%	8.8%	14.0%

APPENDIX L7
Textile Economics – Fashion Goods

| | Jersey Knit | |
	Typical	QR II
Greige Mfg. Cost ($/lb.)		
Yarn	2.15	2.15
Printing	1.05	1.35
Other	0.03	0.03
Total	3.23	3.53
Direct Cost		
Labor	0.26	0.28
Variable	0.12	0.13
Overhead	0.16	0.20
Depreciation	0.03	0.03
Total Mfg. Cost	3.80	4.17
S, G, & A	0.31	0.32
Gross Selling Price	4.69	5.13
Markdowns, etc.	0.14	0.12
Net Selling Price	4.55	5.01
Pre-Tax Profits	0.46	0.53
Investments ($/Ann. Lb.)		
Fixed	0.41	0.38
Inventory	1.61	1.61
Other WC	0.14	0.15
Total Investment	2.16	2.14
ROS	6.3%	6.7%
ROA	13.3%	15.6%

Glossary of Terms

AAMA	American Apparel Manufacturers Association.
ANSI	American National Standards Institute.
ARC	Apparel Research Committee of AAMA.
ATMI	American Textile Manufacturers Institute
BCG	Boston Consulting Group.
BRITE	Basic Research in Industrial Technologies for Europe.
CAD	Computer Assisted Design.
CAM	Computer Assisted Manufacturing.
CIM	Computer Integrated Manufacturing.
CMROI	Contribution Margin Return on Investment.
CVC	Chief Value Cotton.
CVS	Chief Value Synthetic.
CWP	Crafted With Pride In USA Inc.
DL	Direct Labor.
EC	European Community (also referred to as EEC; European Economic Community).
EDI	Electronic Data Interchange.
807	Section of the Customs Code that permits duty free entry to the USA on the assembly value of US made parts assembled off-shore.
FASLINC	Fabric and Suppliers Linkage Council.
FFACT	Fiber, Fabric and Apparel Coalition for Trade.
GMROI	Gross Margin Return on Inventory.
JIT	Just In Time.
KSA	Kurt Salmon Associates.
KTA	Knitted Textiles Association.
LC	Letter of Credit.
M/D	Markdown. (Also MD).
MFA	Multi-Fiber Arrangement.
MITI	Ministry of International Trade and Industry. (Japan).
MRP	Materials Requirement Planning.
MRP II	Manufacturing Resource Planning.
MMFPA	Man-Made Fiber Producers Association. Recently changed to American Fiber Producers Association.
NRMA	National Retail Merchants Association.
OTB	Open-To-Buy.

PBU	Progressive Bundle Unit.
POS	Point-Of-Sale.
QM	Quality Management.
QR	Quick Response.
RITAC	Retail Industry Trade Action Coalition.
SAFLINC	Sundries and Apparel Findings Linkage Council.
SAM	Standard Allowed Minute.
SAH	Standard Allowed Hour
SKU	Stock-Keeping Unit.
S/O	Stockout.
SYE	Square Yard Equivalent.
TALC	Textile Apparel Linkage Council.
(TC)^2	Textile/Clothing Technology Corporation.
UPC	Universal Product Code.
UPS	Unit Production System.
VAP	Value Adding Partnership.
VICS	Voluntary Inter-Industry Communications Standards Committee.
WIP	Work In Process.